MICHAEL CROUCH came to professional writing late in life, after an education at Cambridge and Oxford universities, careers in the British Overseas Service in South Arabia (now Yemen) and in industry and commerce in Western Australia, followed by some years as a school teacher and as a management consultant. This is his fourth book: his autobiography, *An Element of Luck*, was first published in 1993. His first biography, *Bwana Safari*, was released in Kenya in 2003, and his novel, *The Terrorist*, was published in the USA also in 2003. He has also written numerous articles for publications ranging from *Australian Geographic* to the *Australian Financial Review* and the *International Herald Tribune*. Michael Crouch and his wife Jenny live in West Perth.

By the same author

An Element of Luck (autobiography)

Bwana Safari (biography)

The Terrorist (novel)

THE *Literary* LARRIKIN

A CRITICAL BIOGRAPHY OF
T.A.G. HUNGERFORD

MICHAEL CROUCH

UNIVERSITY OF WESTERN AUSTRALIA PRESS

First published in 2005 by
University of Western Australia Press
Crawley, Western Australia 6009
www.uwapress.uwa.edu.au

National Library of Australia
Cataloguing-in-Publication entry:

Crouch, Michael, 1935–
     The literary larrikin: a critical biography of T.A.G. Hungerford.

     Bibliography.
     Includes index.
     ISBN 1 920694 39 0.

     1. Hungerford, T. A. G. (Thomas Arthur Guy), 1915–   .
     2. Authors, Australian — 20th century — Biography. 3.
     Journalists — Australia — 20th century — Biography. 4.
     Australian literature — 20th century. I. Title.

A823.3

Cover: T. A. G. Hungerford, 2003.
Copyright © West Australian Newspapers Ltd 2004

Produced by Benchmark Publications Pty Ltd, Melbourne
Consultant editor: Cathryn Game
Designed by Nada Backovic
Typeset in 11pt Granjon by Lasertype, Perth
Printed by BPA Print Group, Melbourne

To the late Bill Warnock, the author's oldest and dearest friend in Perth, in gratitude for the kindnesses shown to me over the years and for introducing me to Tom Hungerford. I miss him.

And with much love to my wife Jenny, whose support in the preparation of this book has been essential.

FOREWORD

For most of my life Tom Hungerford has been a substantial and significant figure in the Western Australian background. I would have come across him first as author of *The Ridge and the River*, one of my discoveries during a university education that in those halcyon days included plenty of time for voracious reading outside the course of study. Those of us who had been at school during the 1939–45 war encountered a lot of ex-servicemen and women when we arrived at university. Serious about their opportunities and given to firm opinions expressed with great good nature, they were an important maturing influence on the rest of us, but were usually most reticent about discussing their experiences of war. We respected this, and assumed it was something they wanted to put behind them, but we were inevitably curious about what it was — in Libya, or New Guinea, or with the RAAF over German skies — that had shaped their growing up, that gave them an authority and a kind of wisdom beyond our understanding. After reading a book like *The Ridge and the River* we could begin to understand.

Tom Hungerford's life and mine have not intersected very closely since that time, but we have a number of shared experiences from those times in our lives when our trajectories have brought us into Western Australia as well as a number of good friends in common. I remember him as a force for robust common sense in that lively but sometimes ungovernable body, the Fellowship of Australian Writers (WA). He was a publicist for successive Western Australian premiers in the boom years of the early 1970s at a time when it was more than usually important for the state to present the right kind of publicity crafted with the right kind of professionalism.

Above all, through his *Stories from Suburban Road* and its sequels he has been a major contributor to helping Western Australians to define their sense of identity in a rapidly changing world. He has so precisely and deftly delineated the overgrown country town that was the Perth in which the older generation grew up. He knows the sights, the smells, the ways in which people interacted with one another, although, as a North Perth boy, I am bound to take issue with the South Perth myth that we were a lot of 'lairs' on our side of the river. Beyond that accurately etched evocation of a local scene bigger themes lie, most of all the theme of change and mutability and the gradual fading of the insights of childhood and youth. It was a moving experience this year to see the octogenarian Tom Hungerford watching an actor represent his teenage self in a play based on stories written in his middle years. He has not only described the character of old Western Australia, he also embodies the best of it.

Not that he is representative of a type. He has always been a cat who walks by himself, perhaps driven by a disdain for compromise and bullshit, perhaps finding solitude essential to creativity. This makes for an occasional cantankerousness, but it goes with high standards of quality. Everything to which he turns his hand is marked by a passion for good craftsmanship, whether it be in writing, in cooking or in the leadership of men in war. In the case of Michael Crouch's biography this has led to complications, since Michael has written a well-researched and well-crafted account of Tom Hungerford's life and work, but it is not an account that Tom Hungerford feels able to endorse. Speaking as a historian and biographer of some experience, I consider that Michael Crouch has given us an honest and readable biography, balanced in its judgements and judicious in its insights about its subject. It is good that we should have this picture of Tom Hungerford.

One of the themes that emerges from this biography is that although Tom Hungerford, like the rest of us, appreciates recognition, he has a knack of dodging the limelight when it threatens to surround him. A writer who chooses to live and write in Western Australia must expect to find it harder to win recognition than those who operate in the networks of Melbourne and Sydney, but in Tom Hungerford's case there might also be a characteristic distaste for big-noting oneself. Michael Crouch, in writing of him, has been reminded of a Horatius who kept the bridge in the brave days of old. For myself there comes unbidden into my mind those lines of the elderly W. B. Yeats:

> *There's not a fool may call me friend*
> *And I may sup at journey's end*
> *With Landor and with Donne.*

Tom Hungerford would make one of that company.

Geoffrey Bolton
Canberra, May 2004

CONTENTS

PHOTOGRAPHS

Maps

ACKNOWLEDGEMENTS

It was my enjoyable task to assemble as much background as I could, from the circle of T. A. G. Hungerford's family, friends and colleagues, from libraries and archives, to supplement the taped conversations with Hungerford, over a period of some months commencing in 2002. As someone who did not grow up in Australia I am particularly indebted to a wide range of people who have lived all or most of their lives here. I acknowledge their help and warmly thank the following for their comments and advice in researching Hungerford's life. In the order of my having spoken with them:

Dr Jenny Gregory, Director, University of Western Australia Press, and Maureen de la Harpe, also of University of Western Australia Press, both of whom gave me encouragement to press ahead and who commented constructively on earlier drafts—and I am grateful to other UWA Press staff for their help; Professor Dennis Haskell, University of Western Australia, for his advice in the early stages, for his later support and for permission to incorporate an article written for *Westerly* (2003) in this book; Peter Sherlock (editor of the Hungerford and Associated Families Society Inc. publications), Melbourne University; John Hungerford and Betty Crowley, treasurer and then secretary respectively of the Hungerford and Associated Families Society Inc., who have been generous with their time and resources; Nigel Hungerford for family contacts; Emeritus Professor Geoffrey Bolton, AO CitWA, historian and chancellor of Murdoch University, for useful information on Western Australia's social history, for providing the foreword to this book and for picking up errors in the draft he read; the Busselton Genealogical Society for information on

Tom Hungerford's mother and the Hedley family; Ray Coffey, Fremantle Arts Centre Press, for information on the history of the Press and for Hungerford's associations with it; Diana Warnock, for her reminiscences of Perth life from the 1960s to the 1980s and her long friendship with Hungerford; Richard Woldendorp, for his memories of life on the road with Hungerford and for agreeing to lend me certain photographs from that period; Sir Charles Court, AK, KCMG, OBE, for his wartime recollections and his reminiscences of working with Hungerford; Robert and Diana Archdeacon for recounting fond associations with their favourite uncle; John McIlwraith, for background material on working as a journalist in Perth in the 1970s, and for his help with improvements to the manuscript; Shelagh Pascoe, for an account of Hungerford's association with the Curtin University Fitness Centre; Bill Grono, for some pertinent comment on the Perth literary scene from the 1950s to the 1980s; Molly Hungerford, for the privilege of tapping into a razor-sharp memory dating back to her first meeting with her brother-in-law; Win Willis, who served at the Australian consulate-general in New York at the time of Hungerford's posting there; the late Eve Akerman, for the loan of various books and references; Sylvia Carr, National Library of Australia, Canberra, for access to the Hungerford portrait held by the library; Peter Nagle, National Archives of Australia, Canberra, for information on Eastlake Hostel and Hungerford's role as a kitchen-hand and yardman; Mark Whitmore, Lola Wilkins and their colleagues Peter Burness, Madeleine Chaleyer and Simon Forrester of the Australian War Memorial, Canberra, not only for allowing me to climb up inside the tower where Hungerford slaved as an editor but also for their enthusiastic support in accessing material relevant to his time in Canberra; Ian Templeman, Australian National University, for his recollections of Hungerford as an author and as a friend; Jack Harris, who knew Hungerford as a writer and as a friend; Terry Owen on the early days of Fremantle Arts Centre Press and her friendship with Hungerford; Angela Skinner for her recollection of a visit to Canning Vale and of travel in the USSR; the Revd Robin Hungerford, for an accurate account of the origins of the Hungerford family and for permission to quote Lieutenant Colonel R. A. Henderson; Susan Marie, Manager Library and Museum, City of Subiaco, for some research on my behalf; Ivan King, His Majesty's Theatre, Perth, for detail on a Hungerford play; Mark Hancock, Manager Libraries and Heritage, and LaVonne Varendorff, Local Studies Librarian, City of South Perth, for information on the Old Mill Theatre's production of *Stories from Suburban Road* and access to the accompanying exhibition; and Piers Akerman, for memories of encounters with Hungerford in Western Australia. Thank you all.

I acknowledge my use of material from *Stories from Suburban Road* (Fremantle Arts Centre Press, 1983), *A Knockabout with a Slouch Hat* (FACP, 1985) and *Red Rover All Over* (FACP, 1986).

PREFACE

Janet Malcolm, author of *Psychoanalysis: The Impossible Profession* and *In the Freud Archives*, writes,

> [A biography] is to satisfy the reader's curiosity, not to place limits on it. [The biographer] is supposed to go out and bring back the goods — the malevolent secrets that have been quietly burning in archives and libraries and in the minds of contemporaries who have been biding their time, waiting for the biographer's knock on their doors.[1]

It would have been exciting to come across some 'malevolent secrets', but I have discovered none and, other than some frank discussion of Hungerford's personality, the story is as straightforward as might be expected, a story of someone who has led a long and full life. As for knocking on the doors of contemporaries, I have done plenty of that and, as noted earlier, I am grateful to those people. What follows is the life story of the last surviving Grand Old Man of Australian literature.

The book has been compiled primarily from seven sources: first, Tom Hungerford himself, who spent many hours with me, recording his memories. All quotes from Tom Hungerford are taken from my interviews with him, unless otherwise specified in a note; second, members of the Hungerford clan, in Australia and the United Kingdom; third, comments on and reminiscences of Hungerford by his family, friends and colleagues; fourth, his books and short stories, supplemented by contemporary reviews. Much of the book's account of his life story complements his autobiographical trilogy, which I cross-reference where applicable. I have tried not to duplicate what Hungerford has already covered. Where this occurs, it is either because important material needs to be reinforced or because I am able to supplement information provided in his books. My fifth major group of sources was the Battye Library, the Evelyn H. Parker Library (City of Subiaco), the National Archives of Australia (Canberra), the National Library of Australia and the Internet. Sixth was Hungerford's ASIO files, via the National Archives of Australia, Canberra. The security authorities maintained covert observation on him dating from the 'Morotai mutiny' and perhaps even earlier. Most of the ASIO material from 1953 to 1973 was released to me, on request.[2] It is a pleasure incidental to the completion of this book that I have been able to document that ASIO wasted its time and resources in its efforts to paint Tom Hungerford as a dangerous closet communist. It can only be hoped that this expensive organisation is now better skilled at tracking down Australia's contemporary enemies and does not compile dossiers as preposterous as Hungerford's. The seventh major source has been my own observations, based on getting to know the man and reading much of his prodigious output. The colourful story of Hungerford's life has tended to concentrate on the middle years (1942–70) because most of the material will be new to the reader and because that period provides much that is fascinating in observing how the young man matured into middle age.

My focus is primarily on his life story, intertwined of course with his career as a writer. A model for my approach is Eric Hobsbawm's *Interesting Times: A Twentieth-Century Life*,[3] an account that is primarily about him rather than his many books and stories. Some readers, including Tom Hungerford himself, might feel that this approach has in some way diminished his status as a writer, but I consider that placing the emphasis primarily on his writings would have obscured the story of Hungerford as an unique character (as he is in many ways). So I leave it to others to give exclusive attention to Hungerford's immense output of short stories, articles and books. It is 'immense' because for more than twenty years he was also working mighty hard as a journalist. How he laboured as a writer of fiction, much of it autobiographically based, is related in the Introduction.

Hungerford's life story is a 'ripping yarn' in its own right. It is the tale of a man whose long life has spanned most of the two world wars. It recounts how he grew up in the arboreal setting of South Perth, and who returned later to a Perth that has changed out of nearly all recognition, over a span of nearly ninety years. Second, of course, it is a story of one of Australia's most prominent wordsmiths, someone who managed to combine his working life as a soldier and journalist with that of a professional writer of half a dozen books and numerous short stories.

In the main, I have drawn on comment about his work, from formal critiques and the informed observations of others. The latter were made primarily for my personal benefit, to provide a rounded picture of Tom Hungerford, the author and the man, to present his mix of competence and charm, his ego, his stubbornness and prejudices. I have generally not identified the actual sources of such comments, except where these should be attributed to a literary reviewer or are especially pertinent to the context. Any inferences drawn from unattributed comments are of course my sole responsibility.

The idea of my writing the biography emanated from Tom Hungerford, as I would not otherwise have had the audacity to undertake this work during his lifetime. It is a pity therefore that he subsequently made it clear that he did not wish to be associated with the production of this book and that he would have preferred to have written his life story himself. So be it: I like to think that I have done justice to him. It will of course be the critics and the public who decide whether I have succeeded.

Michael Crouch

INTRODUCTION

T. A. G. Hungerford the Author

Fifty years ago, the literary focus on Hungerford, as one of Australia's most promising writers of contemporary fiction, followed publication of *The Ridge and the River* and his three other novels. The latter were never as highly regarded as they might have been by other than the literary cognoscenti, and thereafter Hungerford was seen primarily as a writer of short stories. It is indeed possible that history will remember him only for the one novel, *The Ridge and the River*. His peripatetic lifestyle certainly did not help him to establish a firm base as a writer: he did not settle after the war, going straight from Bougainville to Japan, returning to Canberra to work as a journalist, then to New York and Western Australia, with an interlude in Macau. He really focused on writing full-time only in the mid-1970s. The reading public having lost touch with him after the early 1960s, his reputation rested mainly with his fellow writers, who still recognise his talent to craft and shape sentences.

When Hungerford has something of substance to write about, either from his imagination or, in particular, drawing on his life experiences, he is very good. His first four novels were based vividly on his life, with an emphasis on creative imagination. His autobiographical trilogy *Straightshooter* — comprising *Stories from*

Suburban Road, A Knockabout with a Slouch Hat and *Red Rover All Over* — demonstrates supreme confidence in relating how it was.

It was during World War II that Hungerford started to establish a useful reputation, as a short-story writer and almost exclusively in *The Bulletin* magazine, a primary mark of writing excellence in Australia at the time. He had started to buy *The Bulletin* when he thought he would be a writer, and took out a subscription in 1938 at the age of 23. His first short story, 'Visit to the Lutts', appeared in 1942 and was followed by others for *The Bulletin* that, alas, have been lost to sight, although most of his titles are listed in appendix 2 of this book. While working at the Australian War Memorial a number of his stories appeared in War Memorial publications.

The confidence he acquired from the acceptance of his short stories encouraged him with his first novel, based on his experiences with the Allied occupation forces in Japan from 1946 to 1947. His time in Japan had convinced him that if ever he were to write a novel, the Japanese experience would provide the subject. Someone at the Australian War Memorial had put him in touch with Beatrice Davis, the senior editor at Angus & Robertson, the largest Australian publisher of the 1950s, who would become his mentor. She encouraged him to submit his first full-length manuscript. Hungerford was always grateful to Davis for her help and encouragement. She had told him that their publication program was full for that year, 1949, but advised him to submit *Sowers of the Wind* for the *Sydney Morning Herald* Literary Award, which, much to his surprise, he won. But this first novel was published only in 1954, after Angus & Robertson had released the two novels he wrote subsequently, the famous *The Ridge and the River* (1952) and *Riverslake* (1953), which was published by Angus & Robertson without the formality of a contract.[1]

> Perhaps I discourage easily, but in the three years I had been writing novels, I'd had three accepted and none

published. I'd made the huge sum of fifteen hundred pounds (less tax of course and provisional tax) from my *Herald* prizes. It was not the most promising opener for a long and stable literary career, so when the opportunity came I turned my back on Australian literature. For the time being anyway.[2]

As the title of his first novel *Sowers of the Wind*[3] suggests, Hungerford took a dim view of what eventuated under the Allied occupation of Japan. He felt that the abusive treatment meted out by relatively few occupation troops would provide the basis for another war later on. The Japanese would remember it. That primary motivation for writing his first full-length book is a reminder that Tom Hungerford has always possessed a strong streak of sympathy for the underdog struggling against society's prejudices. This was also to be demonstrated in his third novel, *Riverslake*, an account of life in Canberra's work-camps for displaced persons from Europe.

Hungerford's role while working as literary editor at the Australian War Memorial from 1947 to 1948 was to compile the yearly editions of *As You Were*, a compendium of poetry, articles, short stories and personal experiences, sent in by servicemen and women. This was something he loved doing: editing, and rewriting where necessary. He was also a contributor: 'Splash of Scarlet',[4] 'The Best Boxer' and 'The Nun's Patrol' he thought were among his best short stories ever.

As soon as *Sowers of the Wind* was out of the way, Hungerford was looking for another subject: inevitably it was to focus on his war experiences. He started to draft a novel about fighting in the islands that went through a number of metamorphoses, with what he subsequently recognised as 'the silliest of ideas'. After all, he was just starting out as a novelist. Finally, after three complete drafts, the manuscript was ready to be submitted to Angus & Robertson. *The Ridge and the River* was published in 1952, and has since gone into many editions. He received the *Sydney Morning Herald* Literary Award again and was also awarded the Crouch Gold Medal.[5] Hungerford was interviewed by a journalist from *The Bulletin*, who asked the author why he had written it. He wanted to write about the war, of course. Off the top of his head he said he would like to feel that if in 4,000 years time someone were to dig up the ruins of our civilisation, they might find a copy of this book and read it. They would know exactly how Australian troops had lived and fought in the jungles in the 1940s.[6]

It was the same motivation fifty years later, when he prepared his script for the ABC's *Radio Eye*, 'The Ambush',[7] which described the almost-choreographed preparation for a typical operation in the jungle against the Japanese. He wanted to put into perspective a patrol in which a very diverse group of men had taken part, including incorporation of one aspect of the ugly on-going anti-Aboriginal sentiments of white Australians. Hungerford, with his innate sympathy for the underclass dating back to his childhood, and exacerbated by his experiences in the Northern Territory with Aborigines, included a character of Aboriginal descent in the patrol group. He told the story of how one part-Aboriginal man fared, someone with a mighty chip on his shoulder. This scenario was not entirely fictitious. There was one such person in Hungerford's squadron, but no one knew—except for Hungerford—that the man was from Queensland, and because he was believed to be South American, none of his mates cared: the man was reckoned to be a good bloke.

Hungerford's post-war sojourn in Canberra coincided with the flood of European displaced persons into Australia, who were contracted to work for two years, mainly on heavy construction schemes, as a prelude to being offered Australian residency. In Canberra, after the Australian War Memorial, he went to work at Eastlake, the displaced persons' camp, which housed the explosive mixture of New Australians and itinerant white Australians. There he wrote his third novel, *Riverslake*, the name taken from the two work hostels in Canberra, Riverside and Eastlake. He wanted to expose the xenophobia that existed in migrant camps — the hatred of certain Australians for the post-war refugees — who in turn were amazed by it and could not understand why they were being treated as subhuman.

After he left Canberra, Hungerford's writings from home came to a virtual halt while he was busy travelling and writing for the Australian News and Information Bureau (ANIB). He managed a few short stories, generally unpublished. When he went to the Antarctic in 1954 he was asked why he did not write a novel based on his experiences there. His response was negative: anyone who travels to the Antarctic writes about it. Besides, he felt he could only have produced another group characterisation — a 'Ridge-and-the-River-on-ice', as it were — and he was never a writer of travel books.[8] However, a detailed account of his Antarctic adventures appears in *The Land Beyond the Ice*.[9]

When he was posted to New York in 1957 Hungerford wanted to write his fourth novel. He found his theme through meeting the Australian boxer Tony Madigan there. *Shake the Golden Bough* was partly an attempt to put in focus the post-war generation of young Australians who passed through his office, the predecessors of today's backpackers. Hungerford saw them as antipodean locusts, expecting people to put them up, drive them around and feed them. Tony Madigan himself, however, had some admirable qualities. He was hardworking, ambitious and good company. He and Hungerford developed a strong friendship that still endures.[10]

Hungerford also wanted to write about New York, to describe what it was like to live there, and to discuss the black and white confrontation that was looming. Certainly, if *Shake the Golden Bough* reflects his actual experiences in New York, it is a valuable accessory to his life story.

In the intervening period, he was busy with the ANIB, producing numerous articles for them and later working for the

Western Australian Government from 1971 to 1975. In Perth, he was prominent in writers' circles, sometimes perhaps rather a grand figure, held in some awe by fellow journalists and his younger peers. He had joined the ranks of such luminaries as John K. Ewers, Kenneth Seaforth Mackenzie, Dorothy Hewett, Katharine Susannah Prichard, Mary Durack and Henrietta Drake-Brockman. He still found time to write some short stories, one of which, 'The Voyager', won the Hackett Short Story award in 1961. In 1969 there was *A Million Square*, in conjunction with the celebrated photographer of landscapes from the air, Richard Woldendorp.

During his year in Macau Hungerford was writing articles that he sold to the *South China Morning Post*. While he was there he also compiled a travel book called *Stop-over in Macau*, which he stills think is very good, but he could not place it anywhere, the likely reaction of publishers then being: 'Macau? Where's Macau?' He had also written *Code Word Macau*, making use of his intimate knowledge of the place, and was shocked at the time when he could not find a publisher for it. The story is lightweight. The leading character is an Australian diplomat who is sent to the wrong place. He is supposed to go to Seoul, Korea, and instead is posted to an imaginary place called Saiul. (*Saiul* incidentally is Kanaka for 'vegetable'.)

In 1972 Hungerford wrote a radio play, *Help Me Cut Up a Cat*, and in 1976 there was another radio play, *Looking After Bert*. From the mid-1970s until the late 1980s he was to produce his famous *Stories from Suburban Road* and its companion volumes, to critical acclaim. It was interesting in view of all this success that Hungerford was to make a perhaps invidious comparison of *Stories from Suburban Road* with Albert Facey's *A Fortunate Life*. There was a touch of envy in his ungenerous remark at the runaway triumph of the latter: 'The big thing I had against *A Fortunate Life* — he was successful every time and I thought "Stuff you!" — I couldn't stand him because I have failed so many times — everyone fails so many times.'[11] Perhaps he was also referring to the actual events in *A Fortunate Life* but, if so, his own life is also a story of triumph over the adversities of the time, and Facey's life was by no means plain sailing. If Hungerford was referring to his own publishing fortunes, then certainly he had deserved better with three of the four novels written post-war. He has had similar complaints about Fremantle Arts Centre Press, his relationship with the latter having varied from cordial to cool. Some of his material has been rejected over the years.

Hungerford has never stopped writing. In 1989 Veritas Press, at his own expense, published his *Swagbelly Birdsnatcher and the Prince of Siam*. Swagbelly—an ordinary sort of cat—is dumped in the bush as a kitten. At the house up the hill, there is a splendid Siamese called the Prince of Siam living with a very rich family. The story reflects Hungerford's love of the Australian bush, and the little creatures living in it are very successfully depicted for the reader. One interesting feature is that the kookaburra (a feral species, imported from the eastern states), which has been so enjoyed by many Western Australians and visitors from overseas, is correctly described as a rapacious killer of nestlings. Kookaburras have no natural enemies in Western Australia. Hungerford's use of Australian slang again is interesting, where he has the animals conversing together. It is presumably based on the idiom of his childhood, since much of the phrasing is seldom used today. Rhyming couplets incorporating wise old sayings are also a feature. There is one problem regarding the audience at which the book is aimed. Perhaps it is an older child's book, the text being difficult for young children, although the theme appeals to the young. An unidentified reviewer in Perth's *Sunday Times* commented that, like youth, some books are wasted. Hungerford's descriptive style is so rich that 'you are almost in there with the furry ones'.

Also in 1989 a selection of his short stories were published in an FACP collection, edited by Peter Cowan who, without prior reference to the author, selected the stories and sent him the proofs to edit. Hungerford liked nothing about the way the publishing exercise was conducted; nor did he approve of the title or the cover, but perhaps that is the price of a writer becoming in effect a 'national property'.

In the late 1980s a local poet and writer, Bryn Griffiths, had told Hungerford that he was starting up a small publishing house in the West. He asked the author if he could open his account with *Code Word Macau*. Hungerford had a high regard for Griffiths: if Hungerford had been a young man battling for money he would not have considered Griffiths but, in keeping with his well-deserved reputation for helping his fellow writers and publishers, he wanted to support this new venture. Who knows? It might succeed. He even became a director. Platypus Press published *Code Word Macau* in 1991, but the author made nothing out of it. The book was reviewed by David Lawrence for the *West Australian*.[12] Lawrence, while praising the novel in general terms, was critical of what he saw as Hungerford's 'rampantly sexist and blatantly patriarchal' tone. Lawrence speculated as to whether Hungerford actually saw women like this or whether he wanted the reader to see women in this way. He felt it was an antiquated approach that tended to discriminate against the book's better aspects, which included a climax that lifted the book out of its 'plod' and revived an excitement in the reader. What a shame it was, he concluded, that a man of Hungerford's literary culture had not moved into thriller writing before.

Since then Hungerford has considered using an on-line publisher to handle two more manuscripts, but no distribution could be arranged, so this ambition has withered (although he was still thinking seriously of this approach a couple of years later). In the meantime, he was busy with various other writing initiatives in the 1990s that included editing *Tall Stories: An Anecdotal History of Guildford Grammar School 1896–1996*. Always willing to help out when approached, he had agreed on a purely nominal fee and found himself out of pocket as a result. This venture left a sour taste; after the archivist died, he didn't hear from the school again or receive a copy of the book. He ghosted for a friend *Thine is the Earth* and *The Forgotten Pioneers*, for which he received no monetary recompense or acknowledgement. He got far more pleasure out of three stage plays, the first written partly at the urging of his old friend Bill Warnock, *The Day It All Ended* (a sell-out when performed in Perth). *Prisoner of the Skin* was written for Maggie Anketell but has not been performed, and *Waiting for Andy* followed it.

Then there is his poetry. Tom Hungerford started to write poetry in his pre-teens, but unfortunately little of this very early output has survived.[13] In the last twenty years his poetry has been published at random in various anthologies but not so far as a collection. During his period in Canberra as president of the Canberra branch of the Fellowship of Australian Writers he had helped to edit anthologies of prose and poetry, in which some of his work was included. Poetry continues to be an interest of his, and in June 2003 Jacobyte Press in Adelaide accepted a collection of poetry and short stories for publication in 2005, with the working title of *Emu Dance*.

A film script of *The Ridge and the River* has been prepared, a project first undertaken in the 1970s in conjunction with Bill Warnock. It was a great disappointment that funding was found for *The Odd Angry Shot* yet the proposed Hungerford film missed out. If funding could be made available, the film would be his crowning triumph.

Hungerford has recently been working on three novellas, the manuscripts not too long for him to manage at his age. He confessed to 'writers' block' at one stage. Perhaps it is only natural that after sixty years of output, his brain — still as lucid as ever with his remarkable memories — should be pleading for a break from writing. But Tom Hungerford has had his old typewriter overhauled and is still hard at it. All strength to those aged fingers.

CHAPTER 1

The Brave Days of Old

〜〜〜

'This family, so distinguished in after times, and so fortunate in its intermarriages, with many heiresses.'[1] So wrote an early chronicler of the distinguished Hungerford family that took its name, like so many others, from the city, town or village from where it originated. In this case, the town of Hungerford in Berkshire, England, gave rise to a family known as de Hungerford. The names of various knights, abbots, priors and gentlemen of the de Hungerford family appear in historical records from the twelfth century onwards. But it was not until the late fourteenth century that Hungerfords raised the family to a position of immense wealth and influence. This was through a combination of notable service to the Crown, in peace and war, and a series of opportune and highly profitable marriages with wealthy heiresses of noble families.[2] There is an interesting contemporary portrait of a fighting Hungerford of the fourteenth century that suggests a strong genetic resemblance to at least one of his descendants who has taken a keen interest in the history of his forebears:

> The family crest is a garb of corn, two sickles alongside, surmounting a ducal coronet, and I used to wonder what the ducal coronet was about. I knew there were no dukes

in the family, but it appears that as a reward for captur-
ing this bloke, Sir John was allowed to assume the ducal
coronet, as part of his crest. At the right hand end, a little
figure hanging on a hangman's rope, a gibbet, represented
the Duke, but he wasn't hanged. That stayed there until
my great-grandfather's time.[3]

Apparently the award of the ducal coronet remains a family
fable; it has never been verified, according to the Hungerford family
historian in England. Tom Hungerford's light-hearted and sometimes inaccurate commentary on his antecedents, most of which
is not reproduced here, is a reminder that with his autobiographical trilogy beginning with *Stories from Suburban Road*, and with
Hungerford's quotations in this narrative, there is usually a fictional
element, however much he purports to recount what actually happened. There is nothing wrong with this, of course. The reader
should remember Dr Johnson's comment:

> Above all biography gives pleasure by satisfying curiosity
> and telling good stories. 'No species of writing seems more
> worthy of cultivation of biography, since none can be more
> delightful or more useful, none can more certainly enchain
> the heart by irresistible interest, or more widely diffuse
> instruction to every diversity of condition.'[4]

The Hungerford lineage gradually died out over the centuries,
as often occurred with the great families of England. A collateral
line of the Hungerfords settled in Ireland in the seventeenth century
and preserved the family name that was eventually to take root in
Australia. The Irish connection was due undoubtedly to the English
policy of establishing Protestant families in Ireland, to counter
what English rulers saw as a predominantly Catholic threat from
that unhappy country. The Hungerfords themselves were known

for humane treatment of the locals, by contrast with other great landowners, such as the Binghams (the Earls of Lucan), who were notorious during the Potato Famines of the 1840s for wholesale evictions of starving peasantry. Captain Thomas Hungerford of Rathbarry, who died in 1680, had purchased — rather than just seizing — two estates in County Cork by the mid-1660s. His property was chiefly divided between two of his three surviving sons, Richard Hungerford 'of Foxhall and the Island' (Inchodoney) and Thomas Hungerford of Cahermore. Their descendants retained both properties until the 1920s when, owing to the creation of the Irish Free State, the reapportionment of land to tenants, and the mass emigration of the surviving male heirs, the lands passed out of the family. The Cahermore house was sold to an Irishman in 1921, whereupon the IRA promptly burned it down.[5]

However, the Hungerfords had been looking for other countries in which to make a living many years before 'the Troubles'.[6] Australia was an obvious destination. Captain Emmanuel Hungerford of 'the Island Hungerfords' line, a military man, had emigrated to New South Wales in 1828. His numerous progeny established properties that still exist in the Richmond district of the Blue Mountains and up the North Coast of New South Wales. In 1867 Arthur Townsend Hungerford, Tom Hungerford's father, was born in Ireland. He trained as a medical student in Dublin and was halfway through a medical degree in Cork when he was diagnosed as 'going into a decline', which in those days probably meant contracting tuberculosis. There was only one thing for it: to send the young man to the pure air of the colonies.

In about 1882 Arthur Hungerford was shipped out to a distant cousin in Queensland to recuperate in sunshine and fresh air, with the intention of eventually resuming his medical studies. He mostly recovered his health, but he never returned to Ireland because he suffered agonies of seasickness and could not face the return voyage. Four of his five brothers also emigrated, together with a sister. They left behind their redoubtable mother, a 'stiff-backed old aristocrat', Mary Hungerford, née Boone Cowper. The original Boone was that Daniel Boone who was a scout in the American Civil War.

Arthur Hungerford, her favourite son, this hitherto enfeebled medical student, appeared to thrive in Australia. There is no information on what then happened to him, other than that he first became a jackaroo in Queensland working with cattle on a relative's pastoral spread. This led to an epic feat, on a par with that of the famous Durack family, who took stock overland from New South Wales around the top of Australia to the Kimberley region of Western Australia. Arthur Hungerford drove cattle across the continent from the eastern seaboard to Western Australia. Years later, his son Tom as a young boy happened to say to his father: 'You should have seen the pelicans over the river today!'

His father replied: 'You've never seen pelicans. When I was on the Cooper and Diamantina, you couldn't see the sky for birds. I've seen the Cooper twenty miles wide and running.'

On another occasion the boy and his father were out in the bush, cutting timber for stove wood, and Tom said: 'Dad, I'm thirsty.'

'You don't know what it is to be thirsty. You've never been thirsty until you've been droving cattle and you come towards a water hole, they smell it and they gallop into the waterhole, and by the time you get to it, they've piddled in the water. You get down and drink it.'[7]

According to his son, Arthur Hungerford would have arrived somewhere in Western Australia's Murchison or Gascoyne regions. He was joined there by Dixie Clement, who later became Dr Dixie Clement, the doyen of women's doctors in Perth for many years.[8] The Clement estate ran alongside the Hungerford estate in Ireland, and Dixie had been sent out to Australia when Arthur Hungerford was established, to be looked after until he found his feet. They went gold-mining together and discovered a large low-grade body called the Landsfield in the Pilbara, which they sold for £10,000. Arthur Hungerford then became a cameleer and ran a firm, Hungerford & Kirkpatrick, to supply the early settlements in the goldfields. Theirs was an essential service. Their biggest camel load was a great boiler to be used in the gold-smelting process, which was carried from Lake Way, now Wiluna, to Day Dawn in the Murchison.

While the erstwhile medical student was running his camel teams, a recently widowed woman from Busselton, Mrs Nellie Hedley, and her five children, in company with a friend and her two children, were making their way by rail to Nannine in the Murchison and stage coach to Condon Creek,[9] east-northeast of Port Hedland. Until the latter was developed, the pastoral and mining enterprises in the northern Pilbara were supplied through Condon, which had also been an important link in the telegraph around Australia. Supplies were brought in and wool was sent out by sea. In the 1890s it boasted 200 inhabitants, a pub, store and its own race day.[10] Its importance declined once Port Hedland opened for sea traffic, and it was in decline when the Hedleys wearily climbed out of their coach. Condon is now abandoned.

The 2,000-kilometre journey to Condon was a mammoth expedition overland for a struggling widow, probably still clothed in the ornate mourning dress of the early 1900s, and encumbered by small children. The late Mr Hedley had been behind the bar of his hotel in Busselton in 1905. He was grossly overweight, and one hot day he had a big lunch and then expired, leaving his wife and children with about £1,200. Little else is known of the Hedley family, other than that his English-born widow was no stranger to the northwest, the Hedleys having been married in the 1880s at Hall's Creek, a dusty settlement in the eastern Kimberleys, the site of the earliest gold rush in Western Australia. Later, she had helped to run a hotel with her husband at Roebourne, an early centre for the infant northwest pastoral industry, south of Port Hedland.[11]

Although she would have coped with the dust, the jolting and the demands of bored children, her health suffered.

At the time, that ambitious attempt to keep Australia's major feral scourge out of settled farming and pastoral areas — the rabbit-proof fence — was under construction. The rabbit plague in the eastern states was steadily encroaching on Western Australia, and Condon was the western entry for material to be hauled to the northern sector of the fence. There was no deep water in Condon Creek, so the ships used to offload onto lighters that came alongside the little wharf. Otherwise the ships would have been left high and dry during low tide. Goods were laboriously manhandled on and off the ship. At the settlement there was still a hardware depot, the telegraph station and a boarding house, which was for men working on the rabbit-proof fence and in need of a break from their work. Mrs Hedley took over the boarding house, helped by her friend and the older children, the eldest of whom, Minnie, was about 17.

It was not a successful venture.[12] Mrs Hedley died within a year of arrival, and when Arthur Hungerford with his camel team came into the settlement to load materials for the fence, he was confronted with the news that the boarding house proprietress had succumbed. It happened that Hungerford was also a justice of the peace and hence was required to officiate at the burial. From the other side of the grave he observed a nubile young woman, Minnie Hedley. It appears to have been love at first sight on his part and, after he had courted Minnie for the next few years, they were married in Busselton on 8 April 1910. They returned to Nannine, where Arthur Hungerford was based, then a thriving centre and now another ghost settlement in the Murchison, where the first two of their four children, Mick and Peg, were born.

Arthur Hungerford was twenty years older than his bride, and news of the union had been received with dismay in Ireland, where the redoubtable matriarch wrote in her beautiful, strong and idiosyncratic Gothic handwriting to another son: 'To think that Arthur, the flower of my flock, wrecked himself by marrying a servant!'

Now that the responsibilities of marriage were his principal preoccupation, Arthur Hungerford was forced to consider a gentler way of life. The enormous distances between the remote mining settlements and the coast, the baking heat of the summers and the interludes of howling cyclonic winds followed by torrential rains were not suitable conditions for a young wife and her babies. The Outback was actually dangerous for small children, as the lines of pathetic headstones in old northwest cemeteries today bear mute testimony: dysentery, typhoid, enteric fever, diphtheria…

Arthur Hungerford put the arduous frontier life behind him, sold his camel teams and bought into a choice farming property, Cloverdale, at Beverley in the Western Australian wheat belt, today two hours drive from Perth. This area had been cleared for farming only sixty years earlier and was regarded as prime land, with a reliable rainfall. Unluckily for Arthur, his venture into farming coincided with the period of the great drought in 1911. He carried one other great handicap: he had no head for business.

> He had a deal with the bloke he bought it off. He had a note 'To Pay', and he said to the farmer, 'Look, I can pay you this, but supposing I put another crop in and pay you when the crop comes off…?' The bloke said, 'Oh, fine,' and my poor, silly father, who was like this all his bloody life — he got done so often — did not get anything on paper. It was a gentlemen's agreement, and he was a gentleman. When the note came due, the farmer said, 'Where's the dough?' He couldn't do it now, and my father just walked off the property. The farmer got it.[13]

Arthur Hungerford went to live in what is now South Perth, and his mother in Ireland sent out enough money to set him up in a carrying business and later in a shop. However, Arthur was not bred for a life in trade. In spite of his earlier heroic exploits as a drover, he was defeated by life's challenges. His health was never good; he continued to suffer from a severe 'pneumonic problem for the rest of his life', according to his son. The clothesline in the back garden always carried the red flannel belts Minnie used to make for him, to be strapped around his kidneys, stitched backwards and forwards, about six inches wide and very thick — and purgatory in the summer months. He was eventually forced to look elsewhere to earn his living.

When he had first visited Perth as a good-looking and affluent young man, after successfully droving his cattle from New South Wales, Arthur Hungerford had fitted easily into Perth society. He used to attend what he termed 'soirées' at Government House and, as a result of these social gatherings, he had made some useful contacts. Government appointments in those days generally depended on whom you knew and, after his unsuccessful ventures in South Perth, someone — probably A. O. Neville, the Chief Protector of Aborigines[14] — offered him the position of 'Protector of Aborigines' at Jigalong in the northwest, which is still an Aboriginal settlement today. The Aborigines were already a dispossessed people, having been forced from their ancestral lands and ravaged by the breakdown of their traditional culture and the diseases of the white man. For £3 10s a week Arthur Hungerford ministered to their needs, until he reached retiring age.

His was a fascinating but sad life. He did not long survive Minnie's death in 1938, as will be related later. Mollie Hungerford, his daughter-in-law, the wife of their eldest son Mick, remembered the old gentleman from when she met him shortly before his death in 1939. She was so taken by the striking similarity of the face on a German jug of the time to her father-in-law's that she saved to buy the expensive jug. Apart from the pipe (Arthur Hungerford neither smoke nor drank) and a different moustache, it was him. It still provides an affectionate memory of the old man.[15]

CHAPTER 2

Halcyon Youth

The Hungerfords lived at the less fashionable end of South Perth, and the disparity between the husband and wife's social backgrounds appears to have been of little importance in the simple suburban society of post-colonial Perth. Arthur Hungerford endeavoured to keep the family supplied, and Minnie Hungerford was the quintessential homemaker. Together, they provided a sound and happy foundation for the upbringing of the young Tom Hungerford, one to which he was to return constantly in his later writings. Minnie's sound common sense was the cornerstone of his existence and, together with the mixture of genes inherited from the Hungerford forebears, it was to contribute to the development of a colourful, at times dogmatic and difficult, but straightforward and hardworking individual, Tom Hungerford, who was to make a significant contribution as one of Australia's notable soldiers and writers of the twentieth century.

More than eighty years ago, South Perth was a bucolic suburb around the bend of the Swan River, with cows and horses, orchards and chook yards. It was a beautiful location in which to live and bring up children. Mill Point Road was then called Suburban Road. The name was changed to Mill Point Road apparently at the instigation of Lady Murdoch. It was just a gravel track lined

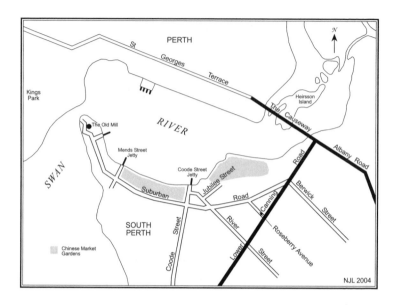

with great hunks of red gravel rolled down hard. The road was flanked on either side by eight or ten Moreton Bay figs, gum trees and lilly pillies.

There were local identities. A Mr Restin who had worked, it was said, as a gardener at Kew Gardens in London was in charge of the trees. He used to clip the fig-trees to a perfect umbrella shape, so that they looked like upturned bowls. Mr Reston invariably wore a collar and tie, a waistcoat and jodhpurs, leather leggings and boots, and an ordinary felt hat. The Roads Board, the precursor to the South Perth Council, employed him, and Arthur Hungerford was a member of the Roads Board. Another local identity was the grocer, Mr Faddy, who parted his hair straight down the middle. He had a neat little moustache, and always wore a round collar, tie, waistcoat and apron.

It was into this suburban normality during World War I, while the horrors of Gallipoli were erupting on the other side of the world, that Thomas Arthur Guy (Tom) Hungerford was born on

5 May 1915, his father's birthday. The arrival of the latest child was, as Tom Hungerford himself commented later, 'some bloody present' to a father already struggling to make a decent living, initially as a carrier, to support a wife and the three elder children. The father's horses were stabled in South Perth and at Nash Street in town by the railway crossing. The four big horses, Darky and Snow, Punch and Judy, pulled loads all around Perth and to Fremantle. But Arthur Hungerford could not make a success of his carrying business, and his mother later financed a shop for him, on the corner of what was then River Street and Suburban Road, now Douglas Avenue and Mill Point Road, just up from the Coode Street ferry. He had to sell the shop because there too he could not make a living, especially during the Depression when his customers were too poor to pay their debts. Hungerford spoke with feeling:

> My father was too old to go to the war. The only family member [who went to war] was my Uncle Tom, my mother's brother, who was very seriously wounded at Gallipoli, and apart from that we weren't in the war. As for what might have happened in South Perth, as part of the war, I was too young to know, but when I was about 10, leading into the Depression, [I met] this chap, father of one of my best friends. His name was Oscar. He was a German. I was playing up at Bobby's place one day, and we were in the kitchen. His father came in, he had a little corn sack and he tipped it out on the table. I remember quite plainly a cabbage, a piece of corn beef, which we often had at home — I recognised corn beef — half a piece of newspaper, some carrots and, I think, potatoes. He stood back and he said, 'That's what I went to the bloody war for.' I've never forgotten that.
>
> Then of course if only a few people had suffered in the Depression, you would have remembered it, but everyone was in the same boat. That's what I grew up in: everyone

had no dough. My father suffered particularly, running the shop and, being the sort of man my father was, he couldn't resist people having provisions without paying. My mother of course, not so much a harder heart, but she could see where it was going. She was very much against it, my father just giving stuff away and putting it down 'in the Book', which mostly meant it was never paid. In those days, every Saturday morning, one of my jobs was to go around to various people who owed my father money. I was 10 or 11, up to 15. I was just a child. Things were tough in the 1920s.

I still remember the humiliation of asking for this money and being told, 'I'm terribly sorry, but I can only give you sixpence.' That ate into my soul, which is why I determined early on that I would never be a poverty-stricken old man. I was determined by hook or by crook that I would be able to pay my way to the grave. Which is why I saved and invested a lot of money I wish now I had spent, because I live on the interest of my investments and I don't live on a pension! When things go bung my income is not influenced by the government as [is] a pension. That's the way I planned it.[1]

With the proceeds from the sale of the shop, Arthur Hungerford bought a little house in Jubilee Street, between Suburban Road and the river. Tom Hungerford was the last of the four children. (Mick was born in 1911; Peg in 1912 and the younger sister, Alice, who was also born in Perth, in 1913.) This was during the period in which his father was working all day with his horses, and that was why Arthur was not around on the two occasions when his younger son nearly died before he was five.

Tom's first brush with death was when he was rescued from drowning in the family horse-trough. He was not quite two years old. His mother told him later that she had been doing the washing. He was playing: he climbed up into the horse-trough and fell into it. His mother called for him and, hearing no reply, found the apparently lifeless infant, face down in the water. The small body, bloated and pale, hung limp in her arms, the skin ashen-grey. The hysterical woman gathered the wet bundle and ran to her neighbour, old Mrs Hollis. The two women lifted their skirts and rushed to the Hortons' corner store, which in 1917 was the only place with a telephone in that area.

> Mrs Hollis was still holding the body while the doctor was rung: the women were standing around saying, 'Oh, poor little soul!' and when the doctor arrived he asked urgently of Mrs Horton: 'Got any chooks?'
>
> 'Yes!'
>
> 'Get me a long feather!'
>
> Mrs Horton rushed out and found a feather, and the doctor stuck it down the boy's throat. He vomited up water, started to move and opened his eyes. He began to cry weakly. 'He's alive!'
>
> The child was taken back to his bed, very ill, and then to the Children's Hospital (which had been opened in 1909 and is now the Princess Margaret Hospital for Children). The near-drowning led to an abscess on the lung, where some of the dirty water had lodged. In hospital, he was laid on his front for three months, with tubes through his back. The doctors had removed part of one rib, and bound it with gold wire, but, even with the treatment, he contracted double pneumonia. The little boy nearly died.[2]

His survival was probably due as much to his mother's devotion as to the medical treatment of the time. His father used to buy 'a whole swag of half-grown chickens in the market', from which his mother killed two and cooked them each evening. After jellying them, she took them daily (with raw eggs she forced him to swallow) to the Children's Hospital at the corner of Thomas and Hay Streets in Subiaco. This was no easy journey. Cradling the boy's precious chicken jelly, she would walk down to the ferry in South Perth, cross the river and catch the tram into the centre of town, where she would connect with the Hay Street tram to the hospital. She returned by the same route and maintained this routine for three months, in between looking after the other three children.

The doctor told Mrs Hungerford that her devotion pulled the boy through, but within a year or two he caught diphtheria, another frightening killer of those times. Diphtheria is an acute infectious disease caused by a bacterium that affects the upper respiratory tract and very occasionally the skin. Virulent strains can damage heart and nervous tissues, and swelling of the throat tissues leads to breathing difficulties. Diphtheria is now rare in Western countries, but in those days about 5 to 10 per cent of diphtheria cases died. This time Tom was nursed at home, but his condition deteriorated so badly that his mother called for the doctor. 'He took one look and said: "Hospital!"

' "Can I wait until Mr Hungerford comes home?"

' "No, he may not get to hospital alive anyway!" '[3]

Once again he was rushed to hospital, where he was put into a steam cot, surrounded by heavy arc lights and jets of steam to melt the mucous blocking his throat. His first real memory is of staring up at the glaring light. And, of course, he survived to live what has now become the fabled childhood of *Stories from Suburban Road*.

There are other more endearing, more tender memories from those early days. As a tiny child Tom used to be playing at the bottom of the garden at the back of the yard, with the cows or the ducks, and suddenly he would think, 'Where's Mum?' He would run up to the house and throw himself at her, and she would cuddle him. He could smell his mother — the womanly sweat wafting from her dress—and the little boy would know that she was his refuge. Minnie Hungerford was also a good neighbour, always doing something for somebody. She used to sew. Later in his life, when the children were going to a party, to a ball or to a school function, 'Her neighbours would call, to ask, "Mrs Hungerford, how do I do this?"' His mother had a sewing machine: '"Oh, I'll run it up." It was a treadle machine and I loved watching her work.'[4] She used to make most of her own clothes and beautiful garments for Tom's sisters, but not for him. He generally inherited his elder brother Mick's hand-me-downs, a sensible economy in those early days of penury.

Mrs Hungerford was not the sort of mother who mollycoddled her children. She might have been their backstop, but she was usually the one who disciplined them. As a small boy, Tom was much addicted to boiled lollies (brightly coloured hunks of solid sugar), and he was thrashed over them once, as were his two sisters. His mother had a jar of the boiled lollies on the shelf in the kitchen.

She was going out, to visit her great friend Mrs Wood. She said, 'Now, don't touch the boiled lollies while I'm out.' Of course, as soon as her back was turned, my eldest sister Peg—she was the biggest—climbed up on a chair. We all gorged ourselves and put them back. When Mother returned home, she said: 'Have you touched the boiled lollies?'

'Oh no, Mum!'

'But you have! I counted them before I went out.'

'Oh…'

She had not, of course. 'Go to your room.'

It was the room I shared with my brother. I felt the boiled lollies were worth it. She had not hurt me—much.[5]

He first came to know his father as the tall, good-looking, quiet but friendly man who was always busy with the horses that heaved the large carts carrying goods around Perth. The boy knew his father went to something he thought he heard referred to as the 'Rose' Board: ' "Where's Dad?"

' "He's down at the 'Rose' Board."

' "Oh…?" I could visualise my father sitting at a table covered with bowls of roses. It was somehow part of how I saw my father, a gentle man.'[6]

But Dad was also someone who physically chastised him, when Tom was still younger than five. There was a little girl visiting the Hungerfords with her mother, who had recently been on a holiday to a farm. She was demure, pretty and dressed for the visit, all bows and pinafore. The little girl was a show-off, and she was happily telling the boy how the kangaroos jumped and how she was the only one to have seen them. The boy felt a childish rage welling up. Who did she think she was? He was so jealous of her experiences that he suddenly pushed her off the veranda, which was about a metre off the ground, into the rose bushes along the front of the veranda. There were shrill screams as the visitor was rescued, scoured by the bushes, red in the face with fury and embarrassment. His father, also embarrassed by this display of inhospitable behaviour, put the small boy across his knee. The miscreant's behind was well and truly smacked. The indignity of it![7]

Tom Hungerford's mother was a good cook, but not of fancy dishes. The family ate well of good solid stews, bakes and roasts, rice puddings and custards. They had a little Jersey cow. Tom would stomp down to the shed when his parents would be milking. His mother used the excess milk to make bowls of junket, with nutmeg sprinkled over. (Tom attributes to his healthy boyhood to these bowls of junket.) If he had been good, he was allowed to scrape the nutmeg onto the junket. His mother used to put the milk in a shallow settling pan, on the back of the wood stove—in the morning, the cream had risen to the top. It was a thick, clotted cream, spooned onto the breakfast porridge. In spite of these delights, the children hated porridge, all excepting Tom's brother

Mick, who would 'stuff it in'. Lunch was usually what they used to call 'a piece': bread-and-butter and jam, or bread-and-butter with something else homemade. They ate dripping that was kept in the brown earthenware crock, and the delicious taste lingered with Hungerford more than eighty years later. The best of it sealed at the bottom, and when he was older and returning home from school, there it was: a piece of bread and dripping with salt and pepper. 'And there were my sisters complaining, "Mum! Tom — he's taken all the brown!"'[8]

His brother was (Mick) Harry Hedley Hungerford, born in 1911. Tom hardly saw Mick, except at mealtimes. Looking back, the younger brother felt he barely knew the older boy, and for much of his early life he envied, even disliked, Mick. Here was he, Tom: fat, red-haired, freckle-faced, who could do nothing well except write poetry and who was always reading. This was of course just sibling rivalry, but the envy persisted for many years. Mick was good at everything and a fine swimmer (although the younger brother was later to become a better swimmer than the older boy), and on one of the few occasions they were together, the small boy learnt to swim in the river with just Mick present.

His elder sister Mary Lorna, called Peg, was born in 1912. The other sister, Alice, was born in 1913 and was the beauty of the family, a mathematician and a pianist. (She never married and died of rheumatic fever in 1943.) In the warm weather the four children slept on the side veranda, the two sisters in one bed and the boys in another double bed.

Outside there were the animals. 'My mother would say: "Look, there's chickens!"

'"Ah, little chickens!"

There was a calf. "Where did the calf come from?"

'"Well...during the night the cow dug a hole and found the calf."

'"Oh...?"'[9]

The family also kept a horse that Arthur Hungerford rode. There was a big peppercorn tree in the horse yard, and it was a constant delight to play under it in cubby houses and in a tree house up above. When he was old enough, Tom took over from Mick the feeding of the horse and cow in the morning, fetching their bran and chaff, mixing them in a can and taking it into the stable. He might have to harness the horse and put it into the cart, feed the chickens and bring up sufficient wood for the stove. Firewood was the great source of fuel, and everyone had wood fires then. If he were asked to, he would water the garden with a hose for his mother. Every now and then, he would rake up the back yard to ensure that there was no rubbish lying about. He used to have to do the washing and drying up. Often, he had to wash and polish the linoleum in the bedroom he shared with his brother, something Tom thought his elder brother was never asked to do. There was a big old-fashioned tin trunk, appropriately called 'the Trunk', in which his mother used to keep the sheets, which his father had probably brought out from Ireland.

> One day my mother said: 'Did you do under the trunk?'
> 'No, Mum.' I was amazed that she would suggest it. She was anything but amazed and her reply was anything but casual. 'You dirty little sweep!' It was a favourite term with her. Maybe she'd been called 'little sweep' in her own childhood. 'I'd rather you were to *clean under the trunk* than *any other part of the room!*'[10]

She was like that. There was also the copper to clean out, and the firebox under it. He used to help his mother with the laundry by turning the mangle.

But there was another really deprived world outside Mrs Hungerford's carefully managed household. The young boy Tom became conscious of Aborigines at an early age. There were families or groups, whom they used to call 'the Blackies', walking along Suburban Road, past their house.

> The males would call, 'Praap, praap!' ('Prop, prop!') The only thing these Aborigines could do for their subsistence was 'go bush' and cut long, slender boughs, with a fork at the top, for holding up the clothes lines, wires strung across the yard. These people had a hopeless, dreadful look and their children were skinny and raggedy.[11]

From those first experiences Hungerford was to develop a strong conscience with regard to Aborigines, which deepened after his first-hand experience, much later in his life, working with them in the Northern Territory and learning how they were treated in northern New South Wales.

Then there were the Chinese market gardens that flourished in Perth, both north and south of the river. Although the Chinese were not perceived to be a real part of the community, in fact there was a good deal of interaction between them and the Europeans. The gardens extended along the entire south bank of the river, except for a narrow band of swamp on the edge of the river. They started on the east side of Mends Street jetty along the riverbank as far as Coode Street. There was a break where Richardson Park is now, and the gardens went as far as Ellen Street in Victoria Park, nearly up to Berwick Street. They were carefully cultivated with every type of vegetable and often fertilised with human waste, which worried some in the European community at the time.

> The warm humid smell of recently watered cauliflower and cabbage drifted up to me with the huge night-flying moths...the dark brown ribbon of riverside swamp squawked and hooted with the noise of birds settling

down for the night…Beyond the swamp the slate-grey
river stretched…away to the east. The hills were no more
than flecked with yellow chips of light, a pale blue line
against the darker blue of the sky.[12]

There would have been fifty or sixty Chinese gardeners in
South Perth. The Hungerford children practically lived with them.
The Chinese had no children, which was why they were so kind
to the youngsters. They were indentured (often to rich merchants
back in China, who subsidised the workers in Perth in return for a
proportion of their earnings). By contrast, in North Perth there was
a Chinese greengrocer who brought his wife out with him to Perth
and, unusually for the Chinese, he stayed, as did his children.[13] In
South Perth if one gardener died, someone, usually a young man,
arrived from China to take his place on the allotments. In the
vegetable gardens, they had lean-to tin shacks, where they did their
cooking and their eating, with a little annex in which there was a
bed. They were up on the high ground, out of reach of any possible
flooding. There was only one flood in Tom Hungerford's childhood,
which submerged the gardens in 1926.

In his adopted garden there were two Chinese, Ah Kim
and Ah Fat, who never minded the children catching their goldfish
out of the pool. The boy helped them pull their onions and pick
the tomatoes. When the tomato season was over, Tom would go
down with what his mother called her 'preserving pan' and fill it
with picked tomatoes, green and ripe, still on the bushes that were
going to be pulled up. Then she made pickles and other preserved
delicacies. For sixpence, Tom would pull out a cauliflower, or cab-
bages, carrots and all sorts of other vegetables, straight out of the
ground. It was a long association for him, from his first memories
of his two friends until the late 1960s, 'when the last of them went
back to China, a dear old man called Wong Chu. He used to say:
"I bling you plesent flom China!" '[14]

On his return from the homeland, the old man brought out six exquisite rice-paper kites in green and red. They were so light that they floated off. Hungerford gave them to various friends of his and regretted never having kept one. By that time the authorities had resumed all the gardens and made a park by the river, which he saw as a poor substitute for a reservoir of fresh vegetables right at the city's door. Wong Chu was by then living at the end of Jubilee Street, with his old horse.

> He used to pass me in Jubilee Street and if the latter was out in the front garden, the little old man would say: 'G'day! Velly nice day!'
>> 'Yeah, very nice day!'
>> 'Maybe lain! Ha Ha Ha!'
> It appalled me that when Wong Chu returned to China to die, the Australian Government apparently stopped his pension.[15]

When Tom was old enough, he had a tricycle. With two or three of his little mates also with tricycles, they would make their way to Roseberry Avenue on the heights of South Perth, only a rough gravel road, and they would speed down that hill on their trikes onto the main road. Luckily for them, in those days there was only about one car a day. As the youngest child at home, he led a solitary existence on the whole: his pleasures including bird-nesting and visiting Clontarf Swamp near Mount Henry and enjoying the wild orchids. Model soldiers were another craze, while his sisters used to get dolls. The boys shared a Meccano set, and that was practically the extent of their toys. Clothing made up the other presents for Christmas and birthdays, a mixture of utilitarianism and fun. It was the river, however, that provided the most enjoyment for the Hungerford children.

At that time in the Perth estuary there were five families on the south bank alone who made a living from fishing. The combined fishing families had an old house down by the river, quite close to the South Perth ferry. Hungerford as a boy went out with them sometimes and, when his mother wanted fish, they would often go down to the river and mainly catch mullet. If the fishing were close inshore, they would take the fish straight out of the net. Otherwise, Hubert Wood, one of the fishermen, would always have some fish at the house so, if his mother wanted some, she would visit the Woods, who lived just behind the Hungerfords. His mother loved oysters, and the river was also teeming with crabs.

In the summer, a couple of times a week after the evening meal (which they still called 'tea')—

> Someone would call, 'Anyone want to go crabbing?' We gathered our scoop nets and one or both of my sisters were dragooned into pulling the bag. We went through the Chinaman's garden, down to the river; we walked out a couple of hundred yards, to near the groyne where there was a shallow bank of seaweed, where the crabs nestled, or could be spotted on the open patches of clean sand.[16]

The river then was clear to the bottom and a veritable playground with swimming off the jetty and, when Tom was older, across the river.

His father had an old wind-up gramophone with a big horn, a constant joy to the boy, with the His Master's Voice dog on the label. When Tom was five years old, he loved that picture of the dog and used to look down the horn to see the tiny chink of light at the bottom. That is where the man sits and sings... The first piece of music he recalled hearing was the Intermezzo from *Cavalleria Rusticana*. It thrilled him, together with a recording of 'Over the Waves' under the title of 'Si Sobre los Olas'. His father also had several other minor classics among a stack of records, which the boy played constantly. That gave him his lasting love of music.

'Another favourite was *The Three Bears* with someone telling the story of the Three Bears, finishing with, "Goldilocks jumped out of the window and ran home! Good night, dears!" I played and replayed it, and every child who came to our place had to listen to *The Three Bears*.'[17]

The Old Mill in South Perth was already a wreck at that time but a favourite place to play. Tom had friends called Kingsbury who lived on the Point, so close to the water that he walked out of their front gate and onto their little beach, where the freeway is now. The children walked everywhere. With his friends he would make his way from his home to play round the Old Mill countless times. There was only one barber in South Perth, and the three of them would walk right down to Mends Street at Mill Point, have a haircut for sixpence and walk home again. Then there were picnics at Como and once the magic journey to Fremantle, when his father had a load to bring from Fremantle to South Perth, off the *Zeelandia* (later torpedoed in World War II). The journey was down what was then Fremantle Road, now Canning Highway. They alighted at the old hotel and walked up the slope, because the load of excited children was too much for the horses. And there — the wonder of Fremantle: going out on the wharf, and thrilling at the sea and the ships. Tom saw the sea again when he was about 10 and a great family friend, Miss Beatrice Cotton,[18] who drove her 'tiny canoe-shaped Citröen bugs, brilliant yellow with a bright fabric hood'[19] up and down Suburban Road, with her Irish terriers in the back, invited him to Cottesloe. It was another world to him. There he stood on a high table on Cottesloe beach and gazed out at the sea … it was magic.

His father's favourite pastime being reading, Tom Hungerford himself had started to read from the time the family moved from their first home to the shop. Someone had talked Arthur Hungerford into buying a collection of books, which he set up as a little lending library for threepence a book. It was in a corner of the shop, and the youngster used to sit on the floor under the shelves of books and become absorbed in reading. He did not care what he read. His early favourites were *Tarzan of the Apes* (which he read again much later while in the United States and was disappointed to think of it then as rubbish). There was *Nomads of the North*, which was set in Canada, and *Tiger Tim* and *Chums*, although his father disapproved of comics and pointed him towards books: 'Read that! Here's a good book...' His father was a great admirer of Zane Grey, with his yarns about the imaginary cowboys and the fictionalised Wild West. Arthur Hungerford loved Edgar Wallace stories, and he spoke to his son about literature, although neither of the parents ever read aloud to the children. Later there was *King Solomon's Mines* and Conan Doyle's Sherlock Holmes and, when he was far too young to really understand what he was reading, Tom ploughed through *The Cloister and the Hearth*.

When they were living in the big old house on the corner of what is now Douglas Avenue and Mill Point Road, he would sit on the tennis court waiting for his elder brother and sisters to come home from school. His two sisters and his mother wanted the girls to learn piano, so they went to St Joseph's Convent, South Perth, later St Columba Primary School. When aged five Tom Hungerford started at his sisters' school. They used to walk nearly two miles there and back.

> [Dr] Dixie Clement had said to my father, 'Arthur: don't send your kids to school in boots, in the winter. They'll sit there all day with wet boots on. Send them with bare feet. It might be cold but they'll be dry.' Otherwise, it was lace-up boots and best clothes when we went to town.[20]

The one item of clothing on which his mother insisted was his school hat. It was a big bone of contention because it was a 'fisher hat' with a brim and a flap down the back. When Tom was older, 12 or 13, he loathed it. Sometimes he used to climb a tree and put the hated hat in the fork on the way to school, and pick it up on the way home.

Initially, his schoolwork was simple. After St Columba, at South Perth Primary, he had to copy something out of a book, in his best writing. They had to learn poetry, too. The tuition in English was excellent, particularly when he was in his early teens.

> I had two or three teachers who used to provide a quote and say, 'Right, five hundred words on that.' They were known as compositions, on a topic such as 'The Storm', or 'A Battle'. The good ones were read out, and mine was always among them. It was the only thing I could do really well.[21]

He was already writing little plays and short stories and trying his hand at poetry.[22]

> I always had a fear of mathematics from the beginning of my school days when I was given little sums to do. This phobia really developed when I was about eight, and although I was a bright boy in a higher class, I was returned to a lower level, because of my inability to comprehend the simplest mathematical concept. That began my fear and horror of figures. Geometry was demonstrable, but algebra and trigonometry were completely beyond me. The trouble was that at the next lesson, everyone knew the first lesson except for me, so I went into the second lesson not knowing the first one. It made my school life a misery. I was always being demeaned, told I was an idiot and made to stand on my chair. 'None right out of 6!'[23]

He attended South Perth Primary School in his tenth year, in 1925, but it was only for a year. He had a row with the headmaster at South Perth because he refused to go to carpentry classes. He said he was no good at carpentry and would never need carpentry, but he knew he had to be better at mathematics. It therefore seemed to him logical to stay at school the day the others went to carpentry and work on mathematics. Here were the first traces of the stubbornness that became a feature of the grown man when faced with a situation to which he objected. The headmaster said no, Tom Hungerford would go to carpentry with the rest of the boys.

> The next carpentry day, on the Thursday, I went to school as usual and sat on in the classroom by myself. In came [the head] and said: 'What are you doing here?'
> 'I'm working on mathematics, Sir.'
> 'You're supposed to be at carpentry!'
> 'I don't want to go to carpentry, Sir.'
> 'I'll fix this!'

He sent for Mrs Hungerford, although their son's schooling was not something in which his parents usually involved themselves. The three of them were in the headmaster's office.

> I put my case, backed up by my mother who asked plaintively: 'What can I do?'
> 'Tom will never get on at this school. He's against it, he's against me,' which I was not—I thought the headmaster was a nice man. 'I suggest that you move him to another school.'
> 'But where?'
> 'He'll have to go to the school in town...' [there was no other state school in South Perth] '...to the James Street school, and I'll fix it so he can go there.'

> So I had to live a lie [that I was actually living with an aunt in town].[24]

So he crossed by ferry and walked up Barrack Street and attended the James Street School for two years from 1927, before completing his secondary education at Perth Boys' School, which was next to James Street School. He was quite content to attend this new establishment but was initially discomfited by being summoned by his surname. 'I worried about what I had done, hearing "Hungerford!" being called out. At South Perth it was, "Tom, Dick, Harry, Bill, Mary!" '[25] This aside, his new school made for a comfortable transition from the familiar surrounds of South Perth to a wider, more cosmopolitan, world.

Leaving the relative isolation of South Perth to be schooled in the city was as big a change to the boy as if he had been living deep in the country as well as an opportunity to explore this strange new culture of bustle and colour. He became acquainted with the exterior of the Perth brothels in Roe Street. One of his new classmates would suggest at lunchtime, 'Let's go down to the "Drums"!' (the name then for these establishments), and they would walk to Roe Street, a block away from his new school. He would also study the menu and curiously eye the bamboo on the window of Perth's only Chinese restaurant, the Shanghai Café, on the corner of William Street. Then there was a remarkable old building built like a pagoda, to walk through, on the corner of William and Wellington Streets, further down from the railway station. It had everything, old second-hand shops and a chicken 'knackery' where chickens were killed, plucked and gutted. There was also the fish market, alongside the railway line, because fish came up from the coast. But all this was just the background to the important business of working towards his Junior Certificate, 'then supposed to open all doors'.[26]

CHAPTER 3

Tickety-boo

The youngster's complete failure to understand mathematics was to dog him during his two years at James Street School (1927–29) and until he left Perth Boys' School in 1931 at the age of 16. He was good at English, French, geography, history and agricultural science, which he particularly enjoyed. This counted for little; he was expected to be competent at mathematics. It was mainly thanks to his English teachers that his competence at and flair for English composition from an early age was to carry him through to his working life. There had been Mr Trippier earlier, who had encouraged him, 'You'll be a writer one day!' and Mr Northam at Perth Boys', who praised the boy, gave him writing assignments and told him of the writer's craft. Hungerford was starting to read widely: he enjoyed the 'Arts and Letters' pages of the *West Australian*, and *Smith's Weekly*. He was not, however, exclusively a bookworm. From an early age, Tom Hungerford liked others' company—including that of girls.

Serious socialising took place away from school, with friends of his sisters and with others whom he had met outside the family circle. When he was about eight, Hungerford had fancied that he had fallen deeply in love with a girl at the convent, Vivienne Stodart, who surfaced again in his life when he was about 19, when she called him up, having had nothing to do with him at school. Later he was to write of trysts under the jetty, all touchingly innocent in that period of his early teens.

In fact, however, socialising was really only a pleasing addition to a life that focused increasingly on the need to get a job, once he had started at Perth Senior Technical College. He had only attended Perth Tech. in the first place to undertake some sort of practical training, but nothing mechanical—he thought he knew that was not his strength—and the fact that he started a clerical course was because there was little employment to be had. He reckoned he must focus on his early ambition—if that was not too strong a word at the time—to become a writer. Shorthand would certainly be useful, bookkeeping less so, but it was part of the course, as well as the abominable maths. However, he did not have to persevere very long with figures. The head of the college came into the class one day where Hungerford was wrestling gloomily with the intricacies of double-entry book-keeping, to announce that there was a job for a boy: he would like some students to be interviewed.

Half a dozen of the class reported to a lighting business at the top of Wellington Street in West Perth, called Aladdin Lamps. There they were put through the sort of investigation into their abilities that suggested the aspirants were being considered for the highest ranks of the diplomatic service. It was in fact for a job that paid 12s 6d a week. The candidates were addressed portentously by their potential employer 'who pointed through the door to a young man who was industriously writing something at the desk: "Now listen! That young man is only 19. He is earning a man's wages now. That's what ahead of you, if you try!" '[1]

It sounded worth a go, and Hungerford was happy to be selected for the position, even if it seemed to be an uninspiring start. The important thing was that it was a job: he agreed to give

10s weekly to his mother and keep 2s 6d for himself. His parents were delighted, and he set to organising his working day. Although there had been a tram service since the mid-1920s from South Perth across the Causeway into the city, he was required to buy his own bicycle, on time payment. Buoyed with optimism, the red-haired youth peddled steadily from South Perth to West Perth via the Causeway on a spring morning, filled with the promise of a new year and a future in the workforce—and this at a time when there were only limited prospects for those of his age.

Even at that early period of his working life, Hungerford showed that he was not prepared to stick at something he disliked, demonstrating an irresponsible stubbornness that was ill-considered, given the shortage of jobs to be had. It did not take him long to resolve that this first job had been a mistake. He decided immediately that he did not like his new boss, an unprepossessing Scot, with 'close-set eyes and shifty demeanour'. His day started with sweeping the stairs, and then he waited in the storeroom until orders arrived for 'Aladdin' lamps, for which the market was mainly in the country where there was no electricity at the time. Towards the end of each day he would receive the orders, pack them up, put them on the trolley and walk them over to the West Perth railway station, where he consigned them to the train and went home. The job itself was certainly menial. This would have been unimportant in itself, but Hungerford made up his mind that it would lead to nothing. It was certainly dull and depressing—a work experience shared by everyone at some stage of their working lives, of course—but he became increasingly despondent as daily he pedalled back across the Causeway to his expectant parents.

His worst suspicions about this apparent dead-end were soon confirmed by the country traveller, a smartly dressed man, who asked kindly if irresponsibly of the latest recruit (Hungerford might have been encouraged to persevere in working towards a position in country travelling): 'Tom, what are you staying here for?'

'Well, it's a job.'

'Get out! There's nothing here. There's nothing ahead of you—get out, do anything.'[2]

The traveller confided that he was earning £12 10s a week—good money in those days. Hungerford's 12s 6d was a pittance. Black despair overwhelmed the younger man. One evening, when there was no one in the office, Hungerford sneaked a look at the wages book and discovered that the young clerk received only £1 a week, and this at the age of 19. It was not worth his while to stay. Anything else—even to continue studying—seemed a better alternative. When he had wearily put away his bicycle that evening he told his parents of his decision to leave. They were understandably upset, and reminded him that it was a paid position and that his mother needed the extra money. He could look for another position elsewhere while he continued packing lamps. But no, Tom Hungerford (as was later typical of the man) thought of himself first and foremost. It was a survival mechanism.

He so disliked his employer that now he had reached the point where he would move on, he wanted it to be on his terms. He brooded for a while, preoccupied as he peddled up the hill to West Perth. His face cleared: he had thought of an appropriate departure that was to be surprisingly malicious, if amusing in the telling. The opportunity arose when he was told to clean the lamps, displayed on two or three rising steps covered with black velvet, so that everything was 'tickety-boo' for an important buyer who was expected. It was a phrase the youngster hated: his boss's favourite order, 'See everything is tickety-boo.' Hungerford cleaned the lamps, carefully filled them and, just as carefully, did not screw the tops back on. He retreated to the storeroom and waited expectantly. The big buyer had arrived and was shown the lamps, gleaming on their stands. The important visitor picked up a lamp: suddenly there was a shout of consternation and anger from the display room as the top fell off and the visitor was covered with kerosene. The result was gratifying. 'Out! Get him out of here! Get him out of here!' He was paid off immediately. He climbed on his bicycle, his pay jingling in his pocket, and suddenly he felt as free as a bird. Now what was he to do? There were apparently no other jobs to be had.

Fortunately, he had a good friend, Graham Walker (who was to be killed in the forthcoming war), son of the printer at the *Daily News*. He asked Hungerford one day whether he was still looking for a job, because there was a vacancy at the *Daily News*, in the printing section. Hungerford was enthusiastic: he had shared with Walker his ideas of becoming a writer. The other agreed to talk to his father, an interview was arranged and Hungerford was employed as a trainee linotype mechanic. As he saw it, this was a real oxymoron—*he* a mechanic, with his slender talent for things mechanical—but needs must. As it happened, he developed into a proficient linotype mechanic and was regarded as the best 'boy' they had ever had, or so the operators told him. He joined the Printing and Allied Trades Union and stayed with the *Daily News* for a decade, settling happily into his new role, at 36s a week, 'the wealth of the Indies', as far as he was concerned, giving his mother a pound a week and keeping 16s for himself.

Finally he had some money with which to enjoy himself. Apart from mingling with his friends, there were the work outings, the annual union picnic at Garden Island and the *Daily News* Angling Club. There was also the ferry to Fremantle wharves after the midnight edition had been 'put to bed'. The young men slept there and were out early the next morning into the Sound for some fishing. For the others it included much drinking, although not Tom Hungerford, who was seasick enough without pouring alcohol into a queasy stomach. He had not been much of a drinker to that point, and this was demonstrated on his twenty-first birthday. His mother had said that she wanted to have a birthday party for him at home, and he demurred. He was not keen on that sort of party, but the family went ahead without his knowledge and invited a number of people to his home.

His prospective brother-in-law, Geoff Archdeacon, who later married his eldest sister Peg, called up the younger man during the day and said, 'How about having a drink this afternoon?' He said a friend of his, Jack Manning, would join them after work. Then they would go to the Hungerford home for dinner. Hungerford agreed, ignorant of the party being arranged. Until then, the only time he had consumed alcohol, and got drunk, was one Easter at Rottnest as an inexperienced 17-year-old. He and a mate of his had bought a bottle of fortified red wine, consumed it all and were 'drunk as skunks and sick as dogs'. That was all he claimed to know about drinking, other than that someone had told him that if he stayed on the same drink, he would not get drunk. He decided he would have only gin squashes and that would be pretty safe 'because of the lemon content'.

Hungerford met the other two after work, at the Royal Hotel, a grand old Perth pub opposite the Savoy, now in the Hay Street mall. On 5 May 1936 it was a cool evening, and he consumed a number of gin squashes in convivial company. His prospective brother-in-law used to sail a yacht on the river, and he had been an experienced drinker for some time. He and his friend were older than Tom. Eventually it was suggested that it was time to go home, and they had to hurry because they were late. As they were running down to the ferry, Hungerford had a funny sensation that he was floating in the air and, by the time he was home, he was vomiting. Of course, he had no idea that after dinner a crowd of people was coming to the house for a big party. All he wanted to do was to go down to the back garden and continue to be sick. 'My sisters were constantly at me: "Come on, Tom! Come up to the house, get cleaned up!" I would reply weakly: "No! Let me go, I wanna ..."'[3] He was, continuously. All he wanted was to go to bed. Finally, they said he was to lie down for a while, which he did, and felt only a little better. But the house was full of guests, and the swaying guest of honour barely recovered as, waxy-faced and gulping convulsively, he retired frequently from the conviviality to throw up. It is one of those memories that faintly embarrasses him, even in old age. So it was hardly surprising that he claimed to drink little at that stage of his life.

Hungerford had enjoyed an energetic physical lifestyle since he first learnt to run down to the river. He joined the Como Swimming Club and probably could have swum for the state.[4] By then, he could certainly beat his brother Mick, no mean swimmer himself. Later there was horse-riding, and the cover of *Straightshooter* shows a red-headed, confident youngster in the peak of condition. It was about the same time, in his late teens, that he started to enjoy visiting the beach regularly. He had also become seriously interested in ballroom dancing.

It was a good way to be with girls, after the initial embarrassment of approaching the partner of his choice, the girls giggling together, watching the would-be swain painfully summoning the courage to ask for a dance. Once he had mastered the basic steps, he attended a dance studio regularly. Both boys and girls took dancing lessons seriously. If he, as the man, knew the basic steps and was light on his feet, he could persuade the prettiest girl to be swept into his arms for a quickstep, a waltz, or—later in the evening—a slow foxtrot, when the lights dimmed, the fragrance of his partner's hair tickled his cheek and the blood quickened, as the two of them moved as one. There were balls, when the boys resembled Fred Astaire, or thought they did, in white tie and tails and could compliment the girls in their beautiful long evening dresses, or 'frocks' as they called them. 'Tails' were almost a second skin to Tom Hungerford in those days.

He had a colleague at the *Daily News* whose girlfriend was Renée Essler, the 'Miss Dancing' of Perth. Hungerford was asked by his friend to help write lyrics for Renée's annual musical show at His Majesty's Theatre. Renée liked him and introduced him to Mary Shaw,[5] who said she would pay him for some lyrics by giving him dancing lessons. This led to his becoming a part-time dance instructor for a time, at 5s a night (when she could afford it) to tutor girls in ballroom dancing.[6] The tall, handsome young man attended every Tuesday and Friday evening, straight from work, when Mary would take him through what he was going to teach the girls that night. He proudly claimed to be recognised as the best dance instructor in the state.[7]

The pre-war years were a busy period of Hungerford's life. This was when he left home each summer, from the age of 17, to live with friends in a flat at Scarborough, which was little more than a shack behind the Silver Bell Tearoom, owned by a Mr Rinaldi. 'During the summer we prowled around the reef, underwater, for hours, picking up shells and bits of coral, watching the fish...Mack...said that if he ever got to Heaven and didn't see something like Triggs just inside the Pearly Gates, he'd turn around and come straight back.'[8] It was the only time he ever had a real difference of opinion with his mother, when he decided to join his friends at the beach from November to March each year. She missed him around the family home, and he was later to regret it, again a single-minded selfishness and typical of the young. It was an idyllic time for him, of convivial evenings, although very decorous by today's standards; the girls sleeping in one area and the boys in another. Unknown to his mother, of course, the youthful Hungerford did, however, manage to enjoy some discreet love affairs with girlfriends of the moment.

It was also the time when he tired of the basic fare produced by his friends and of greasy 'takeaways', when they could not be bothered to light the stove. He decided to prepare some of the simple dishes his mother produced. It was rough cooking at best, and some of his kitchen utensils were unusual, such as a chamber pot he used to brew tea on the stove. Nevertheless from that time at Scarborough grew the Hungerford reputation of being able to serve up a good, nourishing meal, an accomplishment that stayed with him for the next seventy years.

It was also an apocalyptic period for him and his crowd of bronzed, happy-go-lucky friends, which he acknowledged many years later, when writing about those days in Scarborough leading up to the war. As Great Britain and Australia readied for war, however, Hungerford and his mates barely recognised that their life would never be the same, as they partied on or lay in the dark listening to the surf crashing below:

> We were like people in a run-away car charging downhill
> towards a precipice: knowing we were done for, but still
> hoping something would happen to make the brakes work.
> And in another way you hoped after so long mucking about
> it would happen, and in one way another would get you
> off the hook.[9]

Working for a newspaper, Tom Hungerford had as good an idea as most of his peers of the events sweeping the Northern Hemisphere during the 1930s. Whether the so-called phoney war of 1938–39 made a real impression on the young men and women frolicking on Scarborough beach is doubtful. Even in Great Britain where citizens were exhorted to brace themselves against what they feared Hitler might do, in the intervening months before war was declared, the issuing of ration books and gas masks proceeded uneventfully, with little anticipation of what lay ahead. In Australia, there was no shortage of world news about the deteriorating situation in Europe, but it was happening 'over there'. In Western Australia the radio was coming into its own. The ABC's 6WF ('Six Wesfarmers') was broadcasting from the cooperative's head office in Wellington Street, and it was then an important source of information supplementing the three principal newspapers of the time in Perth: the *West Australian*, the *Daily News* and the *Western Mail*.

The Germans invaded Poland, and Great Britain announced that a state of war existed. Great Britain's declaration of war on 3 September 1939 was followed on 6 September by a huge rally in Sydney to bolster support for the British, and it was matched by similar public gatherings throughout the country. Australia was among the first to call for recruits to the armed forces, and a number of young men from the Scarborough gang joined up. In fact, the Royal Air Force had been recruiting trainee Australian and Canadian pilots for a few years before the official declaration of war, anticipating the onslaught of the Luftwaffe on a poorly defended Britain. In 1938 the Australian army had totalled 52,000 of whom only 2,795 were permanent forces. The remainder was 'reserve': members of the Citizen Military Forces (CMF).[10] As a result of the recruiting campaign headed by General Sir Thomas Blamey, by the actual outbreak of the war 80,000 individuals were under arms, in various stages of preparedness, although the authorities were concerned by the slowness of early recruiting. Those who did join up might have been motivated as much by the armed services offering a job in those depressed times as by any sense of patriotism.[11] Then, in 1940, Italy joined Germany. Overnight in Australia thousands of mainly innocent Italians—although there were Fascists among them—were interned, many of them holding British passports as Australian citizens. The country was truly at war, for the second time since Federation.

Chapter 4

Apocalypse Now

The familiar domestic scene had changed forever for Tom Hungerford. When not at the beach, he had still lived at home until 1937, as did his brother and sisters until the elder son and daughter married. It had been a quiet, equable household, and there were seldom rows with his parents, although until Mick the elder brother left, he and Tom used to spar, as young men do. In 1938 the handsome Mick brought his beautiful fiancée Mollie to meet his parents. Minnie lay desperately ill in hospital with the cancer that was to kill her soon after.

She murmured to her devastated younger son at her bedside: 'You were the one I loved best of all.' Tom had never known this. She whispered in a few words how much she had missed his company all those summers he had spent at the beach. In the typical carefree and careless way of a young man enjoying himself, he had taken her for granted and had never guessed. This was heartbreaking enough, but his father survived only for another year. For the remaining four to five years of his retirement, old Arthur Hungerford since retiring as Protector of Aborigines from Jigalong in 1932—in the words of his younger son—'had just sat down quietly and read himself to death. He was always reading.' The old man was already pining for Minnie and had really given up on life. He just faded away in 1939. His old trouble, the weak chest, put him in hospital where little could be done for him as he sank into unconsciousness.

> I went to Royal Perth Hospital and said to the doctor: 'Look, how is my father?'
>
> 'Mr Hungerford, he doesn't want to live. If he doesn't get any better tonight, we're going to put him on the danger list.'
>
> 'OK. Please ring me up if...' My father died in the early morning.[1]

The younger son grieved mightily for his parents. He feels—towards the end of his own long life—that they were never to appreciate that this rather undistinguished, literary boy of theirs, as he appeared to them at home in the shadow of the dashing older brother, was to blossom in ways they could not have imagined.

Tom Hungerford had plans for a life in the military, but he did not join up immediately. He was waiting to see what was going to happen, and he had even done some work towards the hoped-for advancement in the forces, once he had been through basic training. He had passed the Red Cross first aid course, and he had studied wound massage and—something else most unusual at the time—counselling men who were in poor mental condition. He undertook this in his spare time at night with a remarkable Englishwoman, Blanche McGlashen (who appears to have been trained in psychology, although this was not made clear to him). A female friend of his had introduced him to McGlashen when he had confessed to the friend that he had found himself to be very shy when facing those whom he did not know. As he had no intention of remaining a private soldier in the army, he knew he would have to stand up in front of his men and confidently address them. He felt he would not be able to make the words come. For a time he paid Blanche McGlashen half the wages from his newspaper job, and she helped him to overcome his likely shyness, so the expensive exercise was well worth it.

The time came when he decided to enlist. The *Daily News* said it could not let him go because it could not replace him, and he understood that the newspaper was classified as an essential service, its employees exempt from call-up.[2] He never queried this, so he stayed until he received a summons from the Citizen Military Forces. He told the printer that he would at least like to do his three months service in the CMF and that he would assemble all the stocks of type and rules for use in his absence. The printer reluctantly agreed, and Hungerford strove to amass all the material required for his three months away. Yet he never saw the CMF, and he abandoned his job. The CMF was just his excuse to join the army. On 9 July 1941, 14902 Private Hungerford T. A. G. was formally recruited into the Australian Imperial Force (AIF) at Karrakatta, two months after his twenty-sixth birthday.

While Hungerford was taking his time to enlist, friends of his who had joined up as soon as they were able were either in the air force, the navy or the army. The AIF contingent had been sent to the Middle East to combat the Axis push along the North African coastline into Egypt. On 20 January 1940, 3,500 men from Fremantle had left for the Middle East; the majority being in the 20–24 age group.[3] Many of those who survived death, severe injury or capture were to be posted to India or sent to defend the Malayan Peninsula where they faced the Japanese forces that were about to occupy Malaya and to overrun Singapore.

Japanese strategy was divorced from the German and Italian campaigns in Europe. It was based on the peculiar geography of the Pacific Ocean and on the relative weakness and unpreparedness of the Allied military presence there. The western half of the Pacific is dotted with many islands, large and small, while the eastern half of the ocean is, with the exception of the Hawaiian Islands, almost devoid of landmasses (and hence of usable bases). The British, French, American and Dutch military forces in the entire Pacific region west of Hawaii amounted to only about 350,000 troops, most of them lacking combat experience. Allied air power in the Pacific was weak and consisted mostly of obsolete aircraft. If the Japanese, with their large, well-equipped armies, which had been battle-hardened in China, could quickly launch coordinated attacks from their existing bases on certain Japanese-mandated Pacific islands, on Formosa (Taiwan) and from Japan itself, they could overwhelm the Allied forces. They could overrun the entire western Pacific Ocean as well as Southeast Asia, and then develop the resources of those areas to their own military–industrial advantage. If successful in their campaigns, as they were initially, the Japanese planned to establish a strongly fortified defensive perimeter. It would extend from Burma in the west to the southern rim of the Dutch East Indies and northern New Guinea in the south and sweep round to the Gilbert and Marshall Islands in the southeast and east. The Japanese believed that any American and British counter-offensives against this perimeter could be repelled, after which those nations would eventually seek a negotiated peace that would allow Japan to keep her newly won empire.[4]

When Tom Hungerford enlisted in the army in July 1941 as one of more than 14,000 men[5] who had joined the army in Western Australia since the outbreak of war, Singapore had not yet fallen to the Japanese. Although the authorities recognised the vulnerability of the western third of Australia to invasion, it was only after the fall of Singapore in February 1942 that the military in Western Australia faced the prospect of defending the 1.6 million square kilometres of the state. Western Australia was in effect isolated from Australian forces in the eastern states, which were preoccupied with their own defences, although trains across the Nullarbor moved those troops who could be spared for postings either to the east or to the west of the country.

The paucity of manpower with the bulk of the Australian forces committed overseas was to affect the future of those recruits singled out for officer training, one of whom was to be Hungerford. But first he had to learn the basics of being a soldier. Joining the armed forces, even today, is a shock for the eager young men and women hoping to play their part in the latest war for Western values. Those who had attended boarding school and who were familiar with disciplined and institutional routines quickly grasped the idea that they were regarded as being part of a rabble of ignorant and confused people who were discouraged—from the start at least—from thinking of themselves as individuals. The army aimed to reduce all recruits to the lowest common denominator and then to build up each person, according to personal abilities.

Hungerford was inducted at the Claremont Show Ground, the big recruit camp at the time. All that was expected of him there was for him to become used to being in the army. First he had to fill a bag with straw to sleep on—a palliasse—and settle into a tent. He found someone already in the tent who had been inducted several days before and who considered himself already to be a seasoned fighter, rather to Hungerford's contempt, for they never handled any sort of weapon at that basic stage. Foot drill was forced into them in painful detail. They were bellowed at by fearsome corporals and sergeants, until the training squads learnt to move as one. They were also chivvied into the endless fatigues that are part of military life, including the cleaning of latrines and the collection of rubbish.[6]

Shortly after his introduction to the army's mass feeding arrangements, Hungerford had an attack of acute diarrhoea, as did everyone else in the camp. The next day, as if to make a point, he was put on hygiene fatigues, clearing the gully traps and performing other unpleasant tasks. Then it was his turn to be allocated to guard duty, and with other such mundane routines he came to learn part of what he was to face during his military service. In September the same year he was sent for weapons and tactical training to the military camp at Northam, an hour from Perth, from which drafts were posted overseas. The location at that time of year was idyllic.

> It was springtime, and at the bottom of the slope we were sitting on, the beautiful valley of the Avon lay below us, the river purling along strongly with the rains of the winter…The same tiny, yellow flowers which literally carpeted our hill with gold were no more than a yellow dust on the red loam of the distant paddocks from which the bleat of sheep and the lowing of cattle drifted up softly and restfully on the air.[7]

Hungerford himself came to the attention of the authorities soon after his arrival, and he was interviewed by the Commanding Officer (CO). In Hungerford's own words: 'I was big and, I suppose, fairly good-looking, stupid, so very good officer material. The CO said: "Private, I want you to go to an infantry officers' school." ' Being an infantry officer, the trainee soldier replied, was not part of his idealistic dream. He had no wish to serve as an infantryman, commissioned or otherwise. He wanted to be a 'saver-of-life', a stretcher-bearer, in the Australian army's Medical Corps. He had trained for it: he had his Red Cross first aid qualifications, and he had studied wound massage and counselling with Blanche McGlashen before joining up. He said so,

> and the CO, misunderstanding my motives, commented: 'Look, Private, you're just as likely to be shot as a stretcher-bearer as you are as an infantryman.' I said tactfully that the CO had the wrong idea: I was not trying to get out of being shot; stretcher-bearing was what I wanted to do.

The CO replied dismissively that he should give the infantry a try, and Hungerford did so, abandoning his aspirations to be a saver of life.[8]

He attended a pre–officer training school in the lines, performed well there and was promoted to acting corporal on 26 September 1941. Then his CO said he would like Hungerford to attend a physical training (PT) school within the camp, as part of the work-up towards being commissioned. Hungerford liked PT: here too he excelled, and so was sent to the Brigade PT school at the old Ascot racecourse in Perth. He passed out top, was recommended for further PT instructor training and proceeded by train to Frankston on the Mornington Peninsula in Victoria, to attend the army's principal Physical Training Centre. Apart from his now becoming dangerously well qualified in one specialty that might keep him in a permanent training role in Western Australia, he had another potential setback. Just before the end of the course, he was doing a training run up the beach and trod in a hole dug by a child. He so badly damaged his ankle he could not walk, and hopped back to camp. The non-commissioned officer (NCO) in charge of Hungerford's cadre said it was a shame: acting Corporal Hungerford was going to top the school. How bad was it? The NCO felt it, manipulated the ankle a bit and then suggested that if he bandaged it very tightly, Hungerford could pass out from the course. All Corporal Hungerford had to do, the NCO said, was to demonstrate what he had learnt. So Hungerford agreed to have a go, the ankle was tightly strapped and he managed to complete the demonstrations, although it aggravated the ankle injury. He again passed out first, was confirmed as a substantive corporal and returned to Northam.[9]

Singapore having fallen to the Japanese about the time Hungerford was at Frankston, all movement of potential officers to be trained in the eastern states was halted, and as there was no officer school in Western Australia at the time, he was marooned at Northam as a PT corporal instructor. He was also expected to instruct on certain weapons, on which he himself had not been trained. The first day, on the morning parade, Corporal Hungerford took the men for PT. 'When the class broke up the CO said: "Corporal, I want you to take bayonet training." "Sir, I've never done bayonet training. I don't know anything about it." "You'll get through," said the CO unfeelingly.'[10]

There was nothing for it but to instruct those young men, who had all been through bayonet training many times before. When they were assembled, the corporal said simply: 'I'm terribly sorry, fellows, I'm a PT instructor. I know nothing about bayonets! Would you go through your exercises, so I can see what you do.'[11] Being a natural leader, probably older than most of the others, able to communicate with his men and already emanating those powers of leadership that were to distinguish his military service later, he got away with his ignorance, without having to suffer disparaging comments from his men. He also learnt some bayonet training.

It was the same when it came to instructing on the Bren light machine gun (LMG). Hungerford had recognised that he had no affinity with machines, even after his experiences at the printing works, and there he was, confronted with teaching the use of the standard LMG issued to Allied forces at the time. Stolidly, he acquired a pamphlet, read through it and tried to get acquainted with the LMG. He sat with his group of men in the shade of a hut on a hot day, the Bren in front of him. He gulped and repeated his mantra: 'I'm very sorry, I can't instruct you, I've been a PT instructor. I've never handled a Bren, so will you instruct me?' Very happily they did, because they enjoyed showing the corporal what they had to do, and again his natural physical presence and mental strength saw him through. 'It also helped, of course, that this was a group of men who liked me and with whom I hoped to be posted and to lead, in the field.'[12] This was wishful thinking: to his dismay, he was held back from the three drafts for the Middle East, and each time they left the camp for overseas, he was bereft of mates, three times in succession. In retrospect, as far as Hungerford was concerned, it was just as well: many of the men subsequently lost their lives overseas or were made prisoners.

In the meantime he was promoted to acting sergeant in March 1942, and he was told the CO had his eye on Hungerford as the potential sergeant major of the camp, the most senior non-commissioned position. To be kept behind permanently training others was the last thing he wanted. For the next month he was sent as part of a guard detachment to Busselton,[13] even further from potential action, and then in early July came the break for which he had been waiting. He was back in Northam, facing what seemed to him to be a grey future, when there was a call for men to join up in the newly formed 'Independent Companies', to train in southern Victoria for close behind-the-lines work as commandos against the Japanese.

The concept of 'commando' is derived from the South African irregular units that fought the British forces in South Africa at the end of the nineteenth century. Special forces—specialised units, Z and M Forces—were already raiding Japanese shipping in Singapore harbour and were engaged in coastal surveillance, using submarines and kayaks. The British Government had sent a special military mission to Australia in 1940, to train Australian units for guerrilla warfare on the ground. Some of the specialists training the Australians in Hungerford's time were veterans of the British Army's Long Range Desert Group, the precursor to the Special Air Service squadrons that operated behind German and Italian lines in North Africa. Eventually, twelve so-called Independent (Commando) Companies were formed and trained, with 1, 2 and 3 Independent Companies being in action by the end of 1941.[14]

Now volunteers were required to form 9 and 10 Independent Companies. In fact these units were never created, except on paper, and new units were added to the existing Independent Companies (or 'squadrons', as they came to be known) shown by a prefixed number, such as '2' added to the original company, for example, the '2/8th Independent Company'. Commando units were seldom at full strength in the field, and the usual number was maintained at about 120 men in all. In each section there was a lieutenant in command, a sergeant and a corporal or lance corporal. There was a captain for each troop and a headquarters troop with the usual administrative support of clerks, medics and stores. The sergeant major for the company or squadron was normally a warrant officer class I (WOI), the most senior NCO rank in the army. A major commanded the whole unit.

With a couple of his mates at Northam, 'like a chicken on hot shit' (Hungerford's picturesque words), he jumped at the opportunity to volunteer but was told he had no chance. He was far too valuable to the CO at Northam; he was to be retained there to train others. Everyone else seemed to be going away, and Hungerford was frantic to join them. Then by mere chance, the day before the draft was to leave on a Monday, there was a 'pick-up' game of football in the lines. A sergeant who was leaving with that particular draft twisted his knee and was immobilised. As soon as Hungerford heard of it, he went straight to the orderly room. Fortunately the sergeant major was away over the weekend, and someone was on duty there who did not know what he was doing. Hungerford said: 'This sergeant who's busted his knee: you're short of a sergeant on the draft. Can I take over?' The clerk would have looked up dubiously, but this was a sergeant speaking. 'Oh, yeah…suppose you could.'[15] That was how Hungerford escaped from Northam before the CO discovered he had lost a valuable training sergeant.

In early July 1942 the group of volunteers arrived at Darby, situated at the end of Wilson's Promontory in Victoria on a little river, where the training school was established, with Centre Camp and 1, 2 and 3 Camps some distance from Centre Camp.

Hungerford was in 2 Camp, nearest to 'Bloodsweat Beach'. It was peculiar army reasoning to train men to operate in the tropics in one of the coldest parts of Australia and at the chilliest time of the year, but perhaps it was to toughen them up for all conditions. They were put through basic training again and through map-reading, demolitions and handling explosives of all sorts, signals and first aid. Commandos were expected to be totally self-sufficient and to function independently from the usual military specialists who are attached to the standard infantry units. There were route marches—intensive marches over long distances carrying full packs and equipment—an important part of the routine of all armies, but certain other training exercises unique to Wilson's Prom stuck in Hungerford's memory for their sheer unpleasantness.

The trainees were out in all weather for three or four days at a time on the mountainous terrain of the Vereker Range, practising attacks, retreats and ambushes along slopes so steep that they walked on a tilt, carrying their full packs and armaments. The sloping angles did nothing for Hungerford's ankle, but he kept quiet about it. The straps bit cruelly into tired muscles, the cold stung exposed skin until it was numb, and steaming gasps of air rasped from labouring lungs. They ploughed through an area known as Chinaman Creek Swamp, simulating attack conditions. Every morning they had to run more than two kilometres through sand dunes to Bloodsweat Beach. As a professional PT instructor co-opted into the commando school's training team, Hungerford did this twice a day in addition to his other tasks, leading groups of shivering men onto the beach for PT. They would start at six o'clock on a freezing Victorian morning, dive into the river and thrash across, barely swimming a stroke as they sprang off one side and emerged on the opposite bank.

Two drafts graduated and were posted to their units, but not Hungerford, who yet again had been earmarked as one of the permanent training staff, although he was promised he would eventually be posted to active service with the other men. There was then a brief period when no new drafts arrived to be trained. Finally, Hungerford had a group of men with him, most of them Western Australians, who were Middle East veterans but untried in combat, who had been sent to Egypt where they had just idled their time away until they were returned to Australia. Hungerford was instructed to train these men, with the assurance that they were his personal responsibility as he would be posted with them. He was greatly encouraged and, proud to be part of a fine group, persevered with the usual gruelling routine until the Officer Commanding (OC) the training team summoned him. The OC ordered Sergeant Hungerford to report to Centre Camp for his men to be issued with tropical kit. Hungerford's heart lifted. They were away! Then his heart sank.

> The CO said: 'Don't you get fitted out.'
> 'Why not, Sir?'
> 'You won't be going.'
> 'What! You promised me!'
> 'I want you to remain and you will become Sergeant Major of the 9th [Independent Company].' Whether this last assurance was true, I did not know; I had already been promised so much that had never eventuated.[16]

He returned to his little tent on the ridge and brooded darkly and savagely on his future. It so happened that he was not alone in his black despair. There were two others on the training staff: Stan Brohartis, who was working in the quartermaster's store and was a warrant officer class 1, and another sergeant, Harry Hutcheson, who had been a jackaroo at the Overflow Station (immortalised by Banjo Paterson's 'Clancy of the Overflow'). Both were also desperate to escape from Wilson's Promontory. The camp was cleaned out except for a few fatigues, and the three senior NCOs were all three deeply depressed. Then history repeated itself. Hungerford went into the orderly room, not caring whether the OC was away or not.

> I was thinking that I must find a chance, any chance, of getting away and asked: 'Any reinforcements going to any of the companies?'
>
> 'Yes, Sarge: the 2/8th wants six or eight men.'
>
> 'Can I get away?'
>
> 'Well yes, but you'll have to drop your stripes [i.e. abandon his sergeant's rank].'
>
> I raced out and said to the other two: 'We can get away if we drop our stripes!' Off came our badges of rank.[17]

All three men became private soldiers again. They were on their way the next day, and Hungerford often wondered what happened to the poor man in the orderly room when the OC returned to find his birds had flown, the core of his training team. In due course his army record noted on 10 December 1942 that Sergeant Hungerford had reverted to private at his own request.[18]

There was an important highlight of this time at Wilson's Promontory. One day in 1942, Hungerford's first story was published in *The Bulletin*. Hungerford regularly read this publication, the top periodical of the time and an important means then for young authors to be published for the first time. He had subscribed since he was a 23-year-old. He knew he had to start being published somewhere: he had already written all sorts of stories, painstakingly wording and redrafting each piece, as has always been his hallmark. 'I had the feeling I should send them to someone and then I thought what rubbish it all was, and I would discard them in the wastepaper basket.'[19] But on this occasion, although marvelling at his presumption, he finally plucked up courage to send this latest story to *The Bulletin*.

The magazine's practice was not to notify the writer that a piece had been accepted for publication. The author was expected to peruse each issue; if he saw his piece, he then claimed his cheque. Sitting in his little tent on the Prom, Hungerford was idly leafing his way through *The Bulletin* when suddenly he saw it! ' "Visit to the Lutts" by T. A. G. Hungerford.' This great moment in his life was the real start of his writing career. The story had been submitted in longhand like all the early stories, as he had no typewriter then. He received £2 for this first story, a fee that was to rise eventually to £27 per piece.

Some of his stories appeared later under the pseudonym of 'T. Guy' because *The Bulletin* was running a number of his stories. One they rejected, 'Rain at Daybreak', was written when he was depressed at being left behind on Wilson's Promontory. The rejection note commented, 'Great tragedy never depresses.' As with all authors, rejections came as a disappointment and so did any negative reviews, although he valued particularly his army mates' criticism of his writing. One later story, 'It Always Takes Two',[20] was a story of a Japanese ambush, and the hero was debating whether to take the watch off a dead Japanese. The army mate commented that there was no need for any moral tussle: of course the watch would have been taken; a soldier would have 'souvenired' it.

CHAPTER 5

The Dogs of War

Private Hungerford together with the other two 'renegades' took army transport and rail from Wilson's Promontory, up to a little settlement near the Queensland coast called Mudgeeraba. There he reported to the Officer Commanding the 2/8th Independent Company (as is usual, the unit is hereafter referred to as 'the 2/8th'). He found them practising beach landings and other exercises that would be useful for the longed-for action against the enemy. The unit was transferred to Makaranka by train, and by army lorry to Darwin, where they set up their lines in an isolated little gully, about 50 kilometres out of Darwin. In the meantime, Hungerford had been promoted to acting corporal again. Once there, the army tried to decide exactly what to do with the 2/8th, originally tasked with fighting the Japanese in Timor.

Since 1942 Japanese forces had occupied most of Southeast Asia, including Timor, which had been invaded by the Australians in February 1942. 'Sparrow Force'—the Australian troops on Timor—was eventually forced to surrender to the Japanese. A further 250 men of the 2/2nd Independent Company was sent to the Portuguese part of the island (the other part had been under Dutch control). The 2/2nd acted as a guerrilla force, working out of the more rugged terrain and aided by the local Timorese. Attempts were made to support the 2/2nd by landing Dutch troops, and later the 2/4th Independent Company. The Australian and Dutch defenders now numbered about 700 men. However, the Japanese gradually subdued the local population by means of arbitrary arrests, executions and demolition of villages; the local Portuguese administration, nominally neutral, was eliminated; and guerrilla operations became more difficult. In December 1942 the 2/2nd evacuated 190 Dutch troops and 150 Portuguese to Australia before leaving Timor themselves, followed by the 2/4th in January 1943. Apart from the subsequent activities of Z Special Unit to harry the Japanese invaders, the principal gain from Australian operations in Timor was to demonstrate the value of guerrilla tactics against the Japanese.[1] It was also significant for the crucial assistance provided by the local people, something that the 2/8th, in its own operations against the Japanese later, took to heart.

There was an expectation that the Japanese would arrive on the northern Australian coast, so one of the 2/8th's main roles was to patrol nightly up and down the shore. Hungerford's section was responsible for the coastline between a place called Nightcliff and the city of Darwin. It was dangerous work: the soldiers had to cross the mouth of one of the rivers, and the strong tides ebbed and flowed. The patrols linked arms and edged their way across, ignoring the presence of estuarine crocodiles, stingrays and sharks, while swatting at the numerous insects that crawled over and bit any exposed flesh. They were also employed as 'the enemy' when other units in the area were practising their skills and were required to search for downed aircraft. These tasks took Hungerford into areas where the sand-flies were in such numbers that the men were actually frightened to drop their trousers to relieve themselves. Sand-flies excrete an irritant on the skin that is as tormenting as being bitten by mosquitoes, with the resultant persistent itch. Some sufferers react badly to the effect of sand-flies, and many soldiers succumbed to sand-fly fever, with high temperatures and headaches, although Hungerford was fortunate that he did not.

On one occasion Harry Hutcheson and Hungerford had set out to find a track passable for jeeps. It proved hopeless. They had started in an army truck, entered a boggy area, spent a day extracting the vehicle and got no further. It was impossible country for troop transporters. How the Japanese would have managed, if they had landed and pressed inland off the few roads, is hard to imagine. Consequently Hungerford and the others walked for long distances, usually over two to three days, to locate several downed aircraft, both Allied and Japanese, often with the dead pilots in the debris of the aircraft. Such remains were pathetic reminders of what had been living, breathing men, often scorched by fire, the macabre teeth set in a rictus of bizarre welcome, goggles still in place over the staring eyes, the whole fly-blown and putrefying in the hot sun. The patrols had to maintain at least an appearance of indifference as they retrieved valuable maps and other material from the Japanese cockpits.

These patrols brought Hungerford into close contact with the Aborigines, archetypal hunter-gatherers, who guided them, and whom he grew to admire. They were always on the lookout for food.

> On one patrol we were making our way down a creek where the mangroves were loaded with nests crowded with young cormorants, still unfledged. One of the Aborigines crawled out onto a bough and picked two of the fledglings out of the nests. He wrung their necks, slipped the birds by the necks under his belt and carried the two corpses swinging from his waist all day. Then we were walking past a creeper loaded with what looked like green passion-

fruit, and one of the Aborigines said, 'Good tucker!' and
filled his dilly-bag. That night we were sitting round the
campfire and the little cormorant bodies were placed on
the fire just long enough to singe the few downy feathers,
and were eaten, guts and all.[2]

Then they consumed the 'passion-fruit' and the whole party
enjoyed a feast of 'jabiru' stork, also cooked on the coals. 'I tried
to converse with them: "What name this fella...?" and, "You got
girl-friend...lady?" Much laughter.'[3]

He found them to be a people who loved a joke. Later,
he enjoyed writing a story on his experiences with them that he
called 'Lesson by Firelight', which was published in *The Bulletin*.

Otherwise, life was as in any army camp, with the neat
lines of tents, sleeping quarters, the various offices, ablutions
and cookhouse, and the all-important parade ground set out on
the arid, scrub-filled landscape of northern Australia, under the
hot sun. The men arose early, paraded, were detailed for various
fatigues and undertook more training, including mapping. Their
few visits to Darwin were usually for route marches, which
were exercises in stamina as they trudged stoically for the full
distance, sweat in their eyes, full packs on their backs and weapons to hand. The unit also formed a water-polo team that won
the Northern Territory championship in an enclosed swimming
pool at Darwin. Hungerford had never played before. Of course
they also played football and cricket—anything they could find
to pass the time. The only cinema was at Darwin. There was
also a thriving two-up school, two-up being a favourite game
of his.

Tom Hungerford wrote, arranged and presented a concert
party made up of members of his unit, who displayed considerable
talent—singing, dancing and other accomplishments—so much
so that the show did the rounds of the surrounding camps and

was highly praised. As with other forces in war-time, there were seasoned entertainers for the troops, and a professional concert party visited them from Sydney, featuring Jenny Howard, a well-known English artiste, whose performance was greatly enjoyed. It was of course always very hot and, in contravention of standing orders because of mosquitoes, the men were sitting around stripped to the waist. Halfway through the concert there was a quiz: the quiz-master asked whether anyone could tell him the meaning of the word 'palimpsest'. 'Yeah!' called Hungerford. 'So I was invited to the microphone, where I said it was a sort of copy of a manuscript. "Congratulations!" I won a prize and I also received a "Please explain", from my troop commander',[4] who noted that the prize-winner wore no shirt when he stood up to walk to the front: why was he sitting on the hill without a shirt on? He should have been setting an example. Hungerford was fortunate not to be put on a charge and received only a verbal reprimand.[5]

Protection against the various disease-carrying forms of insect life was on-going, if not always effective: at some stage Hungerford went down with dengue fever, another insect-born condition that causes fever, a rash and aching joints and can occasionally be fatal. He was also hospitalised for mumps early in 1943,[6] and later, because he worried about his personal hygiene in the jungle, with little water available for washing, he visited Headquarters in Darwin to see the medical officer and asked to be circumcised. After an embarrassing discussion, Hungerford was sent to the hospital in Darwin for the operation.

'I was sitting in a tent waiting for the young woman at the desk to call me: "Private Smith, pneumonia, Private Jones, sore leg," and then "Sergeant Hungerford! Circumcision!"' He flushed bright red.[7] Suffice to say that it is an unpleasant procedure for an adult, especially for a young man in the prime of life.

Back at camp, Hungerford found life increasingly tedious. In his absence, some of the men had been transferred to a parachute unit, leaving the others feeling unsettled about their future.[8] Moreover, the 2/8th could not have been described as a happy unit at the time. The men had little respect for most of the officers, although each of the latter had had to undergo the strenuous course on Wilson's Promontory. There was a crisis of confidence in their leaders; the men did not look forward to going into action with them. Hungerford was later told why the officers were perceived to be of such indifferent calibre. It is usual of course for enlisted men to complain about their officers, but here it was apparently deserved, with one or two exceptions, although it says little for the loyalty of those NCOs who condoned or even joined in the muttering from the ranks. The scuttlebutt was that apparently one senior officer disliked the major appointed to command the 2/8th Independent Company and made a point of directing poor-quality officers to the unit. This might or might not have been true, but the attitude of the men towards their officers was generally disparaging, and eventually it resulted in an event that could have ruined Hungerford's military career.

He was one of five NCOs who engineered what was in essence a mutiny that arose from disgust at what happened to them, as a result of someone entering the officers' mess and stealing a box of spirits. 'Other ranks' were permitted only a bottle of beer occasionally. The thief could have been anyone. (Hungerford subsequently discovered that it was in fact a corporal of the 2/8th in cahoots with one or two other miscreants.) The 2/8th was camped alongside other units, and there was no internal security, just a guard at the front gate. Anyone could have been the thief, able to walk through the lines of the other units bivouacked there.

At a parade the OC announced that until the culprit owned up, the 2/8th would all be confined to barracks. Confined to barracks was a foolish punishment since there was nothing to go outside for. In effect, they were denied use of what was called the 'amenities tent', a single tent with a few sets of Chinese checkers and other board games, religious tracts and a few books. But the indignity rankled. That afternoon, they were summoned to search a stretch of scrub on the other side of the road from their camp, to locate that missing box of grog. The men were really angry. These were well-trained soldiers who were all being labelled thieves. When they returned to their lines after an abortive search, Hungerford was in his sergeant's tent where he had a visit from four NCOs, from other troops of the 2/8th. Their forthright spokesman, Tim Bannah,[9] said: 'Tom, we're going to put on a "jack-up" [a strike]. Are you going to join us and bring C Troop in?'

'Well, tell me what it's all about.'

Bannah said he did not think they should have been labelled thieves, and they were being punished for something done by someone else, so Hungerford rejoined cautiously: 'OK. Yes. Just give me a little while to think about it.'[10] He rightly recognised this sort of action as being gross indiscipline and very risky for those involved, especially the ringleaders. It could well result in a court martial. His first thought was that he should not involve his men in so dangerous an action as a potential mutiny. He decided he would order an informal 'washing parade', which would ensure that his men were safely out of the way, but he was still in two minds about this, having virtually committed himself to his fellow NCOs. However, his mind was made up for him. One of his men, Frank 'Tanker' O'Neil, who had been a miner in Kalgoorlie,

> and who was as tough as they come, walked into my tent and said: 'Hey Sarge—what's this shit about a washing parade? If we're in this fucking thing, we're going to be in it!' I thought, Jesus! I was being too smart—the men all knew of course. So I said: 'OK, Frank. I see your point,' and I went immediately to Tim Bannah and the other NCOs, to tell them that I and my troop would join them. We then

discussed what form the jack-up should take. There must not be a riot, so we agreed it would be made plain that the protest was going to be conducted in a disciplined manner. All the fatigues would be completed—kitchen, hygiene and guards—but they would refuse to go on parade. That was how we left it.[11]

About mid-morning the next day one of the signalmen—the signals detachment did not join the jack-up—told the striking NCOs that a colleague in Darwin reported the town was buzzing with the news that the 2/8th was on strike. Brigadier Woodford was coming down to investigate the situation that afternoon. It was being taken very seriously, but if Hungerford and the other NCOs had second thoughts, it was too late, and they were convinced that they were in the right. They met to organise their actions and then assembled each troop in its respective area, to inform the men that they were to participate in a formal parade. There would be no noise, no catcalling and no whistling. They would be in their best uniforms—a set of clothes, kept in top condition, ready to go on leave. Their short-sleeved khaki shirts and shorts would be well ironed, and the webbing belt and gaiters would be freshly whitened. Their slouch hats would be immaculate, and boots would be shining. When they were so ordered, they would march on parade as soldiers, and no weapons would be carried.

While they awaited the arrival of the brigadier, the parade drill was hammered into them. After the drill, Hungerford returned to his own lines with his men, who were told not to wander around. 'I soon received the telephone call I was expecting: "Bring your troop on parade!"' He dismissed any disquiet he might have been feeling, put down the handset and turned to form up his men. It was the sergeant major who had rung, and he was not directly involved in the jack-up. The troop commander too was careful not be involved; a captain, he was a spruce, good-looking man but, according to

Hungerford, known to be ineffective, as was the major in charge, who had imposed the confined to barracks order. The OC had done nothing to remedy the situation, other than summoning the NCOs to his tent, to tell them how very displeased and disappointed he was that his senior men had gone on strike. Then he had reported the news to Darwin.

When the soldiers marched onto the parade ground, they showed they had been well drilled and could put on a show, notwithstanding any doubts they might have had about the consequences of their action. At the sharp command, the immaculate ranks came to a perfect halt and turned sharply to face the front, standing stiffly at attention, the NCOs drawn up before their sections. The brigadier was impressed: he had probably expected an unruly mob. He stood the men at ease and proceeded to give them a resounding lecture: he told them that they were 'bloody fools' and were behaving like children. He ended by stating that he would immediately rescind any orders that restricted them from access to the amenities tent or from going outside the lines. They were to resume training for war. That was the end of it—for the men. The brigadier then took the officers to their mess, and the cook there later reported that the brigadier had severely reprimanded them for handling the whole affair so poorly. The only person to suffer from the incident was the major, whose career prospects consequently deteriorated. If the jack-up had been handled sensibly, he would probably have completed his war service with no black mark against him. As with the captain of a ship that goes aground, the stigma follows the individual around, usually putting paid to a more senior command. However, the official military records of the strike's instigators were left unblemished, although if Hungerford's subsequent ASIO record was typical of others, it can be assumed that Army Intelligence took note.

In the meantime, the 2/8th was impatiently waiting to be posted overseas. Originally it had been intended that the unit would take over from the 2/4th in Timor, but by the time Tom Hungerford was posted to the Northern Territory, it was plain that the focus was to be elsewhere: on New Guinea. The Japanese had occupied New Guinea and parts of Papua in January 1942, but a Japanese invasion force, destined for Port Moresby in 1942, had been forced back by the Battle of the Coral Sea. After heavy fighting, mostly under terrible jungle conditions with sickening bloodshed on both sides, the Japanese had been stopped at Myola by Australian forces, on the southern side of the Owen Stanley Range. They were driven back through Kokoda, Wairopi and Gona in September 1941, a historic victory over the apparently invincible invaders and the first land defeats suffered by the Japanese. The fighting moved up the northern coast of New Guinea, and finally the Japanese were driven into isolated pockets by 1944, unable to retreat or advance. Their lines of supply dwindled as Australian and US forces dominated the air, sea and land routes that had been open to the enemy.[12]

To their great relief, the 2/8th was now tasked to move to New Guinea, and the unit went by train to Townsville in Queensland. They were fully equipped for jungle warfare, with .303 rifles and bayonets, Thomson and Owen sub-machine guns, Brens and one two-inch mortar to each section. British HE6 grenades were plentiful, appreciated by the Australians as being markedly superior to the Japanese version. On 5 August 1944 the 2/8th embarked on a 'Liberty ship',[13] as they were known. It was one of the numerous 'rust buckets' that moved troops and supplies. (Liberty ships had been foundering all over the world, breaking in half or just disappearing, without trace.) They disembarked at Lae on the north coast of New Guinea, and were tasked with patrolling up the Busu River. The Japanese had left those parts, but there was still unrest among the indigenous population, and with the Chinese, so patrols were important there for a period. By this time the Allies, mainly the US Marines, were conducting the island campaign, systematically flushing out pockets of Japanese resistance. Later, Hungerford was to work at one stage with the US Marines and was impressed with them, by contrast with the US infantry, whom he found to be less well trained and motivated than the marines. At last the 2/8th Independent Company was actively involved in the war effort.

CHAPTER 6

The Jungle

When they had disembarked at Lae, the 2/8th moved into two-man 'pup tents' with all their personal equipment. It was extremely hot and a malarial area. Before Hungerford's time in New Guinea, 65 per cent of the Australian soldiers posted to New Guinea had been evacuated with malaria—six times the number of battle casualties.[1] The disease was now kept under control by daily doses of Atebrin, the best available prophylactic at the time, which the soldiers disliked. The only apparent side-effect of Atebrin is to turn the recipients' skin yellow, but as the soldiers were living in the bush, away from other troops, they did not recognise this metamorphosis until they mingled with troops from non-malarial areas, who colourfully identified them as 'Wordsworth's fucking daffodils'. The men disliked taking the pills: Hungerford had to line his men up to ensure that they swallowed the tablets, including a vitamin pill of ascorbic acid (vitamin C), lest they throw the pills away. However, once they had stopped taking the drug, months or even years after, many of them succumbed to attacks of malaria, which had lingered, suppressed in their systems. Luckily malaria kills only a few sufferers, but an attack is debilitating, with high temperatures and sweats.

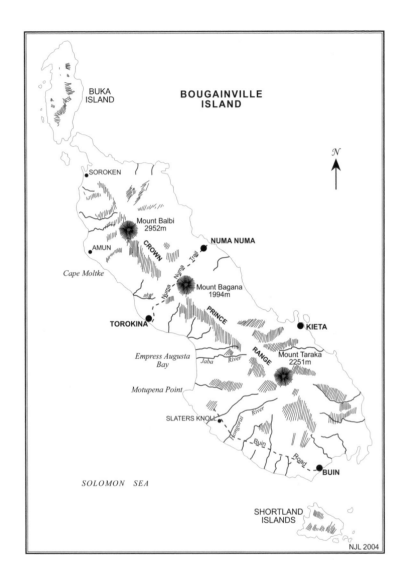

The soldiers lived quite well on the army rations, which were healthy but dull. There were 'goldfish' herrings in tomato sauce, still remembered for the aroma and for the reproachful stare of the neatly packaged fish. Dehydrated vegetables—onions, carrots and potatoes—supplemented the ubiquitous bully beef and biscuits. Ever resourceful, Hungerford improvised to overcome on the lack of fresh vegetables. The heart of the limpom palm, much smaller than a coconut palm, is a hard white-green fibre, the size of a small cabbage. This was cooked into an edible dish, or it could be eaten raw as a 'millionaire's salad'. Alternatively, the very top of a coconut palm could be consumed—reached by shooting it down until the practice was banned. They would acquire *kau-kau* (sweet potatoes) from the locals, and very occasionally there were pawpaws. At one stage they were camped close to an old mission where a lime tree provided buckets full of the small astringent fruit. Occasionally they tossed a block of explosive into the river for fish, but that was heavily frowned upon because the blast killed every fish in the vicinity, depleting the locals' sources of food. Once a large groper was caught off the coast. It was cooked at Headquarters, and there was to be none for Hungerford and his men, until he acquired the backbone and head. Reverting to his Scarborough cooking days, he borrowed a big dixie, threw in onions and other dried vegetables, and made soup for his men. Although there was fresh bread in the early days whenever they were close to a military force with support facilities, it was a rarity. Not until later in the Bougainville campaign, when aerial drops were the principal means of supply, were fresh meat, bread and vegetables more available. While they were on the Busu River in New Guinea their water was transported from Lae. When they were in the bush they drank from the smaller streams, because the local people defecated in the larger rivers. Although the troops were issued with water-purifying tablets, they were not often used.

New Guinea was really just training under jungle conditions for the real conflict that was coming. The patrols up the Busu River were a practice period for Hungerford and his men, but they were given one special task before they left the Lae area. He was ordered to take his section to New Ireland to reconnoitre a Japanese airfield, to confirm whether it had been evacuated. The island is about 340 kilometres long and 600 kilometres northeast of Lae. It had been occupied in 1942 by the Japanese, along with the rest of New Guinea. Hungerford had been running a little weekly news-sheet, typed up at night in the squadron office, to keep everyone informed about what was happening. He used the paper to promulgate gossip that they were just off for a few days on exercise. Instead, fully prepared to meet the enemy, they left by corvette and were offloaded at Malmal on New Ireland from where they trekked for the best part of a day.

Late in the afternoon, they reached a deserted coconut plantation within easy walking distance of the airstrip they had come to reconnoitre. A shark-infested river separated the plantation from the airstrip, and it looked to be a dangerous crossing, especially if the Japanese were lurking on the other side. But one of the local inhabitants, a *tultul* (chief), was canoeing down the river. He offered to guide the commandos to the airstrip. They camped in the old plantation that night, and the next day Hungerford went with the *tultul* and two or three of his men to reconnoitre the airstrip. They crossed the river without incident. Cautiously they crept up to the airstrip's perimeter, to find it was deserted. The state of the buildings indicated that they had been unused for some time. The Japanese were indeed on the run.

The patrol had been allotted a day to carry out the reconnaissance, but a heavy storm blew up and the corvette was unable to manoeuvre near the beach, so no boat could be launched. For two days the section lived stoically on the remainder of their rations. Fortunately there had been a vegetable garden at the plantation and pumpkins proliferated. The men threw whole pumpkins on the fire to roast them. The pumpkins were combined with what was left of their rations, which were also supplemented by coconuts. The troops returned to their camp near Lae, and on 23 November 1944[2] they embarked for Torokina on Bougainville and for the hazardous prospect of harrying the Japanese behind their lines. At last! This was what Tom Hungerford had been waiting for.

Bougainville is the largest of the Solomon Islands group, near the northern end of that chain, in the Southwest Pacific. Together with other small island groups, it is today an uneasy part of Papua New Guinea, after a bloody uprising between 1990 and 1996, which resulted in nominal semi-autonomy being granted. Although not one of the world's larger islands, being only 120 kilometres long and 65 to 95 kilometres wide, it is mountainous along its length. There are active volcanoes in the northern half of the island, and it is thickly forested.[3] It presented problems for military planners: the soldiers had to negotiate thick jungle on steep-sided slopes, often under extreme conditions of heat and isolation.

The Japanese had occupied Bougainville early in 1942. In 1943 Perth's *Daily News* headlined the Allied counter-assaults on Japanese positions in British Borneo and 'the latest Bougainville landing near Chabai within six miles of Bougainville's northern tip'. By March 1944 US troops had established an American enclave protected by minefields and barbed wire at Torokina, at the northern end of the island, later the headquarters of the 3rd Australian Division. Before the arrival of the 3rd Division, the Americans had repelled two major attacks by the Japanese, before the enemy went off the offensive.[4] US Marines sent out occasional patrols to hunt the Japanese, who remained entrenched at the southern end of the island at Buin, near Kieta, the main port in the south. Hungerford commented that it had been reported unofficially that the Japanese garrison had to rely on a submarine for resupply, once the Japanese air force had been defeated.[5]

The Japanese might have stayed there until the end of the war without much harassment from the US forces, but a major contingent of Australian troops was sent to Bougainville to over-run the remaining Japanese. Ahead of the regular troops were the Australian commandos, tasked with being the 'eyes and ears' of the Australian force, and to harass the Japanese by conducting operations behind enemy lines. It was later asserted that the Australians' Bougainville campaign was unnecessary, militarily speaking; however, this is no reflection on the 2/8th and the other Australian units sent.[6] The Japanese were on the run, and it was only a matter of time before Japan capitulated. At the time, however, it made good military sense to pressure Japanese units towards the point of formal surrender, and the Australians were the best troops to achieve that. Certainly the 2/8th performed fully to their American ally's expectation. Nevertheless the Australians were contemptuous of General MacArthur,[7] who had stated earlier that Australia was only useful to the US as a base from which to attack Japan. He also denied the Australians credit for their roles in other campaigns of the Pacific War.[8]

So the move to Bougainville came just in time for the 2/8th to experience actual combat. Inactivity can be deleterious to soldiers' morale, affecting the maintenance of good order and discipline, although the 2/8th was by now generally an integrated, well-behaved body of men. Everyone complained about some-thing, but that was a normal part of being a soldier, accustomed to being moved here and there, apparently at the mere whim of Headquarters. Having been together for three years, most of the men were on first-name terms with each other. Relations between the men and their NCOs were also relaxed and easy. Tom Hungerford was called 'Sarge', and he enjoyed a nickname because of his dark red hair. At that time in the newspapers there was a cartoon character called 'Mopsy the Cheery Redhead' so of course Hungerford was known as 'Mopsy'. Then the character became

'Colonel Mopsy' so Hungerford was called 'Colonel Mopsy' or just 'Tom' or 'Mate'.

At that time, the 2/8th had a change of commanding officer,[9] a man who was greatly liked and respected, by contrast with a predecessor. This was Major Norman 'Steer' ('the Red Steer') Winning.[10] The new OC was not the unit's only notable acquisition. Having been in New Guinea for four months the unit had adopted a big stray black and white dog called Paddy, named after a former OC and which resembled a large fox terrier. Paddy became the unit's mascot and went to Bougainville with the 2/8th. He used to sleep on anybody's bed and was fed the best tucker around. Paddy was 'crimmed' once for consorting with native dogs, but was made a lance corporal by the OC, and this rank appeared on the notice board. 'After we had arrived in Bougainville, Norm Winning had a little parade at which he said: "Listen, fellows: among other things, we can't take Paddy into action with us. It's dangerous. We have to leave him for the Americans to look after." So we lost Paddy.' The OC meant business.[11]

The 2/8th disembarked by lighter from the decrepit Liberty ship that had chugged its dangerous way to Torokina, and was eventually transported to their first camp at the edge of the Jaba River, adjoining territory where the Japanese were still patrolling with forces greatly superior, numerically, to the newcomers. The 2/8th had landed very late in the afternoon with no preparation for their immediate accommodation or supplies. The OC told Hungerford to visit the American headquarters to 'borrow' enough food for the squadron's meal that night. The latter was to acquire a clear insight into the relaxed nature and mores of some of the American troops. Many of them were African Americans in a support capacity, their usual role in World War II. Hungerford acquired a truck with a driver and drove to the Americans' camp where he was greeted by a huge and affable black master sergeant. Hungerford told him who he was and where he had come from.

The American led the new arrival into an enormous warehouse, piled high with food. His visitor was amazed: he asked tentatively whether there was any limit to what he could take. He was genially invited to take the lot.

The 2/8th established themselves in their two-man pup tents for that first night, contrasting their accommodation with that of the Americans, who had large bell tents, erected on drums, with wooden floors. The 2/8th always ensured that a new campsite included adequate and hygienic pit toilets with what they called 'pisser-phones': pipes leading down to a hole filled with stones, so that the urine dissipated into the ground. It was a military crime for a soldier to relieve himself anywhere else in the lines, even behind a bush. As Hungerford was walking through the Americans' camp between those immense tents, an African American walked through the entrance of one of them onto the steps and casually urinated out of the front of his tent. Hungerford was appalled. The resultant smells and flies practically guaranteed stomach complaints in the heat and humidity.

The newcomers had no vehicles, and once they were camped at the first site, Australian foot patrols started to penetrate towards the various Japanese camps, along the tracks known to the local people, to gain a sense of the terrain and of possible enemy contact. Before patrols set out, for a time the 2/8th had a padre available for any soldier who wished to take communion before patrolling. That initiative was not a success, there were few takers, and the padre was allocated to other, more devout, troops. The 2/8th's first area of operation was known as the Jaba Track. Patrols went down there several times to cross the river, and once penetrated right up the watercourse and returned on a raft made of banana trunks. When they had exhausted the Jaba area, they were later moved out to the deserted Savele Mission station and to Niheru. Other locations for the 2/8th base camp followed over the months, as the Japanese gradually withdrew towards Buin. Hungerford accompanied American patrols on a couple of occasions, but the US forces generally preferred to stay behind the safety of their garrison perimeter, which gave the Japanese the virtual run of the island without much opposition—that is, until the arrival of the 2/8th and other Australian units.

As the Japanese were forced down the island towards Buin in the south, the 2/8th was to operate on their eastern flank, working from the high country down to the Japanese lines of communication. Their task was to harass the enemy, as they moved between their various locations, and to attack the smaller Japanese outposts. The 2/8th's role was simple: to give the enemy hell, with demolitions and ambushes. They were to shoot up any static group of the enemy they came across, to map where they went and—whenever they could—to take a Japanese prisoner alive, to be sent back to the coast for interrogation. One of the commandos was actually teaching himself Japanese, and it was Tom Hungerford's task to employ a 'Kanaka' to carry the would-be linguist's books when they shifted camp. Learning other languages is something on which modern Australian and British forces concentrate, and it was this desire to communicate effectively other than in English that so often has made a crucial difference in advancing the military cause, in whatever theatre of war.

The Kanakas were a colourful and major part of the campaign. 'Kanaka' was the generic word for the locals and was the term they themselves preferred then, although it now has pejorative connotations. The Japanese had brutalised the Kanaka men and raped the women, shot up the villages and destroyed their gardens. But the Australians were friendly and respected the Kanakas; the only hangover from the old imperial days being that the locals called the Australians 'Master', which was how they had learnt to speak to a white man. They called Hungerford 'Masta Firegrass', because of his red hair ('grass' being Pidgin English for 'hair'), or 'Masta Tom'.

The Japanese fear of the Kanakas was a great bonus for the newcomers because the Japanese were terrified to leave the main tracks. Once the enemy had the 2/8th to contend with, they were not so easily able to brutalise the Kanakas, who learnt to wait for any Japanese soldier who might come along and put a spear through him. Consequently the Japanese had very limited social access to the local people, who were only too happy to lead the Australian patrols by secret routes through the jungle to the location of Japanese camps, which otherwise would have remained unknown.

At one time the Japanese had at least one Kanaka working with them. He was known to the Australians in the idiom of the time as the 'Red Coon' because he came from Manus, where the people are red-brown in colour, whereas the people of Bougainville are a browner shade. There was a price on his head: he was leading the Japanese to the secret tracks. It was rumoured that the reason he worked for the Japanese was because they were holding his wife hostage.

Although the commandos had a map of the whole island, there were few locality maps. It was the Australians' all-important access to the Kanakas that enabled them to obtain information about tracks and roads, villages and gardens, rivers and river crossings. Fraternising was on mutually easy terms, and the Australians kept the Kanakas' loyalty by learning pidgin. It might have been bowdlerised, but the commandos got their message across and, even more importantly, understood the messages they were given in return. It was drilled into the 2/8th that there must be no interference with what were known as the 'maries', the Kanaka women, one practical reason being that the offender would probably be speared. Such contacts would have jeopardised the friendly relations between the locals and the Australians.

Hungerford had affectionate memories of these attractive people. The men and women wore 'laplaps' (sarongs), and every morning there was a line of Kanaka women doing what they called 'Broom'um—broomin groun' long'. Brandishing *masta*—long brooms made of spines from sago palms—the women would be in a long line, eight or ten of them, sweeping the open ground of the square outside the OC's tent. Not all of the women were young and comely. Others were described in pidgin as 'Susu 'long Mary all same razor strop'. In pidgin *susu* is 'breast' (and, strangely, *susu* also means 'milk' in Japanese and Bahasa Indonesian). The women's breasts swung in unison as they swept backwards and forwards. There were many other exotic sights: once when Hungerford was visiting the Kanakas in their huts he came upon a lovely little girl, in her tiny laplap, sitting contentedly, legs swinging over the edge of the floor raised above the ground, smoking a large pipe crammed with tobacco. Another memorable moment was the exchange with a Kanaka whom Hungerford imagined knew nothing about a firearm. He was pointing to the various trigger settings: ' "Somebody else pres'gun…This-pella no pop. [The weapon was on "Safe".] This pella…pop…one pella! [Single shot.] This pella pop! Pop pop pop!" [Burst of fire.] The response: "Me Savvy!—Safe, Repetition and Automatic!" The Kanaka had been trained in one of the New Guinean battalions.'[12]

The Australians had to do their best to look after the Kanaka people, particularly those who had been treated badly by the Japanese. Later in the campaign, the Australians extracted them from the Japanese areas and kept them on the Australian side within a safe perimeter, until the Kanakas could be conveyed down to the coast. Looking after the (eventually) 2,000 local people, who were suffering from starvation and fever, made for many difficulties, in addition to their active soldiering duties, but it deprived the Japanese of carriers and food supplies. Before the 2/8th had advanced far from Torokina, they too had relied on lines of Kanaka carriers, but that became dangerous, with Japanese forces stationed too close for safety. The 2/8th base was then at Morokai, which was away from the lowlands and therefore cold. The Kanakas had no blankets, and at first the 2/8th kept one blanket per soldier and gave the rest to the Kanakas. Eventually, to keep the increasing number of these people warm at night, blankets were dropped by air.

Being supplied with food for themselves and for the Kanakas was another major problem, and by 1945 the Australians had aerial drops, which created a risk of a different sort. The aircraft used to free-drop steel drums that would not break when they hit the ground. It was a primitive system. In the early days of supply drops, a door was taken off a DC3 Dakota, as there was no aircraft specially built or equipped for that task. The routine was to fly at 500 feet around a supply-drop target, which in itself might be risky, since the underbelly of a Dakota could present a tempting target from below. But because the commandos were adept at selecting the supply-drop areas, no aircraft were lost in this way. Once the door was off, the dispatchers were strapped onto the opposite side of the aircraft. When the pilot was ready, he would push a buzzer; the dispatchers would count one—two—three—push and the heavy drums would roll out of the aircraft. At that moment the pilot would flip the tail, to ensure that the drums leaving the aircraft did not hit the rear of the aircraft. Ammunition, weapons, clothing, food and radios, all were dropped in that way.

The recovery rate initially was poor when drums fell into impenetrable jungle over a wide area, with only 10 per cent being recovered. About 20 to 25 per cent was a good recovery rate. On one occasion the drop not only missed the mark; several of the steel drums of rice hit the Kanaka hospital area, and one cut off a Kanaka's head as he lay in bed. Subsequently the Kanakas were terrified of the aircraft, the 'Baloose',

> the same word for the local pigeons that called at first
> light—'Baloose 'e cry!' When they could hear the aircraft
> approaching from some distance away, the Kanakas

would shout, 'Baloose 'e come! Baloose 'e come!' and run into the jungle. They returned when the drop had been completed.

One day after a scatter of bully beef in cases and rice in drums a bloke in my section said: 'What the hell *they* beefin' about? I been hit by *tons* 'a the bloody stuff since *I* joined the army, and it ain't killed me!'[13]

By that time a number of Australian units were scattered across the island, so basic supply-dropping facilities had to be improved. When the Americans' 'storepedos' (delivery containers) were available, it was a veritable revolution in aerial supply. Stores went down in the storepedo, which, the moment it was ejected from the plane, opened up with a parachute, thus cushioning the blow. The recovery rates went up as high as 80 per cent.

Active patrolling had started on a low key because the 2/8th knew little about the country and they were not used to working with the Kanakas. Reconnaissance was the priority. As their knowledge and confidence expanded, so did their activities. Their initial tasks were to map and to ambush. As they advanced further south, they were sometimes mounting two or three ambushes on the same day, while busily recording mapping data. What was interesting in retrospect about the ambushes was not so much where they took place but some of the varied incidents and the types of ambush. Once they could find their way around, it was unnecessary for the Australians to look far for their enemy, and ambushes were mounted on the main tracks used by the Japanese. If they received information that a track or road was being used, the patrols would wait for them to pass. A patrol usually consisted of a lieutenant, preceded by a scout, then the senior NCO—Hungerford, when he was tasked. Then came the man with the sniper's rifle, the Bren gunner and the remainder of three or four men, each armed with an Owen gun and grenades, with possibly another scout at the rear. On occasion Hungerford commanded the patrol; otherwise, if the lieutenant was young and inexperienced, he 'nursemaided' the youngster while making most of the tactical decisions himself.

As a senior NCO, Hungerford would take with him a pencil and a small notebook, to record anything worth a comment on that particular patrol. He could not take a map but relied on a Kanaka guide. Otherwise, the only item each man wore that might identify him was his 'meat ticket', the identity tag with his blood group recorded. There were no badges of rank or unit identification. Each man wore a green beret, perhaps adorned with twigs or pieces of grass to break the outline. They rubbed dirt on their faces at the ambush site. Apart from their weapons and some basic rations, that was it. They did not carry torches but would insert wooden sticks that glowed with the phosphorus of rotting wood, at the back of each man's pack. The man behind could follow the ghostly gleam, which was the only signal in a darkness that was otherwise like black velvet pulled over their eyes.

An early patrol was nearly a disaster. The men had crossed the river and were proceeding so slowly that at first Hungerford had to remind himself that, in spite of the absence of obvious danger, the intelligence received was that this patrol could encounter active opposition. They had entered Japanese-held territory. Previously they had patrolled, seeking out the enemy. Now they knew the Japanese were there, waiting for the Australians: the hunted would become the hunters. By the time he had rationalised his thoughts, they had covered a considerable distance, very slowly, watching every step, never taking an eye off the side of the track and, he hoped, invisible to the Japanese.

The unseen enemy ahead released a fusillade! It was wild shooting with the bullets coming at an angle from either side of the track. Immediately, the commandos flung themselves to the ground, wriggled into cover and returned the fire, hoping to hit someone. Bursts of lead cracked above their heads, both sides firing blind. All they could see in the dense undergrowth was a quick flitter of the enemy. Then the clatter of firing died away. There was an eerie silence with just the crash of some animal, probably a wild pig, making off in panic. In spite of their caution, the Australians had been caught unawares, and the patrol was fortunate that the entire half dozen of them were not all casualties. Maybe the Japanese ordnance was inferior, or perhaps they were just bad shots, but only one of Hungerford's patrol was hit, his kneecap shattered. Although each patrol carried a supply of sulphur drugs to be powdered onto open wounds, nothing could be done for the wounded man in this instance, and he was helped back to camp immediately, ahead of the rest of the patrol. That was where the Kanakas were superb. If they had the time, they were expert at making a little stretcher out of bush timber and kunda vines. But on this occasion the wounded man put his arms around the shoulders of two of them and hopped his way back, in some agony.

At that stage of the campaign they had no painkillers with them. Later, patrols were issued with morphine syrettes, which were very useful on one occasion, when one of them was bitten by a big centipede. 'He was in agony, screaming and groaning,' and the patrol feared that the noise would make their presence known to the enemy. Each of the men donated their syrettes to calm him. As a result the unfortunate man became a drug addict after the war, which was not uncommon when there was easy access to morphine.

When the firing died after this first contact with the enemy, Hungerford had been looking around for any further sign of action and something to shoot at, when he suddenly thought how hungry he was. The patrol had had a very early breakfast at about 5 a.m., and it was now nearly lunchtime. He remembered that he had put a piece of Christmas cake, sent by his sister Peg, in his little bag. Sitting there in the jungle, having just tried to kill his fellow human beings, he munched contently on this reminder of goodwill towards all men.

Apart from being attacked by the Japanese, the wild pigs were another cause of sudden alarm. The patrol would be sitting at night, overlooking a track in the middle of Japanese territory waiting for the enemy to pass, and, about 25 metres away, there would be a loud crash in the bush. A sudden surge of adrenaline among the hidden men and then the realisation, fingers off triggers...wild pigs! It was a shame that the Australians could not even eat them, because they were full of diseases and worms. Whenever they visited a Kanaka village, their hosts would barbecue a wild pig, and the guests' response always had to be a regretful shake of the head. If they had decided to eat the meat and became ill, it was regarded as a self-inflicted wound and a military crime, so they left the wild pigs alone. But the threat of infected pork was the least of the ills that threatened them.

The principal 'self-inflicted wound' they could do nothing about, except seek treatment, was hookworm. This is an unpleasant endemic tropical infection of parasitic worms that make their way to the small intestine. The larvae enter the skin via the sweat glands, where the female lays thousands of eggs that pass out of the body, turn into larvae in infected soil that seek the next host to be in contact. The patrol once visited a hut in a clearing where two graves indicated a previous concentration of Japanese troops in residence. The hookworm was in immense infestation on the grave mounds. As usual, the Australians had approached very quietly, crawling on their fronts, over the graves. By the time they were back in camp, some of the men had come out in rashes. Hungerford himself became infected very badly with about 80,000 of them, he was later told, and eight or ten of the men most stricken, he among them, were evacuated to the coast. There they were administered with what was called the 'hookworm bomb'. They were starved for 24 hours, then given the hookworm bomb, 'akin to drinking a glass of petrol, a packet of Epsom salts and a cup of very strong, sweet tea'. The worms having been starved for a day were hungry, and the host's blood was sluggish from the enforced starvation. Then the hookworm bomb hit the unwelcome 'guests', and the Epsom salts with the tea expelled them from the body.

Malaria was subdued by Atebrin, and hookworm, 'prickly heat', impetigo and fungus that affected the crotch, under the arms and between the toes, added to the men's discomfort. Sometimes the sufferers could not walk as a result. The medics had a brutal way of treating prickly heat. When the little pustules came up, the Regimental Aid Post (RAP) orderly used to break them with a rough cloth and apply methylated spirits. It worked up to a point. Gentian violet, a dye much in vogue at one stage for treating burns, was popular until it was discovered that infection flourished under the coating. Red mercurochrome and peroxide were useful for various conditions, and much in demand by the Kanakas for hair colouring. If they could obtain a supply of gentian violet or mer-curochrome, and another that was brilliant green, the Australians were treated to the colourful sight of great heads of purple, red, green or even white hair.

Chapter 7

Alarums and Excursions

The Japanese had been mainly living off the land. A favourite ploy of the Australians was to shoot them up in the gardens, having done a reconnaissance the evening before. At first light the next morning the only sounds were the crowing of the cocks and the shrills of the native birds in the tall trees surrounding the clearings. Keen eyes scanned the sleepy Japanese soldiery as they stumbled from their beds and walked outside to relieve themselves—and that was the last they knew. They would fall, kicking and screaming, in a hail of bullets, while their assailants faded back into the jungle, making good their escape before an avenging force could be organised to follow them up. But the 2/8th preferred to set up ambushes on small groups, moving between camps and preferably those caught carrying stores. The aim was not so much to inflict casualties, although that was good if they could, as to discomfit the Japanese and make them feel that nowhere was safe for them. There were some notable successes, notably the night of the 'wheely-wheely' ambush. 'Wheely-wheely' was what the Kanakas called any vehicle on wheels.

A Kanaka came into the 2/8th camp and reportedly excitedly: 'Long harp ['The other side of the island'] one-pella wheely-wheely go walkabout come' ['At night a truck goes up the road']…'Bring 'em 'e come some-pella man' ['men in the back of the truck']. 'Long night-time 'e come.' So it was decided to take out this wheely-wheely.[1]

A patrol of about ten or twelve men was mounted. Bruce Killen, the young and rather inexperienced lieutenant, was in command, supported by Sergeant Hungerford, a corporal and eight or nine troopers. They arrived in the afternoon and were in position on the first night. It was raining heavily at the chosen location, and Hungerford stretched out with his head on his pack, fully dressed in the downpour, wondering idly to himself what on earth he was doing there. They lay at the side of the road until nearly midnight, before the Japanese truck arrived, travelling very fast downhill. Hungerford urgently passed the word along the line: 'Stop! Stop—Stop!'

They held their fire, and there was no ambush that night. They reckoned that on the next night the truck would be toiling uphill the other way. They would hide in the jungle for another day and wait for the truck to return that night as it was a regular run, or so the Kanaka told them. Sure enough, they heard it approaching from some distance away, its engine labouring as it tackled the steep gradient. The patrol waited tensely, fingers on triggers, until the vehicle was right in front of Hungerford. Then the Bren opened up, straight into the cab, killing everyone in front. The rest of the ambush concentrated on the men in the back of the truck. The screams of agony gradually ebbed away. Shattered glass was everywhere. The patrol was lucky: if the truck had plunged on top of the Australians, it could have been serious, but the stricken driver had wrenched the vehicle away from their side of the track. It had come to an abrupt halt across from them.

There was dead silence, the Japanese victims lay quiet and the blackness in the cover of the trees was intense. The truck had no headlights and had been steered by the white clay of the road, which gleamed slightly in the starlight. The adrenaline slowly ebbing, the patrol waited long enough to make sure they had all survived, but the Japanese had been taken completely unawares, with no chance to respond. The attackers melted back into the black jungle, in case a rescue party was sent out. They had no idea where the nearest Japanese base was located, and it could have been that the dead men were part of a small group of Japanese military based in Kanaka gardens that provided them with fruit and vegetables.

The next day, a couple of the Australians returned to the ambush site with two Kanaka scouts, to count the dead. Nineteen Japanese infantry had been killed. Their bodies were searched for anything that could identify them. After snatching what sleep they could in hiding, and buoyed by the success of the 'wheely-wheely' operation, the Australians went into what was to be the most dangerous raid of all.

It started well; it was a beautiful day, following on the earlier downpour. As Lieutenant Killen was still inexperienced, it was Sergeant Hungerford who suggested that some of the patrol mount another ambush, instead of them all just walking back to camp. Four troopers stayed with their sergeant. Killen agreed to the plan and returned to camp with the others. Hungerford and his party—'Chick' Parsons, Alan Cobb, Slim Cater and Peter Pinney (himself, incidentally, later an author of note)—walked cautiously along the track until they came to an ideal spot: a long-dead tree. It lay parallel with the road, more than a metre high on its side, perfect for hiding behind while waiting for someone to come along the track. There was a clump of banana palms just out in front, and Peter Pinney said he would position himself behind the banana palms. Hungerford disagreed: Pinney would mask the fire of those behind the log and could be shot himself. The patrol commander emphasised that as they were only a small group and a long way from base, they could not afford to engage a large detachment of the enemy. They would let four or five walk past, and if there were still a few coming up behind, they would shoot up those in the middle and withdraw smartly. That was the arrangement.

In time, a column of Japanese troops was sighted, well-built men, moving briskly. They foolishly announced their presence by loud talk and the clanking of the utensils they carried, unlike their opponents, who always kept silence and masked the billy and dixies by wrapping them in rags. The ambushers should have known that this was a big party of troops, just by their noise, and it was later learnt that they were marines from the large contingent down at Buin. Because of Hungerford's stricture that they would open up only on a small group, they let six or eight of these well-equipped men through, followed by a raggle-taggle of regular soldiers, and Hungerford thought it was sensible that they had not fired. There were marines at the rear of the column. Then—to everyone's shock, both the enemy and the Australians—Peter Pinney released a burst of fire.

Two of the Japanese fell, jerked feebly and lay silent. By then everyone had opened fire. Immediately the marines at the rear did a 'box trick', diving straight back into the jungle on either side of the track to move up on either side of the Australians. It was apparent that these were no ordinary infantry: the patrol had to retire immediately if they were to save themselves. The Japanese were almost alongside them, and there was much whistling and shouting as their pursuers crashed on into the dense jungle. The handful of Australians plunged ahead of them, hearts pounding, their packs, ammunition and firearms weighing them down. They gradually widened the distance between themselves and the enemy.

Soon the tumult had died behind them as they penetrated deeper into the jungle and, since it was each man for himself at that stage, it was inevitable that the patrol broke up. Once Hungerford and the one other with him, Slim Cater, had decided they had shaken off the Japanese, they headed for camp. On this occasion they had no Kanaka with them, but they knew that if they went straight back they would strike the track from the camp. There they caught up with three of the others, but there was still one missing: Alan Cobb, the lance corporal. He was a capable young man, at home in the jungle. He knew his way around, he had a compass and Hungerford was not unduly worried; Cobb would find his way back on his own. They eventually walked into the camp by mid-afternoon without incident and, as they had had no sleep for two nights, they went straight to their tents.

Hungerford had not been on his bed very long when an old Kanaka named Kumba[2] asked to talk to him urgently. Kumba was in great distress and said: 'Masta Tom, me look 'um 'long Masta Alan. ['I've seen Alan.'] Emi dai tasol—emi no dai pinis.' ['He died a little bit but is not really dead.'] It sounded as if Cobb was in a bad way. Hungerford hurried to tell Major Winning that he, Hungerford, had to rescue Cobb. It was urgent. The party consisted of Lieutenant Clifton, Sergeant Hungerford with twelve troopers including 'Spud' Murphy, a medic, six Kanakas to make and carry a stretcher, and two good scouts. The major knew Hungerford had already been out for two days, but Cobb was one of the sergeant's men and Hungerford was determined to help retrieve him.

Kumba briefed the scouts on that one spot in the jungle where the wounded man was lying, and the scouts led them straight to Alan Cobb, in the last light of the day. He lay under the dewar tree where Kumba had found him and covered him with leaves. Cobb was still alive but deeply unconscious. A shot had sliced the front of his skull, skimming the front of his brain and leaving a hideous gash. The Kanakas constructed a stretcher out of bush timber, tied it up with kunda vine, lifted Cobb onto it and set off. On this rescue they had taken a torch for the first time and were forcing a path through what the Kanakas called 'bush nothing', meaning terrain unfamiliar to them. After some hours there was a problem:

how were they going to make their way through the thickest part, encumbered with the wounded man on his improvised stretcher? It was solved by two of the Kanakas walking ahead with machetes, laboriously clearing a path, cutting away any boughs that might hit the unconscious man.

They plodded along all night in a miasma of exhaustion, the blackness alleviated solely by the gleam of the torch, the only sounds the crash of the machetes ahead and their own laboured breathing. At one stage they reached a *garamut* (a 'sing-sing' house with big drums made of hollowed-out logs), a local hall for the Kanakas, a beautiful building made long ago out of bush timber. The beams were constructed from great trees, and a very high hard slope on the roof was made of *sac-sac*, sago leaves or thatch, attached to a long pole with orchids growing along the beams. Alan Cobb was lowered into the *garamut*. Two Kanakas were still sitting up, chewing betel nut, as was their habit. The party collapsed to the ground for a short rest.

It was well into the morning by the time a fresh team from the camp found them and took over the burden. By later that day they were back in camp. Cobb was placed in the RAP tent, and for a long while remained comatose. 'I regularly went to his bedside, as did everyone else when they had time, hoping to find an improvement: "G'day Alan! How are you?" '[3] At first there was no response. At last the wounded man stirred: Cobb waggled a finger. He could now survive a 'casevac' (a medical evacuation). An Auster aircraft bounced into the little landing strip cut by the Kanakas in the jungle on top of the hill. Alan Cobb was flown to Torokina and back to Australia. He was permanently disabled, but was eventually able to walk. He subsequently married and held down a job, in charge of a lift in a big office in Melbourne. As for Kumba, he was rewarded with a dozen bully beef tins and three sticks of tobacco. He was also released from patrolling and—his greatest delight—presented with an Australian slouch hat.

That was the most stressful ambush Tom Hungerford undertook personally and one that could have had even worse consequences. The 2/8th suffered other, more disastrous incidents. On one occasion it was the fault of the young officer,[4] someone not best respected by the men, in charge of a particular patrol looking for Japanese, up a track that zigzagged the side of a hill. Hungerford happened to be back in camp on that occasion. The officer set up the ambush with one group at the top of the track and one below, a thoughtless decision, given what then occurred. One of the patrol at the top was the same 'Chick' Parsons who had been with Hungerford previously. A tough timber-cutter from the north coast of New South Wales, he was much liked. All Parsons saw through the greenery was someone dressed in khaki, and yellow in hue, walking up the side of the hill carrying a Japanese aluminium dixie. Parsons did not hesitate: it had to be a Japanese. He aimed—and shot the man dead. Tragically, it was another Australian, 'Slats' Slater, also highly regarded by the others. He had been carrying a Japanese dixie, souvenired from a dead Japanese, to carry water (a practice stopped immediately thereafter), and of course his skin was yellow from the Atebrin taken for malaria prevention.

To shoot one of the enemy was undertaken without regard, without the slightest feeling for the other's life. The enemy was dehumanised; he had to be, otherwise how could one shoot him down and leave him, lying in his bloody entrails? But to kill your own friend, that was tragedy beyond consolation. The men would hold someone responsible for it—not Parsons, but the officer who had set the ambush. There would surely be trouble. 'When I heard of the incident, I hurried to Major Winning and said urgently: "Major, we've got to get [Lieutenant Jones] out of the camp, other-wise Chick Parsons is going to kill him!" '[5]

Major Winning understood immediately: he summoned the officer concerned, told him briefly of his decision and arranged for him to be sent down to the coast at once, with a convoy of Kanakas. Parsons was grief-stricken, and Hungerford stayed awake that night in Parsons' tent, to calm him down. Whether he ever got over it fully Hungerford never knew. Nobody would have minded so much if it had been the man responsible for siting the ambush who had been shot; that would have been poetic justice.

The poor quality of some officers was one reason why Hungerford claimed he was happy not to take a commission, whatever mixed feelings he might have had about his prospects for a commission, at the start of his training. He felt he could not take sole charge of such capable men, as is the role of a commissioned officer. He would be responsible for their lives. Hungerford did not acknowledge to himself the other qualities that had made him a good NCO: his powers of leadership, his physical presence, his wit, his practical education and his overall experience. It so happened that about three months before the end of the war, two of them, Lee Clarke and himself, were nominated for commissions in the field, but the war ended before the commissions came through. At least Hungerford knew that the army thought he was worth it.

As the campaign ground on through 1945, the 2/8th was determined to kill or capture as many Japanese as possible, working in small efficient groups and refining their ambushes. Stories of Japanese treatment of Australian prisoners of war were by now common knowledge, after a US submarine had torpedoed a Japanese transport in 1944. The vessel had been carrying Allied prisoners of war from the infamous Burma Railway for forced labour in Japan, and the world learnt of their barbarous treatment from the survivors. Nearly fifty years later, it is hard to relate this cold-blooded, impersonal hatred and revenge to the jovial old men gathered for successive Anzac Day reunions, although there is always one at least who comes up with a blood-thirsty recollection.[6]

Perhaps the ultimate refinement in their ambushing technique was demonstrated when it was determined to waylay a

Japanese convoy carrying *kau-kau* (sweet potato). Information had been received from a Kanaka who spoke of one particular road occasionally used by the Japanese to carry packs of *kau-kau*, in among which—so it was reported—they carried documents. A patrol was tasked with visiting the road by the evening, establishing an ambush position, and lying awake all night watching the track. They were in position by 4 p.m., having eaten in the jungle en route to avoid movement at the ambush site. This was at a bend in the road: Japanese foot patrols tended to negotiate bends in a loosely extended line. There was also a large dead tree lying partly across the road. This was also ideal: the enemy would likely bunch up as they negotiated the tree.

The ambush was carefully choreographed, almost like the moves in a ballet. Hungerford with one or two others would secure the tracks into the scrub on the opposite side of the road from where the rest of the patrol was in hiding. Once the first blast went off, the plan was to follow up with a devastating fire on the rest. Those Japanese not killed in the initial encounter would scatter into the scrub, to hide or run away. Sometimes the frightened survivors would throw grenades if they managed to reach the scrub on the other side, but it was fortunate that the Japanese grenades were very poor quality, compared with the British Mills bomb, the HE36.

At first, all went to plan. The Japanese scout cautiously advanced around the bend, saw that the track was clear and beckoned to the others to follow him. As the Japanese negotiated the bend and the dead tree, each Australian hidden at the side, slowly and methodically, aimed at an unsuspecting target. There was the thunder of fire, and the wretched Japanese spun as the bullets hit them, shrieking as they collapsed. They flapped and then lay still in the contortions of sudden death. As soon as the first blast had gone off, those not hit in the fusillade had scattered and the firing stopped. There was the sudden contrast of silence. The smoke blew away.

I lifted my head. All was quiet. With my Owen gun held ready to fire, I walked down the track. I was intent on searching the bags of *kau-kau* for documents and [for two to three metres] I picked up the packs of *kau-kau* and threw them to the side. I had just reached the big tree trunk, about a metre high, when my corporal, Jimmy Nolan, suddenly yelled: 'Get off the track, you silly bastard! You'll get hit!'[7]

Hungerford ducked below the trunk as he saw a khaki cap with the Rising Sun emblem looming on the other side of the tree. He pulled the Owen's trigger right in the face of the startled Japanese—nothing happened. He had forgotten to refill his magazine. He swung the butt around automatically and smacked the unfortunate Japanese in the face. At that moment, Hungerford felt a swish past him as Jimmy Nolan put a burst of bullets into the man, who toppled over dead. And after all that, there was nothing in the bags except *kau-kau*. There were about ten dead Japanese crumpled in the road, and in the excitement no one noticed whether others had escaped into the bush on the other side of the track. They did not investigate and abandoned the *kau-kau*.

Sometimes members of a patrol would return to the scene of an ambush at a later date, often when the corpses of the slain Japanese were putrefying, an accelerated process in the jungle heat. On one occasion Hungerford's patrol had been overlooking three bodies for some hours, unwilling to reveal their position until it was clear that no other Japanese were in the vicinity. They were only 10 metres from the bodies, which were visibly deteriorating from mortality to decay, with that accompanying unforgettable, heavy, sweet, cloying odour of human corruption. In the meantime, in spite of the unedifying spectacle stretched out before them, the Australians had to eat. Hungerford reached for the small reserve of rations he carried, a can of bully beef and some biscuits. He was using a stick to scrape out the fat from the can—at that time he had a craving for fat—when a large green blowfly clung to the edge of the can. He was nearly sick when he thought where it had come from.

In addition to ambushing and mapping, the other task of the 2/8th was to capture Japanese for interrogation, and Hungerford managed that, once. The standard procedure was for a patrol to settle themselves between two enemy camps, in the expectation that a single Japanese soldier would walk from one camp to the other, perhaps with a message. After two or three days this happened. The target was strolling casually along the track, with his firearm slung over his shoulder. The Japanese soldier had no idea that Australians were in the area. No ambushes had been mounted down that way. As the unsuspecting soldier came opposite the hidden men, they sprang out. One of the patrol hit the Japanese on the head with a grenade in a sock, which was enough to knock him unconscious. Helpless and dizzy when he came to, he was too heavy to carry so he was escorted on foot back to camp. The man offered no resistance and seemed more or less resigned to his fate and even glad to be out of the conflict. In camp, he was fed all the bully beef he could eat and put to bed in the little RAP tent with a guard outside. The 2/8th then had to escort him down to the coast for interrogation out of Japanese-occupied territory, and that meant crossing the Taar River.

Two commandos were detailed to escort him and two Kanakas, one at each end of the file. It was necessary according to international protocol to hang a small sign round the prisoner's neck inscribed with 'I AM A PW' so he would not be shot on sight. As they reached the Taar River they were ambushed by a Japanese patrol and were fortunate not to be killed outright. One of the Australians dived into the river and hid up against the bank under an overhang of grass. The other fled back towards the camp, which was half a day's walk away, and the two Kanakas just faded into the jungle. The Japanese patrol came out of the ambush position and waded back across the river, two or three of them in front, the prisoner, still with the sign around his neck, and two or three behind, to near where the first commando was hiding. They escorted the prisoner to a dead tree and, after a couple of minutes, the Australian hiding in the river heard a shot. He waited for a lengthy period to check that the Japanese were no longer in the area and crept along the track to find that the erstwhile prisoner had been executed by his rescuers. That seemed an extraordinary action: here was someone who could have told the Japanese the location of the Australian camp and what it contained. However, because of the Japanese belief that to be a prisoner was dishonour, the unfortunate man was eliminated.

For their part, although the 2/8th captured no more live prisoners, they did acquire many useful maps and papers during their months on Bougainville, and that was really their principal contribution to the campaign.

CHAPTER 8

Anticlimax

The end of the war came as a great surprise to Tom Hungerford and his mates. One day they were out patrolling, and the next day they were told to stay in camp. The army distributed an army newspaper by aerial drop with the food, announcing that an atom bomb had been dropped on Hiroshima. What was an atom bomb? It sounded final, but they were left with a problem locally. As far as it was known, the Japanese on Bougainville had not heard of the Japanese capitulation. In fact, although the Australians had been told that the Japanese had sued for peace on 10 August 1945, the surrender of Bougainville did not commence until 6 September 1945. In the interim all Australian patrols were suspended, to avoid unnecessary clashes.

> For the last time I...walked along the ridge-top path away from the hole we had lived in for four or five weeks. On the other side the sharp drop to the plain, the swamps we'd never had to charge across in our deathless assault on Buin, the thin blue line of the sea meeting the solid green land at the very edge of my vision. It never meant anything. It was just another place in the jungle.[1]

When hostilities formally ceased on Bougainville, the 2/8th helped to muster the Japanese prisoners of war at the end of the campaign and, in spite of the Australians' ingrained hatred for them after the stories of Japanese brutality, their captors on the whole behaved decently towards the prisoners.[2] After the final formal surrender of the 20,000 Japanese on the island on 9 September 1945, the latter were interned on small islands off the coast where they were left to fend for themselves until disarmed Japanese warships took them back them to Japan.[3]

The 2/8th was finally ordered out of the jungle to the coast where they waited to be taken down to the main base to be shipped, as they thought, back to Australia. They were settled into swampy tent lines at Torokina, enjoying the sunshine and sea on the beach after their months in the jungle, but impatient to be repatriated. With the enforced idleness there were inevitably some outbreaks of high spirits and unruly behaviour.[4] The authorities were plainly concerned that the group was being left to its own devices and, accordingly, a Brigadier (later Major General) Bridgeford visited them. He found Tom Hungerford and the others standing around on the beach, either naked or in their laplaps. 'The brigadier appeared to be unfazed by the informality of the occasion. He said: "I want to tell you, this campaign could not have been fought if it had not been for the information the 2/8th handed over to Div." '[5]

The 2/8th had certainly done its job. Hungerford was mentioned in dispatches,[6] the emblem of an oak leaf worn on a campaign medal ribbon, for his service on the island, and another soldier was awarded a British Empire Medal. The Distinguished Conduct Medal (DCM) was the most prestigious decoration awarded to a member of the unit. As a British award, after the Victoria Cross it was the next highest decoration for heroism in action that could be presented to someone not commissioned. This award of the DCM marked the only time that the 2/8th had fought in a mass engagement, one named Commando Hill, against a large and aggressive group of Japanese, on the Hongarai River. There were air strikes by Australian aircraft based at Torokina on the Japanese dug in, on the ridge above the river, and when the 2/8th moved in it was to find that, apart from a small group, the Japanese had withdrawn. The remaining Japanese were armed with a Woodpecker, a heavy machine-gun. One of the two men who had escaped with Hungerford from the Mornington Peninsula, Stan Brohartis, went in to silence the Woodpecker, close enough to throw a grenade over, in the face of the Woodpecker's fire. For that he was awarded the DCM.

The meeting on the beach with Brigadier Bridgeforth was really a turning point for Hungerford and thereafter an appalling anticlimax to his service on Bougainville. The brigadier had promised them that they would go home as a unit, but the 3rd Division, doubtless concerned at increasing indiscipline, and with no respect for the soldiers having grown into a cohesive family over the three years they had been together, disbanded the unit. A month after the Japanese had formally surrendered Bougainville,

> the men of the 2/8th Independent Company were arbitrarily lined up along the side of the road. 'Right. You, you and you to that truck, you and you go to that truck, and you and you go to that truck…' Callously cutting across deep friendships that had developed during the years of war, the men were sent to different units in camps all over the island.[7]

Not only was the unit broken up physically but so also were the men, mentally. Sergeant Hungerford was posted to 8th Infantry Battalion of 3rd Australian Division on 13 October 1945.[8] There he was expected to give basic training all over again to men who had been in action. 'It was preposterous, but the problem was that the army simply did not know what to do with this specialist group of intelligent men',[9] who had been highly trained to kill in the service of their country and who were now idle.

This was bad enough, but Tom Hungerford was deeply depressed for other reasons. Vivienne Stodart, his childhood sweetheart, had been corresponding regularly with him throughout the war. Before he had left Perth to join up, Vivienne and Tom had been keeping company for quite some time. It was a very innocent 'boy and girl' relationship that was never consummated, but they fancied themselves to be in love, and of course they had discussed the possibility of getting married before Hungerford went to war. He was the one who said no. Whether he was just making excuses to put off marriage when he made this decision, or whether he really believed it was for the best, is unclear. It was true he was worried that he might return disabled, a poor basis for a marriage, or that he might not survive at all. In the meantime he could dream of when he returned to Perth. Towards the end of the war when he was on guard duty at night, he imagined himself walking up Hay Street and entering Foys, where Vivienne worked, and saying, 'Let's go and have lunch!' He would then escort her into a jeweller's shop and buy her an engagement ring… That night they might have enjoyed Irene Dunne and Charles Boyer in *Together Again* (which was screening at Perth's Capitol cinema).[10] But it was not to be. Before the war finished Hungerford had received what was known as a 'Dear John' letter, carefully composed and full of compassion.

Vivienne wrote that she was terribly sorry to have to write like this. He had been away a long while, and she had met someone else with whom she had fallen deeply in love. They were going to get married. Tom Hungerford was shattered: he had never imagined that would happen to him, although he knew of others in his unit who had received such letters. The circumstances of his receiving the letter were also painful. One of the men in Hungerford's section, who knew about his devotion to his girl, recognised her writing.

The mail came and my mate said jokingly: 'A letter from
Viv—it's to tell you that she's dumped you!' That was it
exactly. Holding the open letter in my hand, the colour
drained from my face, I walked unsteadily towards another
friend of mine who started when he saw my demeanour:
'What the...what's wrong with you? You're white as a
ghost.'[11]

In retrospect, the jilted man had severe doubts as to whether
the marriage would have worked. Viv was an intelligent and
delightful woman in many ways, but she had a strong, puritan,
strait-laced conviction that what she said, and what her old mother
said, was right. He would have met dogmatic opposition. He was
inclined to be more laid-back in his behaviour and attitudes. It
might have been a stressful union. The man who had replaced
him in Viv's affections was a mate on a Norwegian freighter, and
he would be away much of the time she was at home. When he
returned to Perth, Hungerford could not help but meet her, because
they had mutual friends. He bore this in mind when he considered
his options, now that the war had ended.

He decided that the breakdown of the relationship was a
good reason to leave Perth, for the time being at least, but the
alternative was dreary. He was now facing an immediate future of
putting soldiers through more basic training, men who had been
in action and who were longing to be released from the army. On
20 November 1945[12] they were embarked at Torokina for the island
of Morotai, in the Celebes group, now part of Indonesia and originally under Dutch rule. There seemed to be no option but to stick at
the pointless task of basic training until, sick at heart, he had the first
opportunity to transfer from being an infantryman and decide on a
future when he was discharged. The opportunity came up.

One of the sergeants had come into the mess with the news
that the Australian Army Canteens Service (AACS) was look-

ing for NCOs. The AACS was responsible for the storage and distribution of troops' food and drink, made available to messes and canteens to purchase many of the items usually available in civilian shops in peacetime. It did not matter whether applicants had AACS training or not. They would soon learn. That was what they had been waiting for. The senior NCOs left in a body to apply: the quartermaster sergeant, the orderly room sergeant and Hungerford, with about five others.

> We were first paraded before the CO and explained our situation. He said: 'You mustn't do that!'
>
> We replied promptly: 'We're going to, Sir!'
>
> He said resignedly: 'Very well, gentlemen, if you'd prefer to be grocers than soldiers, you may go.' Soldiers! That was a laugh. Our real soldering was behind us.[13]

It was a full six months before Hungerford was able to embark on the next phase of his life but, before then, he was to put his career and his reputation on the line, all over again, by challenging authority. On Morotai, he had been put in charge of what they call an issue point, from which the units collected their supplies of beer, 'lolly-water', biscuits and toiletries. He knew nothing about what was involved; no one had told him anything, and the existing staff, who had been running it before Hungerford arrived, continued with their duties. Hungerford did practically nothing. He found his most unusual job at one stage was to be in charge of a store for the AACS that contained 60,000 bottles of gin, with just two other happy-go-lucky sergeants to help. He lived in a battered caravan, originally US property, with an ancient refrigerator. He seldom touched a bottle because unfortunately (he felt at the time) he did not like gin. It sounds like someone's heaven, but it was not his, although he came up with a recipe that combined chilled wild pawpaw and AACS tinned cream doused with sugar, the whole soaked in gin.

The enforced inactivity continued for more than three months, and it was as demoralising as being based at Torokina. A prospectus was circulated about joining 'Japforce', the occupation force in Japan, formally known as the British Commonwealth Occupation Force (BCOF). It sounded interesting: Hungerford applied and was accepted. But General MacArthur had not yet made up his mind whether the British Commonwealth forces, which included the Australians, would be permitted to take part in the occupation of Japan. The men did not know where they were going or when they were leaving. To add to the deteriorating morale, some of the men reported that they had letters from home, passing on the rumour in Australia that 'Japforce' was composed of malcontents and others who had caught diseases from the Kanakas. Of course it was ridiculous, but it upset the bored troops on Morotai. There had been other trouble brewing: many soldiers due to return to Australia were long-service men who had accumulated sufficient demobilisation points to warrant early discharge. Carrying banners with slogans like 'WE WANT SHIPS NOT ASSURANCES', 4,500 of them marched on local headquarters, where they were assured by two colonels that they would be shipped home as soon as possible.[14]

Late one night four or five NCOs came to Hungerford's little hut and told him that they were planning a 'jack-up'. Hungerford's standing with the first jack-up at Darwin was known. Would he lead it? Hungerford sympathised, but with his reputation as a troublemaker, he was concerned by the possible consequences for him if he led another potential mutiny. The others understood: there was a major who was sympathetic to their woes and who might represent them, if Hungerford declined, but the NCOs returned later with the news that the major had had second thoughts. Would Hungerford speak for them? He rationalised that he would get as much out of it as anybody, so why should he not go along with it? He certainly knew how to run a jack-up…he agreed, but he stipulated that it must be on the basis of his experiences with the Darwin strike.

As before, all the fatigues were to be carried out and there would be no larrikinism. There would be a formal parade. He arranged for the engineers to erect a public address system outside the brigadier's tent headquarters and told each NCO to march his section over, at 7.30 in the morning. No arms were to be carried. Hungerford arrived at the parade site early, 'the coconut-palms holding up a cloudless blue sky over a world cool and sunny with the promise of another perfect Morotai day'.[15] He was amazed to see that there were already no fewer than 1,300 men[16] formed up in a hollow square, with the PA system in the middle.

> They [had] swung rhythmically into the area in front of the HQ tents, all brown boots, brown skin, khaki drill and sun-warmed dust, the pale green feathers of the palms floating in the air above them. No noise but the tramp of their coming and the shouts of their NCOs as they were formed up into the huge capital 'U' which I had stipulated.[17]

What had he let himself in for? But it was too late to worry about the consequences, and Hungerford was convinced that they were in the right.

When the men had been stood at ease, Hungerford addressed them. He told them what he expected of their behaviour: there were to be no catcalls, no bad behaviour of any sort. A spokesman for the troops presented Hungerford with a list of their complaints, and he announced that he would take the list to the commander, Brigadier Nimmo, and see what could be done. So he entered the tent, heart pounding—but there was no brigadier. It was typical of the unit's poor communications that the men had no idea their CO was away in Australia. A cold-eyed officer, Colonel Colby, was sitting at the desk. Hungerford saluted, handed him the list, written on a sheet of Salvation Army paper, and the following exchange took place:[18]

> 'Colonel: these are the demands that the men have presented to you.'
> 'Demands, Sergeant?'
> 'Requests.'
> 'I can have you shot for this!'
> 'Yes, but you won't, Sir. Times have changed.'
> Colonel Colby read the list and said shortly: 'Yes, I'll come and address the men.' This he did and, in spite of his earlier demeanour when presented with the 'demands', it was in an easy, conversational and avuncular way. He went down through the list of complaints, such as, 'We want new uniforms...Some sort of amusement...We want sporting teams arranged...We want to know if we're going to Japan or not...We want something done about these rumours drifting back from Australia, that we're a bum lot.' The last complaint concerned a driver, who had been put in detention for something he had not done, and the men wanted him released. The colonel went through the whole list: 'I can do something about [this], I can't do anything about [that]...'

The big red-haired sergeant flung him a salute, and the colonel retired to his tent.

> I then addressed the men: 'Now you've heard the colonel. The brigadier's in Australia, so the colonel's in charge. You've heard what he said. He's treated you very fairly and he's been very logical about it. Now: you will all return

to your lines.' I said to the NCOs, who were all in a line behind me: 'Get your blokes back to the lines to begin your normal duties.'

The men all dispersed happily enough, 'a shuffling caterpillar of dust wriggling away under the soaring palms',[19]

except for another red-haired man, a nuggety corporal, and his little group of maybe twenty men, who were plainly filled with the blood of martyrs. I enquired: 'What's the matter, Corporal?'

The corporal replied truculently: 'We're not going back. We've got nothing out of this. That bloke didn't say anything, and Driver [So-and-So] is still in the boob!'

Hungerford said quietly: 'The colonel said he'd do what he can about the driver, and if you don't get your men back to your lines now, I'll put you under my arm and pull your fucking head off!'[20]

Sergeant Hungerford was a big man and looked as if he meant it. The corporal and his men moved away smartly. And that was it, the one of the biggest mutinies in the Australian army defused. Hungerford thought he had got away with it again: he heard nothing more from anyone in authority over the next few days.[21] Not that the daily routine had changed; time still passed slowly with nothing to do except to laze the hours away. 'One lovely morning I was relaxing on a chaise-longue, originally the property, I thought, of some poor Dutchman who had been chased out by the Japanese. I was not a pretty sight: my outfit consisted of a pair of boots, a lap-lap and a topi helmet.'[22]

A jeep pulled up with a jerk alongside him. It contained the new officer commanding the army canteens, a major who went by the sobriquet of 'Eyes-and-Teeth' in recognition of his flashing eyes and copious display of gleaming dentures.

Recoiling in shock at the unlovely apparition before him, the major enquired: 'Can you tell me where I can find Sergeant Hungerford?' 'I'm Sergeant Hungerford, Sir.' This shook the major, who rallied himself and said: 'Sergeant, go and have a shave, get dressed and come out here, quick time.' I did so and when I was in the jeep, the major said with evident sincerity: 'Sergeant, it's a terrible shock for me to come up here and find one of my senior NCOs is running a strike!'[23]

The major drove him over to the brigadier's headquarters, and Hungerford entered the tent to face Brigadier Nimmo. The moment Hungerford saw him, he thought he was on safe ground: the brigadier was an impressive figure but one who looked as if he were prepared to listen. Hungerford was introduced, and Nimmo said he wanted to know all about it. Hungerford recounted how he had been asked to head the demonstration and what had eventuated. This done, the brigadier reminded him of the consequences of having led a mutiny, particularly while the troops were still on active service.

After being harangued for a while, I interjected: 'With respect, Sir: that parade was carried out in a perfectly military fashion. There was no trouble, there was no hooting or barracking, or carrying-on. The men heard what the Colonel said and went back to their lines, to resume their duties. During that parade, none of the duties was pigeonholed. Everything carried on in the camps, except we didn't go on parade. It might have been very different if I hadn't taken control of it.'

Nimmo asked: 'Sergeant, why do you think the men chose you to lead this thing?'[24]

Hungerford thought quickly—did the brigadier know or not know about Darwin? His face impassive, he said:

> 'As a matter of fact, I had a similar experience…' 'Um, yes…Anyway, Sergeant, thank you for what you've done. I realise what it might have been, if it had not been well arranged. Now: if you have any further complaints, here's my tent. Don't go through the red tape. Just let my orderly know you're coming and I'll see you.' This was too good an opportunity to let slip. We had Japanese prisoners of war in the lines who performed the fatigues, such as cleaning out the lavatories. I said: 'As a matter of fact, Sir, there is a complaint right now. The Japanese are using the men's lavatories and the men are very worried about it.'
>
> The men had an idea they could catch venereal disease off the seats and everyone thought the Japanese were infected with VD. His manner now stern, the brigadier turned to one of several of the officers standing behind. 'Is that so, Major? Are the Japanese using the men's latrines?' 'Yes, Sir. They are.' 'Get out now, and dig latrines for the Japs!' It was after that he added: 'Sergeant: if you have any further questions, come back and see me.'[25]

So the major drove Hungerford back to the issue point, and that was practically the last that was heard about the incident.

> One day when I was being driven in Japan, the Australian driver from the motor pool said: 'I seem to know your face.'
>
> 'Oh…?'
>
> 'Did you lead that mutiny in Morotai?'
>
> 'Yes.'

'Jesus Christ, you've got guts!'

It was the only accolade I received from that bit of theatre in the raw.[26]

It was remarkable that news of the mutiny never appeared in the Australian press, such was the degree of censorship the army was able to impose. Nor was there any mention of the incident in Hungerford's army record, although details of the two events were to be noted elsewhere: he was later recorded on an ASIO list of suspected subversives.[27]

On 9 March 1946[28] Hungerford, the only volunteer from an Independent Company and the forty or so others of the AACS recruits, all NCOs like himself, were on their way from Morotai to Kure in Japan, on the Liberty ship *Stanford Victory*, another very old vessel. Hungerford never felt safe on that ship. It was a relief to step ashore, onto the war-ravaged wharves of Kure where snow was falling. As expected, nothing had been prepared for their arrival. The town was mainly in ruins, and the gaunt shapes of the bombed houses loomed in the dusk. They camped in a semi-demolished warehouse, on the second floor, and for the first few nights they slept on the concrete floor. There was no heating; there were no facilities of any sort. Later on, they were moved into billets and lived fairly comfortably, but Japan was a country reduced to extreme penury by the exigencies of war, defeat and invasion. Gangs of hungry children, desperate women and elderly men frantically sought the means of keeping themselves fed.

He was in Japan for just over nine months, over the worst part of two winters. Hungerford's OC was 'Eyes-and-Teeth', the same major who had escorted him to Brigadier Nimmo on Morotai, and they became friendly. Because of his organisational ability and leadership, wherever there was a problem, Hungerford was given charge of the issue points. He organised the gangs to work on the wharves and in the stores and oversaw the dispatch of goods to outlying areas. The local people unloaded the vessels and stored the enormous quantity and range of consumable goods being imported, to feed the occupation troops and to enable the country to recover towards self-sufficiency. He relied on interpreters, as the only Japanese word he really knew was '*Ishoge!*' ('Hurry!') Some of the Japanese labourers and clerks were demobbed servicemen, but largely they were middle-aged civilians, because the young ones had been killed or were still interned.

Generally, their attitude to him at the beginning was one of subservience, which did not prevent them from pilfering anything to which they had access. Hungerford found out later that they were leaving the store with whatever they could stuff into their under-pants. It was understandable, and forgivable in a way, because the Japanese were on starvation rations. For his part, Hungerford was not part of the thriving black market in Japan, known as 'wogging'. Some Australian servicemen made fortunes just by exchanging overseas currencies into Japanese yen.

The contrast of arriving from the tropics into snow was hard on him and his army colleagues. The change of climate was one thing, but their health was another. When they left the islands they had stopped taking Atebrin. Collapsing in the Japanese winter, Hungerford himself was hospitalised twice with malaria, as were others. It was difficult initially for the medical authorities to recognise the problem, as is often the case across the Western world, when someone suffering from malaria presents himself to a doctor who is unfamiliar with the symptoms. On the first occasion Hungerford was sitting at his desk, trying to cope with a rising temperature. Eventually he abandoned his work and reported to the doctor, who gave him a cursory examination, did not do a blood test, and gave him aspirin for the blinding headaches associated with a malaria attack. Hungerford tried to tell him why he thought he was ill, but he was shown the door and accused of malingering. He returned to his desk, but at the end of the day he collapsed on his bed. He boiled with fever and delirium, followed by cycles of intense shivering. Eventually he was taken to hospital, where it was suspected that he had malaria, but the parasite in his blood could not be isolated. He was in hospital for four days as the doctors puzzled around his bed. Finally they decided he definitely had malaria, because the fever broke. He lay soaked in sweat, 'weak as a kitten'. A few days later he had returned to full-time work.

He did not see much of Japan, but as part of his job of overseeing distribution, he did some travelling, from Kure to Tokyo, Kobe and Kyoto. He also visited Hiroshima on two occasions, the first early in his tour of duty, to call on a brewery for a load of beer. The unbelievable desert of destruction, a wasteland of desolation, the few buildings standing and the blasted, scorched vegetation shocked him immensely. He would have liked to have discussed his feelings with someone, but in all his time in Japan, no Japanese ever spoke to him about the atomic bomb. It was as though the subject was taboo, and life had to move on.[29]

Hungerford had left for Japan hating the Japanese and what he imagined they stood for, and by the time he had been there for just two weeks, he found they were just people, like those he had left behind. They were even likeable, too: he made a number of friends. His middle-aged Japanese head storeman, Yosh, he found to be a good man. They came to learn something of each other's character and temperament, and the feelings of affection were mutual. Yosh was forlorn when Hungerford eventually left for Australia. Such relationships, although they were perhaps uncommon, were indicative of the fact that the thousand or more Australians generally behaved well in Japan, certainly in contrast to other Commonwealth occupation forces, such as Indian troops, who were accused of rape and pillage.

Like the other Australians stationed far away from home, Hungerford occasionally sought female solace at the dance halls-cum-brothels, set up especially for the foreigners. Many of the women had come from good homes and were now destitute. The authorities attempted to prevent the spread of VD, and the women were medically examined regularly at the officially sanctioned brothels. Some Australians troops spent all their spare time there, and not always in those brothels that were properly inspected. They were young men who had been in the jungle for years, and the readily available, pretty young women represented a form of heaven to them. On the few occasions he visited these establishments, Hungerford found the women delightful in themselves, quite apart from the more obvious pleasures on offer.

This led to a more permanent relationship: for about two months he moved in with a Japanese girl whom he had met at the dance hall. She was upper middle class. Her grandfather, father and husband had been in the Japanese navy. She had been married to a young man whom, she believed, had been lost in a submarine off Singapore. Whether the Japanese used submarines at Singapore is debatable, but that was what she said: 'Shonan…' ('Singapore, "City of Light" '). She was sweet, tender and—it may be surmised—more than a little in love with the handsome Australian who, for his part, enjoyed a relationship that was to be the most sexually fulfilling period of his long life. Perhaps he loved her in return. But in spite of the mutual attraction, unlike some of his colleagues, Tom Hungerford never considered returning to marry and settle in Japan. He made his position plain at the start of his relationship. Marriage to a Japanese woman was generally a success for Australians who committed themselves to a formal relationship. They were taken into big families and found good jobs.[30]

He also enjoyed a brief relationship with one of the Australian secretaries posted with the Australian forces, but nothing came of it, although it was her advice that prevented Hungerford from being court-martialled for insubordination before he left for Australia. As president of the sergeants' mess, Hungerford had asked for some free liquor supplies for a party at the mess. The captain who could have approved what was a reasonable request to support the inauguration of the mess was unconvinced by the assurance that there would be no drunkenness and refused to approve the requisition. Incensed, Hungerford wrote to the captain, to the effect that although the captain might be 'an Officer and a Gentleman by King's Command', he was no gentleman. 'The secretary told me to look out for myself: "He spends his whole day going through MR and Os [the manual of military discipline], looking for something he can hang you on." '[31]

Hungerford sailed on 22 January 1947 for Sydney,[32] before the formal request for an inquiry into his insubordination, the possible prelude to a court martial, could be instituted. The voyage home was in a packed ship, some sleeping on the deck, the latest detachment of servicemen anxious for demobilisation and new lives. Hungerford breezed through Sydney, where there was no official welcome—that had occurred much earlier when the first of the troops had returned—just a greeting from some members of his old unit who came down to the wharf. They had been demobbed earlier, as soon as they had been released from Bougainville. Returning to Australia was another anticlimax. He was about to become a civilian again.

CHAPTER 9

Reorientation

~~~

As a member of a big family, soon-to-be ex-soldier Hungerford had enjoyed the army. He had been responsible for the care and comfort of his men and had come to know everything about them. It had been an interesting time for him; he had found the routine highly satisfying. Every aspect of his physical wellbeing had been looked after. In its way, it was a comfortable existence, once he had come to terms with what he had regarded as the sometimes outrageous expectations and omissions of the military hierarchy. But he had no thoughts at any point of staying on and making a military career. Not that it would have been a realistic option: the Australian Government was desperate to reduce the expense of maintaining a large force at war-time level. No, Hungerford was looking forward to making his way as a civilian and was already regarding himself as one. He took the train straight through from Sydney to Melbourne, en route to Perth.

He had made one particularly good friend in the AACS, who lived in Melbourne, and the Western Australian contingent was due to spend a couple of days there before boarding the train to Perth. The friend invited Hungerford to stay with him, instead of being based in tented accommodation on one of the football ovals.

But two days only? He decided to take a week off in Melbourne and, in the military jargon, go 'absent without leave'. After all, he rationalised, the army could not do anything serious to him as he was about to be discharged. This was typical of a man who carefully thought out the consequences and did not act on mere impulse, a feature of Hungerford's make-up. Here was also the strong rebellious streak in him emerging. Yes, they could remove his sergeant's stripes and reduce him to being a private soldier again. Well, he had been there before, although at his own request, but otherwise there was little else they could do, other than throw him out of the army. He had never seen Melbourne so—with the help of his friend's attractive sister—he thoroughly enjoyed the unauthorised break.

> But at some stage I had to draw some money, and the moment I produced my paybook [to record the transaction] I was accosted and escorted to the major-in-charge. The major said sadly: 'Sergeant: it's a terrible shame, spoiling this clean record after four years of service! You have besmirched your paybook.' After four years in the army and in spite of my various brushes with authority, I did not have a single military misdemeanour recorded in my paybook. I thought, God, the silly old bugger. I said: 'Look Sir, I've done the right thing, I am in the army now, but not of it. I am virtually a civilian on the way out. I am endangering nobody; I live on the other side of the continent. I wanted to have a week here in Melbourne, which I've never really seen, and I have a good mate here to knock around with.' I was fined £10 and was not reduced in rank.[1]

Once again, Hungerford rationalised a potentially serious situation by talking himself out of trouble. However, he was immediately detailed to be part of a burial guard for a deceased soldier. It was a nuisance, a punishment of a sort, just to let him know that the powers-that-be were displeased with him and that he was still in the army.

When he arrived in Adelaide they camped out again, awaiting the next train across the Nullarbor. He arranged to visit another friend, Bob West, ex-2/8th. It was a long bus trip out to West's house in the suburbs. Hungerford was feeling a bit sick as he entered the bus, and on the way he was very ill indeed, to the point that when he alighted, he could hardly walk from the bus stop to the house. As he walked unsteadily up to the little suburban house, he found Bob's wife Peg working at a sewing machine on the open back veranda. She noticed his condition and asked what was wrong with him. Hungerford just groaned and collapsed onto an old couch, where he stayed for two days, until yet another attack of malaria had passed. He had had only one day's official leave in Adelaide, and once the rigor and sweat had passed and the fever abated, he returned to the camp, to explain his second unauthorised absence. This time there was no trouble; he was dosed up for the remaining journey to Perth.

Somewhere near the settlement of Cook, one of the tiny maintenance centres on the long straight stretch of rail into Western Australia, the train was held up by a wash-away. It was near a fettlers' camp, and one of the fettlers must have known there was a troop train coming through that would be stopped. He had trapped or shot bags of rabbits that were in plague proportions then, in even the most remote regions. The train had hardly pulled up when Hungerford heard a voice outside the train, 'Roast stuffed rabbits! Roast stuffed rabbits! Two bob a top!' Luckily this enterprising entrepreneur was right outside Hungerford's carriage. He wondered how the fettler's wife had managed to cook so many rabbits and bought one for each of the eight hungry soldiers, a blessed change from army rations. Despite the fact that they were back in Australia, they had been still living on bully beef, beans and biscuits.

Once in Perth they went straight to Karrakatta to be formally discharged from the army. As Hungerford was being processed he had to be passed by the medical officer (MO), who asked:

'Have you got any problems?'

'None really, Sir. I've had hookworm, malaria, dengue fever, that stuff,' and almost as an afterthought I added: 'My ankle's very sore.'

'Let's have a look at it,' and the MO examined it. He said: 'Ummm, I think I'll put you under [a general anaesthetic] and have a good look at it.'

When I came to, the MO said: 'I've got news for you. You've had an unresolved fracture of your ankle for two or three years.'[2]

This meant that all his commando work had been accomplished on a broken ankle and, yes, it had been sore…

I said, startled: 'Hell—I know it had been bad. What do you do?'

The MO replied casually: 'Oh well, we just put you back into hospital: we'll break the ankle and reset it.'

'How long will that take?'

'Three months.'

'No, I can't do it!' I was about to shed my uniform after four years and felt I just could not stay in the army, much as I had liked it. I was tasting freedom, rather like a bird escaping its cage, and I wanted more of it.

The MO said resignedly: 'Well, that's your business. I can't force you.' However, being classed as a war-induced injury, the doctor must have recommended me for a limited disability pension because later, I received a communication from the army saying I would be awarded a pension of 7/6d a fortnight.[3]

What was more important was that now he was on the veterans' pension records. When the ankle really started to deteriorate in later life, it would have cost him heavily if he had not been entitled to veterans' benefits.

He was formally discharged from the army on 11 April 1947.[4] Initially it felt very strange to be a civilian again. Carrying his demob civilian suit (which he never wore) he went to stay at his sister Peg's.

Jubilee Street was still as shabby-genteel as ever behind its white-laced front-room curtains…People I met, for the first time in years, said: 'G'day! Nice to see ya!' or: 'Where ya been? Most 'a boys been home for ages!' or 'Well, you won't find much changed around here!' In some way which I didn't even bother to think about, I resented South Perth's complacency—when I should have treasured it. I'd changed—that I knew. The world had changed. South Perth hadn't, and moreover, wasn't about to change. I felt that if I wanted to come back to it, I'd have to squeeze myself, somehow, into the old mould I knew I'd discarded forever. I had a mental picture of myself as a full-grown cray trying to get back into the shell it had shed when it was a kaka.[5]

Peg was actually living in Hungerford's old home, married to Geoff Archdeacon with the first of their little boys. She was an authentic, good-hearted Western Australian woman, with a Western Australian inevitability about the way she looked and dressed. As with her younger brother, there was a stable rock-solid agelessness to her. She was a woman who maintained an innocence about life that was also typical of Tom Hungerford himself.[6] As noted earlier, his younger sister Alice had died in 1942 of rheumatic fever.

He caught up with his elder brother Mick, who had returned as a captain after marrying Mollie and going away to the war, and they already had the first of two girls. Mick had settled down, and now the brothers got on well together. In the early days, of course, Hungerford had been jealous of him and resented the position Mick held as the older brother, good-looking, capable and an athlete. Before the war Mick had been a good golfer and became president of the Karrinyup Golf Club. Mick had been a salesman for Yalumba Wines, and he continued as state manager after he returned. He was a socially conscious man and a prominent member of Legacy. Mick's problem was that in time he became fatally addicted to his own product, which was to contribute to his early death in 1977.

What should Tom Hungerford do next? He was not badly off at this stage of his life, with more than £700 in the bank. Of course, Vivienne was still on the Perth scene, which was one reason Hungerford felt he should leave. Two employment options had emerged. Jim McCartney of the *West Australian* offered him a D grade journalist position, on the basis of his previous writing experience. Another idea was of perhaps returning to New Guinea, to work as an overseer on plantations, along with a couple of friends, both ex-sergeants and proficient in pidgin. Hungerford had been in touch with his mate Wal; he put it to him that they should return to the islands. Wal was enthusiastic, so with Viv in mind and the thought of returning to New Guinea, he decided to turn down the McCartney offer and leave Perth after staying with Peg for only two or three weeks. He flew across to Sydney, the first time he had ever been in an aircraft. It was also a momentous occasion for his sister and brother-in-law with their little boy who saw him off in a Douglas DC10. It seemed a huge aircraft to them then, the reliable workhorse of the time, but it was a long flight of ten hours.

Once he had landed in Sydney it soon became apparent that the New Guinea plans would not eventuate, because Wal's mother objected: Wal was her only support. Hungerford wondered what he should do with his life. When he was still in the army, he had vowed to take a month's holiday for every year he spent in uniform, to compensate for all the toil and danger. That meant he owed himself four months holiday. He found a bed in Castlecrag, a beautiful part of the world, a long funnel of land running out into Sydney Harbour, in the Roseville area. He was staying in the boathouse of a family who were the uncle and aunt of a mate of his in the army who 'adopted' Hungerford on his arrival in Sydney. They lived in their house on the hill and Hungerford lived by the water. At first, he had a marvellous time swimming and fishing. Not long after he had been there, he had just dived off the front of the boathouse into the harbour.

> I suddenly noticed 'Auntie' Ol leaning out of the window and screaming for me, and my first thought was that something had happened to 'Uncle' Ern, so I raced up seventy steps to the house. 'Auntie' Ol gasped, 'Oh, never do that!' She took me to the window and pointed—there, there and there—where people had been taken by sharks, in the very spot where I had dived, so of course I never did it again.[7]

Instead, he used to row a little skiff over to the Spit Bridge and fish from there. He became a member of a good water polo team, organised a swimming carnival and in the winter played basketball.

In between enjoying himself, he continued to write a few short stories, just as he had done while still in the army, mostly published in *The Bulletin*. He had written one article on the occupation of Japan for the *West Australian*, which was probably never published. He also took a job as a junior subeditor for two Sydney publications, *Truth* and *Sportsman*, at £9 12s a week.[8] A writer friend was later to recall meeting Hungerford in Sydney a few years later: he saw him as the apotheosis of 'the warrior returned'. Hungerford radiated power. He had the biggest arms his friend had ever seen on a man; he was built like a wrestler, with huge sloping shoulders. When this friend was corresponding with an agent in London, he remarked that Tom Hungerford wrote the most beautiful poetry, but was the quintessential wharf labourer to look at.[9]

Whenever a ship was due from Japan, Hungerford went into Sydney to meet the returning soldiers. On one occasion after a convivial night at Marrickville with a number of men who had just docked, he got very drunk, drinking spirits as well as beer. He had felt quite normal in the pub, but when they went outside it was very cold and he came to in the back of a police car, with two others. He was gaoled until about midnight. Coping with the aftermath of heavy drinking he was dimly aware that he was in trouble, although there was a lighter moment.

> There was one man locked up with me, who kept repeat-ing, 'I don't mind—the missus will keep the saveloys warm for me.' Then, quite suddenly, I was released. The police were straightforward: 'You can demand a trial, or you can give us ten shillings now, and you're out.'
>
> 'Make it ten shillings!' They probably used to pocket that kind of back-hander, I thought, but I had no way of knowing. I did not care. I was free.[10]

About this time one of his friends from the army, Frank Norton, the artist,[11] wrote to Tom Hungerford and asked if he would like a good job. Norton had been doing artwork for Colonel Treloar, director of the Australian War Memorial, who had asked him if he knew of anyone who could take over the editorship of a War Memorial publication, *As You Were*. Hungerford was intrigued by the thought of handling the written experiences of other returned soldiers. He had always wanted to visit Canberra, if only to see what happened in the national capital, and was put in touch with Treloar.

Treloar's idiosyncratic reputation lingers today. His whole working life had been at the Memorial, starting in Melbourne and continued until his death, except during World War II when he was posted to the Middle East in a clerical role, from which he returned as a lieutenant colonel to resume his work as director. His pre-war forté had been raising considerable funds for the Memorial through the sale of publications, such as *As You Were*, the celebrated 'Christmas Books' series that sold so well to ex-servicemen and their families. After the war, however, Treloar became obsessive in his desire to control every aspect of the Memorial's administration, insisting on seeing all correspondence and issuing reams of lengthy memoranda.[12] He asked Hungerford to forward two or three pieces he had written. Hungerford responded enthusiastically and, after a lengthy exchange of correspondence, was invited to take the job, at £1,100 a year. He sent a cable to confirm he was ready to leave Sydney—EVERYTHING IN GARDEN LOVELY: TOM HUNGERFORD—and shortly after his thirty-first birthday, on 1 June 1947,[13] he travelled by rail to work in Canberra, his first proper job after leaving the army.

The train stopped at an attractive little station that dates from the 1860s. He was amazed that all he could see from the train were paddocks, a couple of houses, a few sheep, goats...where was he? Colonel Treloar had said that Hungerford would have to commute into Canberra daily—but where was the capital of Australia? He was reassured that this was only the small (as it was then) town of Queanbeyan on the outskirts of the capital, and he took a room there, in Walsh's Hotel. This was also a shock, the first time he had lived in a pub. His was a small, cold, impersonal room. But the woman in charge was a 'charmer', and she made the tall red-headed newcomer welcome. Every night there was a big fire in the lounge room, where Hungerford sat and talked to people, his lifetime pleasure. He had brought little money with him; he had a savings account at the time and thought to draw money on arrival. Friday came and the transfer had not come through. 'I had to pay my rent and I apologised to the landlady, "I'm terribly sorry, but I have no money. They haven't sent my account up here." "Mr Hungerford, don't worry. Can I lend you some?" It warmed my heart.'[14]

He used the pub as a base, travelling by bus into and out of Canberra, for two or three weeks. Then he decided to base himself closer to the job, and on 24 July 1948[15] he moved to the Karrawarra Guesthouse, near the Manuka shops. Karrawarra was run by Miss Cassie Thompson, who hailed originally from a dairy farm at Nimmitabel, in the Australian Alps. She was a fat, jolly business-like woman, who earned plenty of money from her 'Young men taken and done for', and she had eight or ten young men living there. Hungerford was one of them for quite some time, but he relates that Miss Cassie came to fancy him sexually and that made life very uncomfortable. Until then, however, she showed her worth as a mother figure. One of the young men had asthma. He would sit up in bed coughing until Cassie came down the corridor into the two-man bedroom to look after him. She would do the same for Hungerford when he was up late writing and could not sleep. A glass of hot milk would induce slumber. He left Cassie when things got 'too hot', and took a room in a hostel and later stayed with some friends of his in the Canberra suburb of O'Connor.

He enjoyed an energetic social life after work and at some later stage became deeply involved with a woman in Canberra, a physical education teacher at Canberra High School, whom initially he found sensual and delightful after the barren post-Japan years. By then he had started on the three novels he was to complete while he was in Canberra over three years. His girlfriend used to stay at his place for the weekend, and at the time he was fully occupied with writing. 'The relationship did not last, mainly because she would come and look over my shoulder and say, "Oh, why did he say that? What's he going to do next?" That constituted serious interference with my work.'[16]

He suspected then that he could never share his writing craft with a partner, although she was probably not the right woman for him in any event. Perhaps no one could ever be right for him, he had concluded. Novels aside, however, the principal focus then had to be on what he was being paid for.

> The Australian War Memorial stood in splendid isola-
> tion among the gullies of Mount Ainslie's ochre-coloured
> foothills. When I first saw it, I thought it must be the most
> beautiful, most beautifully sited, building in Australia, and
> I never tired of gazing at it. In that clear-glass upland air
> its vast angled surfaces of plain grey stone changed from
> alabaster to honey to ice as the light of morning, noon and
> evening flowed over and about it.[17]

Just below the cupola itself, a series of beautifully finished windows, each with its expensive handcrafted latch, opens out on the glorious vistas of Canberra, the surrounding hills and, these days, straight down Anzac Parade to the magnificent Parliament House across the lake. Regrettably no one is allowed up there to appreciate the view. It is still a very lonely vantage point. When the weather really warmed up Hungerford would sneak out of the window, take his clothes off and lie out in the sun, with only the heavens to look down on him.

However, Hungerford's actual role at the Memorial provided a rather different perspective. The physical impediments to the job were formidable, in a most peculiar work environment. Away from the public display areas and the administrative offices at the rear of the building, there are levels of small cold rooms within the cupola itself, now completely unused. His office was one of these monk-like cells, reached by many flights of stairs that only he used. For a gregarious person it was somewhat of a culture shock to sit in a solitary space up in the tower, although Hungerford enjoyed being away from everybody while he concentrated on his editing. But having no secretary was a big problem.

So was his boss. Hungerford very soon came to the realisation that this was no place for him on any long-term basis. He discovered that Colonel Treloar was a cold and unapproachable, 'do-it-by-rote' man, whom Hungerford never saw outside his office. The colonel actually lived on the premises, although he had a family in Melbourne. Treloar used to spend each weekend in his office with a Dictaphone, the latest office equipment then, filling a couple of tapes with letters. His secretary, Miss Elizabeth Southern, who also dedicated her life to the Memorial[18]—and to the colonel—typed them on Mondays and Tuesdays, generating vast numbers of letters, reports and confusing memoranda.

In addition to his editing role, Hungerford was also required to liaise with the contributors and with the printers. He would bound down the endless stairs to the colonel's office with the galleys, all neatly annotated (as they still are today in the Memorial's records). Apparently, however, Treloar had no idea of the exigencies of dealing with printers. Halstead Press in Sydney required copy by a certain date to meet deadlines. But everything had to go through the colonel. If he had trusted the younger man to know what he was doing and had given him the go-ahead, all would have been well, but, no, the director had to read everything. In the meantime, Hungerford would beg Miss Southern to have some urgent copy released so that it could be sent to Sydney.

> Gently but firmly, writhing with regret, she would produce fifteen reasons why the Colonel must not be disturbed, even though the printer in Sydney might be hanging on the line for a decision about any one of half-a-dozen

Memorial publications: even, I'm certain, if the building were on fire and the typewriters melting in the main office outside hers.[19]

The thin smile and the regretful shake of the head drove him to clamber dejectedly again up those endless stairs to his office. However, he was determined to get his name on the edition of *As You Were*, so he persevered. When he had done all he could and the galleys were still with the colonel, he took some leave to Sydney, to attend a gathering of ex-commandos, from where he pleaded by cable with Treloar to forward the material to the printers. Hungerford took extra (unpaid) leave while he persisted with persuading the colonel to release the material. Eventually the 1949 edition of *As You Were* was released for printing, with acknowledgements to him and to Frank Norton for their work, but Hungerford had had enough. He handed in his resignation on 21 October 1949.[20] The other staff had a small party to see him off, in the tea room adjacent to the director's office, and Colonel Treloar sent a note from next door, saying he was sorry he could not be present.

———

Hungerford was actually ebullient as he left: since arriving in Canberra he had written his first book, *Sowers of the Wind*, the novel about Australian troops in Japan, which received a prize of £1,000 for fiction awarded by the *Sydney Morning Herald*, in 1949, a tremendous fillip to his ego. Incidentally, £500 of the prize money was taken in taxation, and there was a demand for provisional tax of another £500, in case there was a competition in the following year that he might win. Hungerford is still outraged about this demand more than fifty years later.

The four-year delay in publishing *Sowers of the Wind* was caused by Angus & Robertson's wariness of the censor, after it had published a novel called *Love Me Sailor* that contained sex scenes. *Sowers of the*

Wind contained some sexual content, and much of the book is set in brothels. A 1950 comment in the Australian War Memorial's *Stand-To* stated—somewhat exaggeratedly by today's standards—that *Sowers of the Wind* made *Love Me Sailor* look like Mrs Beeton's cookery book. The delay in publishing cost him money, although Hungerford was to comment in retrospect that what he would have made on three of his novels was 'fruit for the sideboard'.[21]

Sowers of the Wind is a gripping post-war episode, gritty in its detail and very black in its focus on the ghastly situation in Japan under occupation. It is a strange combination of sordid detail and Hungerford's inimitable ability to write about the countryside that presents so well. The colour and vigour of the author himself comes through in the intense descriptions of the events that were intrinsic to the tale—from the settling in of the troops to the final denouement and confrontation between the principal character, Sergeant McNaughton, and the evil colonel. There is a powerful characterisation of this central figure, plainly an amalgam of the author himself and other role models.

Perhaps Hungerford is less successful with some of the other characters, who at times tend almost to be caricatures. Their conversations, physical yearnings and behaviour swamp the reader with almost overwhelming detail, leaving little to the reader's imagination. Reading the novel more than fifty years later, it seems overwritten by today's standards. However, the love story of McNaughton and Fumie is beautifully handled, enough to confirm that it was based on fact, which perhaps makes the point that Hungerford has been criticised for not handling love scenes in other novels so effectively, although it is recognised as notoriously hard to write such scenes.

He had started on his famous war novel *The Ridge and the River*, to be published in 1952 ahead of *Sowers of the Wind*, which was published in 1953. Hungerford first titled the book 'Tononoi Ridge', because that was the fictitious name he gave to the camp where they were stationed.

[The commissioning editor] Beatrice Davis did not like the
title: 'What does it mean—Tononoi Ridge?' At the time
I had been reading Bemelman's book, *King's Row*, which
was selling well: 'What does *King's Row* mean? It means
no more than *Tononoi Ridge*!' But Davis repeated that they
would like me to change it. So I said: 'Oh hell—well, the
ridge is very big in the thing, and the river was big in it.
It's a euphonious title.'

'Oh, that's wonderful! You mightn't know but if there
is "wind" or "river" in the title, it sells the book!'

'I didn't know that. OK: my next book is going to be
called *The Wind on the River*!'[22]

The Ridge and the River caused a stir when the novel was
released. It was reprinted three times and was widely reviewed.
Langlen Stewart, a New Zealander working at the time on *The
Bulletin*'s Red Page, the focal point for book reviews, pleased
Hungerford the most with his comment: 'This book is illuminated
by its complete sincerity.'[23] Of the many other reviewers, there
were two who summarised the overall sentiment of the critics.
Geoffrey Dutton wrote of the survival of humanity in war-time
being the deep sad subject of *The Ridge and the River*, indicated
in the end by stoicism rather than heroism.[24] Douglas Stewart, a
recognised poet and writer, identified the admirable portrayal of
men and officers, a perfect understanding of the soldier's outlook,
its humour and its toughness, its pathos and its courage, its nights
of rain and slush, and its days of sudden violence. He concluded
that it was a grim story of savagery and exuberance but with a
profound pride in the men who fought in the jungle, again in the
clear light of 'complete sincerity'.[25]

There were only two negative 'crits': one was Vance Palmer, a
member of a group of Australian writers prominent in the first half
of the twentieth century. Hungerford was convinced that Palmer's

review had been prepared from the book's publicity material and that Palmer had not actually read the book. Palmer wrote: 'This is good reportage, but not a novel.'[26] He went on to comment that the reader had no idea of what the men in the patrol were like, which was nonsense. Hungerford had gone to immense trouble to provide an understanding of the nature and background of each one of them. Surprisingly, a similar comment came from Osmar White in the Melbourne *Herald* who, while praising the novel, wrote that it was 'still not the novel of jungle warfare we have been waiting for. It reports almost faultlessly but it says nothing of private things, hidden things the jungle did to the very texture of the human spirit. It may move some to tears, but it will carry none beyond them.'[27] However, an anonymous reviewer in *Stand-To* concluded that it was true to life, 'free from glamour or melodrama...with all the compelling urgency of a thriller or whodunnit'. Hungerford would have appreciated that.

It is interesting that in a long review Hungerford wrote for *Stand-To* of *The Veterans* by Eric Lambert,[28] he was critical of the savage scenes that, he felt, could not be excused as an on-going paean of hatred against the former foes ten years on. His senti-mental attitude towards the past was chronicled in a poem 'On an Island Beach' published in *Stand-To* in July 1950. With its use of almost Victorian phraseology—'his lips are tightly curled' and 'here where the questing bullet sped', to take two quotations at random—it is fair comment that Hungerford's distaste for savagery at that period of his budding career was in danger of ruining his ability to tell it how it was. Luckily this saccharine style did not manifest itself later.

His publisher, Angus & Robertson, then contacted him to say that Billy Hughes, the former prime minister, was looking for someone to write his biography. Did Hungerford want to do it? It sounded interesting. He was required to go to Sydney to be interviewed, and dressed up very smartly for it in the one of the two suits not eaten by 'silverfish' that had cost him 26 guineas each. He was introduced to Billy Hughes in the publisher's office. After meeting the man and gaining an impression of a wizened gnome, he decided he would take the job of Billy Hughes' private-cum-press secretary. The salary looked as if it might be a sticking point. 'I said tentatively: "About payment…?" "Oh Mr Hungerford! I'm a very poor man…"' Squinting, querulous, abrupt, obviously hating the prospect of having to pay someone for doing what he lacked the capacity to do for himself.'[29] 'Doing a Shylock', thought Hungerford to himself, oh yes, you're a poor man! It was eventually decided that he would be paid about £12 a week, that Hughes would pay half his salary and the Prime Minister's Department would pay the rest.

Billy Hughes was 88 but claimed to be 86 (early in his life he had knocked two years off his age and never corrected it[30]). Hungerford was 33 years old, and initially trusting when they met. Hughes was a truly memorable character, with a name for vituperation, revenge and manipulation of those who trusted him, to say nothing of his reputation with his political enemies. But Hughes was also a remarkable man who had enjoyed an extraordinary political career. He was prime minister continuously from October 1915 to February 1923, having been a member of the first Commonwealth Government after Federation and in the first Labor cabinet in 1904. He was expelled twice from the Labor Party over his support for conscription. He went to two referenda over the issue but was defeated both times. For about three months at the end of 1917 the government was in total disarray over this issue. Hughes resigned as prime minister after many of his cabinet resigned but was recommissioned by the governor-general. He continued to sit as a backbencher for the rest of his life. He was pro-British and openly racist (then common), and inclined sentimentally towards the Left, yet allied with the Right.[31]

It should have been a fascinating biography, particularly as the Labor Party's 'greatest rat' (as he was referred to in orthodox Labor circles) died only six years after the meeting and Hungerford would have had free rein to write up a memorable life. But 'W. M. H. was as cold as sea ice, vain as a peacock, cruel as a butcher-bird, sly as a weasel and mean as catshit…'.[32] The appointment was a mistake, but an unforgettable experience. The contract lasted from 5 to 29 May 1948 and was to prove impossible from the start.

CHAPTER 10

In His Element

~~~

Initially, the up-and-coming writer was excited about this great break, the opportunity to record for posterity the definitive life story of the founder of the Labor Party, one of Australia's most interesting public figures. But it soon became clear that the commission was going to be anything but straightforward. Hungerford started his new job by preparing a number of draft questions-and-answers for his employer. Dismayed, he would sit in the House of Representatives watching Hughes, as he stumbled through the typescript, lost his place and finally ad-libbed so incoherently that he was an embarrassment to listen to.[1] This would have been an irrelevance to what Hungerford thought he was contracted to do, but he could not gain access to Hughes to interview him on his life. It soon became clear that the old man had no intention of cooperating with Hungerford in systematically recording material. Instead, in his rambling and incoherent manner,

> Hughes said: 'Mr Hungerford, there's a little job I want you to do...like you to get started on a book...take them from the articles, the papers from the library...another book on the Case for Labor.' He then promised to sit down with

me to provide material for the biography. So that was why I was there, I thought, to ghost another book for the old curmudgeon, taken out of what was known as the famous Case for Labor articles. Hughes had no intention of my writing his biography, and although researching old stories about the birth of the Labor Party was interesting, it was not what I had contracted to do. 'Mr Hughes, I didn't come up here to waste my time poking around in old newspaper files for you or for anyone else. I was hired to write your biography. It looks as if I'm never going to get the chance to do that, so I'm quitting.' Billy Hughes was instantly all charm: 'Now, Mr Hungerford, you and I mustn't be bad friends. Sit down, and we'll talk it over.' For an hour or so he reminisced about his life, providing some of the material the prospective biographer was so desperate to learn, but it was all at random. [I said, determinedly and rather frantically:] 'Mr Hughes, this is what I want from you on a regular basis.'

'Yes, Mr Hungerford, we'll fix that up.'

Exhilarated, I walked out. There was no promised meeting.[2]

The impasse came to a head some days later when Hughes suddenly addressed Hungerford in the vicious tone he employed with his devoted secretary and his long-suffering wife: 'You've done nothing since you've been here.'

'I've done what I've been asked to do!'

'Mr Hungerford, a cat could have done that!'

'Get a fucking cat to do it!'[3]

Hungerford walked out and slammed the door. This grand gesture was somewhat spoilt by the door-arrester nearly breaking his wrist, but he was slightly inebriated at the time. He returned to the bar where he had been discussing his troubles with Massey

Stanley, a well-respected journalist of the period. When Hungerford returned to his office at about six o'clock, his rage only slightly ameliorated, he noticed there was a reply to the resignation note he had put on Billy Hughes' desk. He had typed that he was leaving and that he was owed three weeks wages—he had received nothing at all since he had started.

> The note from Billy Hughes read: 'Dear Mr Hungerford, I am sorry to see you are going. I owe you for three weeks, at £5 a week, and if you leave a note for my secretary, she will see you are paid. And as Miss Mae West says, come up and see me some time. W. M. Hughes.' I tossed the note into the basket and placed another note on the table: 'Dear Mr Hughes, Thank you for your note. If you want me to come up and have a talk with you, I'd love to, but if you want me to work for you in any way, I'd rather go to bed with a sabre-tooth tiger. Yours sincerely, Tom Hungerford.' And that was that. I was never paid.[4]

When Hungerford was working at the Parliament House Library he had made a friend of the clerk of the house, Frank Green, who was something of an institution in his own right, having been there since Federal Parliament operated out of Melbourne before 1927.[5] It was he who had previously persuaded Hungerford to stay on with Billy Hughes when the latter despaired of working with the old man. Green had told him that he had a wonderful opportunity and urged him on three occasions to persevere. Eventually of course Hungerford insisted on leaving, and Green asked him what he intended to do next. Hungerford said he had heard that a very dangerous situation was arising in the migrant camps in Canberra and that he would like to write a novel about it. He explained.

At the Australian War Memorial, he had met an interesting man who worked as a storeman at Eastlake. This was one of the migrant hostels in Canberra, set up at the height of the arrival in Australia of displaced persons from European countries that had been ravaged by World War II. The first influx was mostly from the three Baltic countries, Latvia, Lithuania and Estonia, forced out by German and Russian pressure, and they were later supplemented by Ukrainians, Poles, southern Italians and Germans. With a fine disregard for detail they were all known then by the pejorative epithet of the 'bloody Balts' or 'reffos'. Since 1947 Australia, along with Canada and New Zealand, had been taking in displaced persons to work on infrastructure projects, as a prelude to being allowed to settle in the country of choice, after completing the two years work to which they were allocated. In Canberra the men were usually accommodated in the two hostels, Riverside and Eastlake, both old service depots from the war (now in the modern suburb of Kingston).[6] They mainly worked on large development and building projects, the most famous being the Snowy Mountains Scheme, the ambitious undertaking commenced in 1948 to divert water from the Snowy River to power irrigation projects in New South Wales and Victoria. The first power was generated in 1955 and more than fifty years on, the Snowy Mountains Scheme is still recognised as one of Australia's great engineering projects, although overuse of the Snowy's water has resulted in severe environmental degradation.

The hothouse milieu of the migrant camp had also attracted the worst type of white Australian, itinerant labourers who cared nothing for anyone, loathing the newcomers who were arriving, many of whom were well qualified in their own countries, and who were eager to work. There were many stories of success among the newcomers, but some found the two years of hard physical labour very taxing. There was the member of the Czech aristocracy who had fled his ancestral castle to Vienna, where he had been quizzed about his experience and abilities. He had been trained for nothing except to manage the ancestral estates, so he expressed a hesitant interest in 'trees'. He found himself employed as a tree-feller. He was later to become a distinguished entomologist.[7]

From the inception of the migration scheme, new arrivals were subject to resentment and abuse from xenophobic Australian labourers on the Snowy. 'They're takin' all the jobs and takin' all the sheilas' was the chorus at the time, and it reflected the common Australian reaction to the arrival of any large group of foreigners from overseas. Hungerford remembered the 'Pommies' of his childhood being exposed to similar intolerance, and then the Italians, whom he personally felt deserved support and sympathy. He had always sympathised with the underdog. Frank Green told him something of what happened at Eastlake, which he described as 'a bloody jungle!' In 1950 Hungerford determined to base his third novel on what he might find at the camp, and this he put to Green with a request for an approach to the camp manager.

> Green nodded and picked up the telephone to call the manager of Eastlake hostel. 'Oh Bill—I have in my office a Mr Tom Hungerford...he wants to get a job in the kitchen at Eastlake.' I wondered what the manager must think of being asked by the clerk of the house to find a job for a kitchen hand.[8]

But that was where he would experience the life of the ordinary migrant. It was arranged. Two days later he reported for work, a tough routine from 6 a.m. to 2 p.m., then off until 6 p.m. when he started again. There was plenty of colourful material for the book, and he also learnt some recipes from the cook in charge, to widen his culinary repertoire, but he was so tired at night that he simply could not write. He also became increasingly concerned about his 'undercover' role and decided eventually to seek an interview with the manager, who was known as 'the Bastard' by the camp inmates.

But Hungerford found Ferrier, the manager, to be a very fair if stern man. He did his best to protect the European migrants from those Hungerford referred to as 'the Roughies' at Eastlake, who constantly moved from construction scheme to construction scheme, taking advantage of the chronic shortage of labour, tough Australian-born labourers who so resented the newcomers from Europe. The manager received him in his office.

> I felt rather foolish and did not really know what to say. 'What is it, Mr Hungerford?'
>
> 'Mr Ferrier, I'm not what you think I am.'
>
> 'What are you?'
>
> 'I'm a journalist, I'm not a kitchen hand. I'm here to do a novel on what goes on in the migrant camps.'
>
> 'Mr Hungerford, I know that, I know that.' He leaned over and pulled out a thick file. 'Here's your file.' He flipped through it and he said casually: 'Oh, you've had troubles in the army, a couple of mutinies? Then there's [this and that and something else].'[9]

The file was an up-to-date record of Hungerford's life initially compiled by military intelligence, and it had followed him around. ASIO has since released part of it into the public record, although the material dates only from 1953. The contents are a curious mishmash of accusations against him, of being inspired by communists to lead the Morotai 'mutiny' and later of being guilty of communistic leanings by belonging to the Fellowship of Australian Writers.[10] It was still being used against him when, some years later, Hungerford was under consideration for a posting to Djakarta as press officer at the Australian Embassy. The then ambassador, Walter Crocker,[11] was believed to have said that 'he was not having that "bloody red rag Hungerford loose in my embassy!"'[12]

Given Hungerford's reputation from Army Intelligence, it was perhaps natural that Ferrier was advised to monitor his activities, but the allegedly dangerous subversive was momentarily stunned. He felt he was a very easy-going man—although others might well have regarded him as intolerant and set in his ways—but he considered he had shown that he would do the work put in front of him, without causing any trouble. 'Ferrier continued: "You don't know what goes on here. This is a hotbed of political and other intrigues, and you've walked right into it!" '[13]

Hungerford rallied himself, recounted how it was just these circumstances that had led him to Eastlake, but explained that his kitchen-hand duties left him no time to write.

> I was going to end by saying I thought it best if I resigned.
> Ferrier, as if reading my mind, said: 'Can we fit you up
> in another job? What do you want to do?'
>
> 'I don't mind. What have you got to offer me?'
>
> 'Well, we want a yardman.'
>
> 'What does a yardman do?'
>
> 'He cleans out the lavatories, the showers, the wash-
> room and the laundry and, if you do that, the rest of the
> day is your own.'[14]

Hungerford took the job, which he held for the remainder of the seven to eight months he spent at Eastlake. He received £5 10s a week and 'all found', which was adequate for his needs. He was also given his own accommodation in a hut behind the administrative centre, in one of about eight or ten rooms reserved for men working at the camp on educational jobs who required the quiet and order absent in the rest of the camp. Strangely, in view of what he was required to do for his wage and keep, it turned out to be one of the happiest periods of his life. For a start,

Hungerford liked cleaning; perhaps a relic of his mother's earlier training coupled with what the army had taught him.

That first Saturday morning was to be imprinted indelibly on his memory when he walked into the main toilet block. Whoever was meant to have done the cleaning before him had just not bothered, and whoever was responsible for overseeing it had also failed. He just could not believe what he saw. Men had returned drunk from an evening's carousing and vomited everywhere. Hungerford went straight to the storeroom and obtained a hard broom, a big can of Phenyl—the disinfectant cleaner of the day—a bucket of tar with a brush, a hose, rubber gloves and Wellington boots. Breathing heavily through his mouth, he stood at the door of the toilets with the hose and sprayed the urinals clean. With steel wool and cleaner, he scrubbed the seats and the bowls. He 'broomed' the floor and the walls. He waited until they had dried, and then he painted the surfaces with tar. Then he moved into the showers, which were coated with a film of old soap, and eventually had them gleaming.

> I got my recognition one afternoon after work, when I was having a shower myself, and there were two men on the other side also taking a shower. One said to the other: 'Jesus Christ! There must be a new bloke cleaning these places! Never seen them so clean!' I thought to myself, a very nice job, Tom![15]

Even allowing for this degree of hubris, it was understandable that having been appointed to the most menial of positions he took great satisfaction in looking back at this achievement. There was still the laundry to tackle, which was also disgusting: departing inmates had left coppers full of dirty, sweaty clothes. He dumped the contents, cleaned out the coppers and troughs, and started on the floor, which was caked with soap and was dangerous to walk on, but he got it so clean that the whole laundry also sparkled. From then on, the inmates kept the toilets and laundry very clean. Hungerford had learnt in the army that once a standard was set, the men kept it up.

Thereafter, starting at 7 a.m. and well finished by lunchtime, he was able to maintain the facilities easily and quickly, so that he had time to write in the afternoon. The hard labour also restored his physical condition to nearly what it had been when he was swimming in Sydney. He made friends with an entertaining old man, Mick Shear, who was the Eastlake gardener, born on the Monaro, and someone who knew all the local history. Mick hardly did a stroke of work. He would stand in the road and talk, while keeping an eye out for one of the hierarchy, whereupon he would start to scrape his hoe lethargically. Hungerford has always liked gardening and enjoyed helping him to prune the roses. Outside Eastlake duties, his focus remained his writing to the exclusion of all else, including female company.

But he did have another life, away from the camp. It was during the Eastlake period that Hungerford became increasingly involved with other writers in Canberra. He was acquiring something of a reputation as a young lion of literary fiction. His first three novels, *The Ridge and the River*, *Riverslake* and *Sowers of the Wind* were still to be published—in 1952, 1953 and 1954 respectively—but his burgeoning literary status among the cognoscenti was acknowledged by the invitation to edit two anthologies of prose and poetry, *Australian Signpost: An Anthology of Poetry and Short Stories*[16] for the Canberra branch of the Fellowship of Australian Writers, of which he was elected president. He was also editor overall for *Australian Writers*. The Canberra branch of the FAW had some illustrious members then, including Professor Manning Clark, the farmer–poet David Campbell and the poet Tom Inglis Moore of Canberra University College.

The Hungerford name was not, however, just associated with Tom Hungerford the Writer when he was based in Canberra.

There were two other Hungerfords, both with similar initials, one a distinguished veterinarian. He was puzzled one day to receive a cheque for £60, for delivering a calf.

This mixture of his daytime menial work and evening literary-cum-social pursuits led to some amusing situations. On one occasion, the wife of the Canadian high commissioner, a fellow member of the FAW, offered him a lift home to Eastlake. She was horrified to find out where he lived and what he did for a living. A fuller but necessarily fictionalised account of the eclectic society in which he mingled emerges from the pages of *Riverslake*, to which another entertaining story is attached. Eastlake was highly unionised, and Hungerford himself became a member of the union. 'The secretary of the union in Canberra was a strange man called Shamus McVee, otherwise known as "Humus" McVee, who, small and furtive, was not unlike a little animal found under a hedge.' For the purposes of the book's narrative, Hungerford depicted the union secretary as the antithesis of McVee, a crisp, intelligent, hard-working young man studying for a degree in his spare time. 'One day some years after publication of the book, I was having a drink at Eastlake camp's back-bar, after work at the Australian News and Information Bureau. "Humus" came up to me and gave me a nudge in the ribs. He said complaisantly: "I see you got me into your book!" '[17]

By February 1951 Hungerford again reached the point where he felt he was still not finding enough time to write. He now had all the material that he needed to write his book *Riverslake*. The result is a magnificent depiction of an important period of post-war Australian history and is an immensely powerful book, a valuable account of a period when post-war reconstruction depended on the physical labour of a misunderstood and reviled group of foreigners. One reviewer, Marjorie Barnard, described it as 'rough and chunky, the story of emotions worked out not in tranquillity but in anger and bitterness'.[18] As Barnard comments, with overtones of Vance

Palmer's earlier review, it is more a documentary than a novel; it has little that is nourishing for the reader and much that is an educative indictment of Australian attitudes of the time.

Although the book was not a commercial success, it caused a stir in Canberra circles. Some scandalised readers believed they could discern real people behind Hungerford's fictional characters. More importantly, it was an opportunity lost to educate the wider post-war Australian public about the horrors faced by the new immigrants who made up so much of the itinerant labour force on the big projects, such as the Snowy Mountains Scheme. In *Riverslake* the majority of the native-born Australians are shown as being racist and introverted, with the grossest of social habits. One particularly vivid and unpleasant incident, based on fact, has one of the Australian itinerants throwing a cat belonging to one of the 'Balts' into a furnace. The 'bloody Balts' by contrast were civilised and only wanted to be accepted for their contribution to their new country. The key figure in the novel and commentator on the social scene, Randolph, provides a stereotype of the ex-serviceman, fiercely proud of his country but despairing of its future. There is much of the author in the character's make-up.

In addition to the problems of assimilation faced by the newcomers, Hungerford's other themes were the exaggerated threats of civil war in Australia, if Australia could not reconcile the different parts of its society, and the 'Yellow Peril', with the suggestion that Asian hordes would sweep into Australia from the north, a recurrent theme in Australian mythology. When Hungerford spoke fifty years later of his period at Eastlake, little of the savagery of the time came through in his recollections. Canberra was still a relatively 'raw' place: the contrast of educated and cultured Canberrans with the virtual dregs of society, as pictured in *Riverslake*, made for a startling and vivid story. Even the appropriate slang for the period reads more easily than it does in *Sowers of the Wind*.

As always, his descriptions of the scenery and the sometimes violent interactions of the characters are what he does best. His love scenes and related touches of intimacy are somewhat forced, although Marjorie Barnard was wrong when she criticised the depiction of Linda Spain, the so-called nymphomaniac, as not being drawn from life. In fact, she was.[19] There is still some over-description of characters that can be compared unfavourably with Nevil Shute's writings on Australia in the 1950s. The latter's portraits of his stories' characters leave enough unsaid for the reader to complete a mental word picture. Shute is a bit like Somerset Maugham (who, incidentally—according to Hungerford—favourably reviewed *The Ridge and the River* in the UK), and they both share a simple direct-ness with Hungerford, who makes more social observation but perhaps not as delicately as Maugham. Hungerford in effect forces the reader to share his perspective and allows little opportunity to form personal judgements.

Two further reviews of *Riverslake* gave conflicting perspectives. The first, by Geoffrey Dutton, wrote of the book being 'hot, topical and important…urgent…sincere', suggesting that the 'whole migrant scheme is a tragic fiasco'.[20] The other by Geoffrey Tubbutt wrote of the book's themes of 'gloom, savagery and despair'. The reviewer was plainly looking for entertainment rather than enlightenment: 'something less negative and more complete than a sunless novel of disillusion…'. He too had problems with the slang Hungerford used, which he thought was 'likely to baffle even people who thought they knew the Australian language'.[21]

—•—

Before Hungerford decided to leave Eastlake, he had applied for a lowly position at the Commonwealth Scientific and Industrial Research Organisation (CSIRO). It was undertaking a pasture inspection, sorting the two sorts of grass in a paddock. Sorting grasses all day was not really his vocation, but it was a job and he enjoyed the prospect of working out of doors. Luckily, before he was committed to the CSIRO position and while he was still at Eastlake, news of his literary prowess had gone before him. He received a call from the Australian News and Information Bureau (ANIB), now the Australian Information Service. It was Mel Pratt, the editor, who enquired whether he would work for the ANIB.

Hungerford was not at all sure that he wanted the ANIB position. One of the reasons he had considered the CSIRO job was that he had set his heart on visiting London the following June. He had £500 saved, and London was the place for an up-and-coming writer to be. So he put this to Pratt, who asked if Hungerford would work for the ANIB until he left for London. He agreed somewhat reluctantly to join them—and was still working for the ANIB in 1967. The ANIB was in effect a public relations exercise for Australia, 'issuing in one typical year 187,000 written and pictorial items for overseas consumption, via San Francisco, New York, London and Bonn, where the ANIB then maintained offices'.[22] By agreement with the Australian Journalists' Association, no pieces were to be used in Australia, although some of Hungerford's work was later circulated within the country.

Pratt said, 'We want some special stories. The first thing we want you to do is a story on myxomatosis.' Actually, the first job given to Hungerford was to prepare imaginative captions to a series of 200 photographs of North Queensland, which he really enjoyed. Then the CSIRO reports about the effects of myxomatosis on the rabbit population were received. Hungerford was told to monitor the various outbreaks as they were reported and prepare a story. His article on myxomatosis was circulated worldwide. This project was the ideal journalistic combination of research into a story and writing it up, as one of the four journalists in the big ANIB office. The doyen was Stan East, experienced and worldly wise. He was 'subbing' Hungerford's article, and he said:

'Well, that's the sort of article I like to do. You don't have to do a fucking thing to it!' I heard him from the other side of the room, and it gave me confidence, because what I was writing was for the first time at someone else's request; previously I wrote what I chose. [Stan East had an idiosyncratic work style.] He used to say to me: 'Tom, stop clacking that bloody typewriter. I can't sleep!' I never knew whether he was joking.[23]

Hungerford's first major assignment out of town was to drive in his own vehicle up the north coast of New South Wales as far as Wauchope, doing stories on the way. Then on to the Narrabri area, the black soil plains of northern New South Wales, where he had a good friend, from the old 2/8th, who had bought a 'soldier's farm'. This was Harry Hutcheson, one of the two NCOs who had escaped with him from the depths of the Mornington Peninsula to join the 2/8th. Hungerford's brief was to write up the young returned soldiers resettled on a big station. The pastoral spread of Old Edgeroi had been resumed from the absentee English landlords, who had done nothing with the land, and it had been divided into farming blocks. Hutcheson had the original fattening paddock of a thousand acres, with the elderly out-station homestead and a big water tank. It was a beautiful place. When Hungerford had completed the stories he returned to Canberra via Kiama on the south coast. He had been away several weeks.

After I had been back in Canberra for a while, Mel Pratt said to me: 'What about your expenses?'

I thought, oh, what do I have to pay? 'What expenses?'

'You get expenses when you're out in the paddock, you know.'

'What?'

'OK…you run your own car. That's worth [so much]
a mile, of course all your expenses: staying in a hotel and
everything, laundry and newspapers and anything else you
regard as an expense for the job.'

'That's wonderful!' Of course I received a substantial
cheque, on top of nearly £12 a week salary.[24]

That persuaded him to stay on with the ANIB. He thought
that he had an excellent job—travelling, being paid for it and not
required to stay much in Canberra. He was still a young, carefree
individual. He appreciated a peripatetic life and the pleasures of
one or two brief relationships on his journeys with lonely single
women who enjoyed a night with the debonair stranger, who was
here today, gone tomorrow.

I went along the Murray Valley, right down to Goolwa,
up into the Snowy Mountains, through the Centre in
all directions, all over Victoria. I went to Maralinga and
Millingimbi, the Dampier Archipelago and the Gulf of
Carpentaria, the Hawkesbury, the Gascoyne and Cooper's
Creek…by train, plane, car and boat, for short distances
by horse and for much shorter spins by camel…I slept
in posh hotels and bush pubs, in historic homesteads of
three-foot wide pisé walls, in settlers' shanties and chaff
sheds, at construction camps and mission stations, once in
a monastery and many times under the stars.[25]

Generally he was received very hospitably, although his visit
to Hermannsburg, 124 km southwest of Alice Springs, in 1954 was
an exception. He was to provide readers with a picture of how this
mission station coped with its responsibilities and, with his innate
sympathy for the Aboriginal population, he was well placed to
undertake this assignment. Pastor Albrecht, head of the mission,

met him, and he made it clear that he disliked visiting journalists, following an unfortunate write-up by a previous visitor. After being allowed grudging and limited access to the settlement, Hungerford happened to comment on the poor physical condition of some of the Aborigines sitting around. The pastor's reply was: 'Their bodies are their own business. We're interested in their souls.'[26] Hungerford compared this coldness with what he observed of the Aborigines in the Kimberleys of northwestern Australia years later, when he was touched by the deep and mutual affection between the Durack sisters and the local people. Both were examples of paternalistic relationships, but there was a world of difference in their expression.

In 1954 Tom Hungerford covered the Queen's tour for the ANIB, the last occasion on which he was to wear his white tie-and-tails from the dancing days in Perth. Thereafter he vowed never again to dress up in an outmoded garb that was bearable only in the cold season. His royal tour experience was to stand him in good stead. Some years later, he was to manage the press arrangements for Princess Margaret's visit to Western Australia. He had acquired a reputation as a seasoned organiser, fashioned by his time in the army, although someone at the time did not think Hungerford was particularly well suited to being a public relations organiser. He was permanently unforgiving of one young journalist whom he saw as having broken the rigid schedule that he had drawn up.[27]

Mel Pratt in 1954 casually asked Hungerford whether he would like to accompany an Australian expedition to the Antarctic. The Mawson Base had been established on MacRobertson Land when the Australian Antarctic Territory Act in 1954 declared that the laws in force in the Australian Capital Territory, as far as they were applicable, would apply in the Australian Antarctic Territory.[28] The ANIB had permission to send someone to write up the scientific programs and any human interest stories that might arise. 'Until that day I had never given much thought to the Antarctic—who had? I knew it was large and white and cold, that it had penguins but no polar bears.'[29] He jumped at the opportunity and attended an interview with Phillip Law, director of the Australian National Antarctic Research Expedition (ANARE). Law questioned him closely on his abilities and motivation and finally asked whether he could cook, which of course he could, from his Scarborough days, with additional culinary skills acquired at Eastlake. It was all pretty basic, however.

> I could hash up a stew…in the time honoured Australian style of those days I could boil the guts out of any vegetable ever grown. I could grill meat, make a custard (with custard power), knock up a salad of lettuce and tomato or lettuce and onion, plentifully doused with vinegar—was there any other sort in those days?[30]

He was accepted for the 1955 expedition, and his cooking skills were at once in demand. The official expedition cook was prostrate from seasickness and, on the way south, Hungerford, with the assistance of two men in the galley, became expedition cook for the time being. The expedition vessel was the Danish icebreaker *Kista Dan*, similar in size to the smaller Manly ferries. She was 1,200 tons, with two-thirds of her hull taken up by immense engines, built not to plough through ice but to ride up on them and shatter the ice sheets. The expedition sailed out of Melbourne for Macquarie Island. Hungerford started by cooking six chickens for the twenty-five men aboard. He really did not know what he was doing much of the time, because he had been used to knocking up a very rough meal for four or five of his mates who hardly cared what they ate as long as it was food. But the locker was well stocked, and he gained in confidence. He would tell his assistants to fetch him fifty lamb chops, a ham or four or five dozen eggs.

They always enjoyed fish on Fridays, frozen because they caught nothing on passage.

> I made this immense fruitcake for Christmas. I put half a bottle of rum in it when I mixed it. I put half a bottle of rum in the icing, which I didn't know how to make, and I forgot to put eggs in it, and I thought as it was a pretty thick mixture I'd better have a pretty hot oven. Right down in the tail of the ship there was a great big oven, heated by an enormous blowtorch. So I got this piping hot and I put the goo in it. I remembered what my mother had done, really. She used to put in a piece of brown paper and put the stuff on it. So I stuck it into the oven and went back to the galley to get something else ready for the Christmas lunch. After a while I thought I'd better go and have a look at the cake. It was on fire! The paper was burning and the top of the cake was flaming, so I dragged it out and beat the flames out. I thought I didn't know what to do, really, so I turned the blowtorch off and put it back in. It was pretty well cooked, but like a pudding.
>
> Then it came to making the bloody icing: I had no idea—you put icing and milk or something, but I never thought of mixing it with butter, like I know now. I had no idea of the affinity of icing for water; I'd get a nice mixture and I'd think it mustn't get too thick, so I'd better water it, and all of a sudden it got watery. It needs some more icing—and I finished up with a bloody great bowl of icing that you could whitewash the chook-house with![31] I had put in half a bottle of rum and I just kept ladling it over the cake until I got a reasonable thickness. It went as hard as bloody iron but I can tell you, mate, there wasn't more than a little wedge of that cake left. The blokes loved it—because of the rum, I suppose.[32]

Shortly after, the ship received a signal from Heard base to say their cook had nearly cut his thumb off, and did they have someone on board who could cook? So Hungerford went off the ship straight into a kitchen on the island and started cooking.

The Heard Island station was being closed down, and the huskies, bred for sledge-drawing, were evacuated to Mawson, the new base on the mainland. They could take only so many dogs there, and they were not allowed to bring the dogs back to Australia because of the quarantine laws, so those not needed were shot. That really upset Hungerford, a dog lover all his life. It was a thousand kilometres by ship to Mawson, and en route they landed on the Antarctic coast at the Vestfold Hills, a hundred kilometres east of Macquarie, where there was a freshwater lake. They put in at Pridz ('Shit') Bay, where the scientists examined the local seals to measure the iron content in their blood. Hungerford was thrilled at being among the very first visitors to Pridz Bay. The dogs were held on the ice while the ship was cleaned up, anchored to the sea ice. While the dogs were being lowered onto the ice, the top dog, George, was dropped in error onto Hungerford's face as he stood below on the sea ice. The weight of the animal and the forcible contact with its dirty rear end temporarily overwhelmed the dog lover.

When it had become known in Canberra that Hungerford was going to the Antarctic, several of his friends told him he was mad, he could be killed. He scorned their worries, but his friends were nearly proved right. Initially it was other members of the expedition who had a narrow escape. At Pridz Bay, Phillip Law had decided to go ashore from the edge of the sea ice where they were moored. He took a dog sled and, with three or four other expedition members, explored the nearby terrain. While he was away, the sea ice started to break into great fissures, which forced Law and his party to manoeuvre from one floe to another. Those left on the ship watched, their hearts in their mouths. The team safely recovered, the ship attempted to reach the open sea. They were nearly frozen in for the year there, and it took four or five hours to break their way out of Pridz Bay to clear water.

Before the expedition had left Mawson, Hungerford had two particularly dangerous experiences. The station was on a little plateau with a small bay behind, where the seals used to gather. They were food for the dogs. Seals were killed, left on the ice and sawn up like a log as they were needed. Each dog was given a round of seal about 20 centimetres thick for its weekly meal.

On this occasion, they had taken several light cane sleds to bring the seal carcasses home. Hungerford had work to do at the station, so he told the others that he would return ahead of them. He took one of the sleds to ride down the slope to avoid walking back and mounted the sled, which took off like lightning down the slope, increasing its speed. He could see the rapidly approaching sea and was certain he could not alight before crashing into the water, which was a good two metres below the ice ledge. Drowning or just freezing to death was imminent, and no one knew where he was. Luckily he was wearing heavy rubber boots. He put his right foot down and dragged hard on that side. The sled gradually turned around, and he finished up not a metre from the edge of the ledge. It was a while before he could control his shaking and carefully return to the camp.

On another occasion he was with a party that climbed a peak in the Casey Range, two or three hours travel by DUKW, an amphibious jeep. By the time they decided to return it was late. On the return journey, the DUKW's back wheel jammed tight in a crevasse. They were marooned there for the night, concerned that if a blizzard blew up they would probably be overwhelmed. The five of them huddled together 'like pups in a box', the engine running all night to keep warm. The base had been notified, but nothing could be done until first thing in the morning, when a tractor dug the DUKW out of the crevasse.

The waves in the Southern Ocean were terrifying in their size and intensity but, much to his surprise, given his father's intolerance of high seas, Hungerford seldom suffered from seasickness. 'I was seasick only three times—and then very briefly. Twice it was from the effects of spirituous and fermented liquors, and once from frying sixty pieces of fish in a very small galley going up and down like a lift, and sometimes sideways.'[33]

The return to Melbourne should have been without incident. True, the short-range radar was unserviceable, but no one worried very much: it would be repaired before it was needed. Hungerford was down in his cabin, banging out on his typewriter the twenty stories he was to produce. Suddenly there was a scraping sound and a judder. The *Kista* leaned over and faltered. In that huge ocean the ship had run against an isolated spire of rock that was not shown in the charts. Hungerford's first thought was how far they were from Melbourne. He knew that a minute in the water meant death. Fortunately the vessel was only scraped. The master warped her off, and they returned to Australia without further incident. Antarctica was undoubtedly Hungerford's most exciting assignment with the ANIB.

In between various forays to outlying parts of Australia in search of stories for the ANIB his next major assignment was to work on publicity in 1955 for the Olympic Games, which were staged in Melbourne in 1956. For him, this was a bit of a holiday, because the international press corps produced copious material of their own, and although he enjoyed being part of what was for Australia a momentous occasion, he was not particularly drawn to any of the events. The ANIB then came up with a new assignment for him.

CHAPTER 11

The New World

~~~

In 1957, after six years with the Australian News and Information Bureau in Australia, Tom Hungerford was asked if he would like to take over as federal press officer in New York for a four-year posting, although he had been promised London after three years in Australia. The USA sounded exciting and he agreed, flying to the US West Coast. He spent a few days in San Francisco, soaking in its unique mixture of colour and contrast, the Golden Gate Bridge, the fogs rolling in, the trolley cars being hauled up the steep hills and the sinister complex of Alcatraz out in the bay. It was an invigorating start to a new life, but thousands of kilometres separated him from his new posting in New York, and he arranged to drive across the country with another Australian.

Although the distances did not overwhelm the Australians, Hungerford was unused to the fast pace of the States and to a strange mixture of culture shock and the absurd. His first scare was driving along the highway: a Greyhound bus travelling at 110 mph nearly drove them off the road, the vast shape of the vehicle suddenly looming alongside. Then sheer fright was relieved by absurdity: they were bowling along a magnificent highway through empty country, and—ever aware of the written word—he read a billboard: 'Get in touch with your Congressman about adding a lane.'

Crossing the Rocky Mountains was nearly their last experience of driving in the States. Hungerford was at the wheel as they climbed higher and higher, until there was ice on the roads. They had no chains, and it was almost impossible to control the car, which was sliding on the glassy surface. He slowed to a slippery crawl. The narrow road snaked down the side of the hill to a bench-cut, then down steeply into a river. He very carefully nursed the car along, wondering where they were going to stay for the night. 'Then, suddenly: "Oh Jesus! Here comes a truck!" A huge vehicle was coming down the hill ahead of us, luckily lit up like the New York skyline! Dan had the door open: he was certain they would be knocked off the road.'[1]

Fortunately on the right-hand side of the road, there was a small flat indent in the side of the hill. There were already two cars there, and Hungerford put his foot down. Swerving wildly, they just inched into the space as the truck howled by on their tail. Shaken, they sedately followed their would-be Nemesis down the hill to equip themselves with chains. They celebrated their narrow escape with many drinks that night. The next day, subdued by their narrow escape and by celebratory excess the evening before, they drove over deep snow; the road was covered and the trees weighed down. Driving very cautiously they made their way over the mountains, to be faced by the endless plains of the American Midwest.

In their innocence, they had assumed they would just drive to New York to the specific address Hungerford had been given, 11 Locustwood Boulevard in Westchester County on Long Island. Days later, they started asking the way, when they could see from 30 kilometres away the dramatic skyline of New York floating on the horizon. As soon as they were negotiating the outer urban areas, they were lost. Finally, they reached the Hudson River, crossed it gingerly and then traversed Manhattan to head towards Long

Island, where Hungerford's Australian friend was living. (She had married an American during World War II.) They finally found the house. When Ella answered the door she asked in some amazement where they had come from, and Hungerford said laconically that they had just arrived from San Francisco.

> 'How?' 'We drove.' 'You drove? All the way to here?' 'Sure.'
> 'My God!' She turned and shouted into the house. 'Fred!
> It's Tom! They drove all the way. Right across Manhattan.'
> 'Goddamn!' said Fred, ex-Marines sergeant. 'You guys
> drove, yourselves, right across Manhattan?' 'Well…yes.'
> I'd begun to wonder whether we'd broken some local law
> of trespass or something like that.[2]

Tom Hungerford breathed in the ambience of New York. It is in his novel *Shake the Golden Bough* that readers best experience some of New York's atmosphere as they picture the streets of Manhattan downtown with its tang of disintegration of the old houses and the sensual impact of new developments, of daily frenetic living and the 'harbour-bitter breath of the sea'. The ANIB operated out of the Manhattan offices of the Australian consul-general in New York, at that time Sir Josiah Francis, an ex-Queensland politician 'of the old school and a consummate operator'. As with the US foreign service, albeit on a necessarily smaller scale, it has been customary for many years for Australian ex-politicians to be found comfortable berths as senior consuls and ambassadors. The ANIB staff itself was small, consisting of Hungerford and the director, their secretaries and an elderly lady on the switchboard, whose length of service was picturesquely described by Hungerford as her having been there 'since Christ was a lance corporal'.[3]

He worked relentlessly. Apart from his written pieces for the ANIB, looking after official visitors after hours and visits to schools, he produced a daily news sheet of Australian news that was circulated to other missions in New York, from material his secretary took down from Radio Australia. He showed movies of his country, generally educating his audiences and promoting the country to New Yorkers, many of whom had never heard of Australia, unless their fathers had been stationed there during the war. Generally, ordinary Americans had no idea where Australia was, 'and soon after I had arrived in New York and was having a haircut, the barber said: "Where you from, Buddy? You a Limey [British]?"

'"No, I'm from Australia."

'"How long have you been here?"

'"Six weeks."

'"Gee, you learned the language quickly!"'[4]

American insularity is still a recognisable trait, with no apparent wish to know much about the rest of the world, but it always astonished Hungerford. Some New Yorkers confused Australia with Austria. The Austrian offices were used to receiving the Australians' mail, because the US Postal Service knew of Austria. Then there was the barman: 'Hey Aussie! When you goin' to get your ass out from under that stupid goddam Queen 'a yours? Payin' taxes jus' to buy her palaces and crowns and all that shit?'[5]

He was in demand to talk to colleges and schools in New York. The type and social setting of the schools he was asked to visit varied widely. One was a very up-market school, in Westchester County. Hungerford had arrived early. The teacher had not returned from lunch, and the classroom door was closed. The students, aged in their early teens, were lined up along the wall. He decided to make a start; he entered, followed by the class, and started to address them.

> Then I noticed my audience was just talking to each other, paying no attention to the guest speaker. I stopped. After a while, they realised I was silent, and gradually they stopped

talking. I said: 'I've been in many schools in a number of countries and I have never, ever met anyone quite so discourteous as you children!' I continued in like vein and had their attention.[6]

By contrast with that occasion, Hungerford visited an all-black school at the 'bottom end of New York'. They were perfectly behaved, and he noted that these young people enjoyed none of the wealthy school's facilities. His disillusion with aspects of upper-class American upbringing was reinforced when he stayed at the home of affluent educated friends who had two little boys. The older one was what Hungerford described feelingly as 'a swine of a child'. One weekend, while the husband was away,

> his wife and I were sitting in the living room, talking. The boys were in their own rooms and from one of them there was a shout and a commotion. The elder boy came out, flounced through the room, and as he walked past the table he brushed a book off. His mother said: 'Jake, honey—pick up that book.'
> 'Fuck the book!'
> I was as shocked as I had ever been to hear the mother spoken to in that way, and the casual manner in which it was uttered. The boy then deliberately farted at the table and nothing was said about it.[7]

Perhaps these social solecisms are more commonplace in some circles now, but in the late 1950s they were an outrage to him. Americans were such a mix, he thought. The other side of the coin was that Americans were forthright, generous to a fault, wonderful hosts, and full of humour and fun. He made good friends.

He was asked to all sorts of functions in his role as a press officer. Once it was to Toots Shaw's famous 'drinkery 'n eatery', where he met someone he liked very much. Barbara ran Toots Shaw's public relations, and she too was struck by the tall Australian. It resulted in what Hungerford described—somewhat inappropriately, perhaps, given his age at the time—as a very nice 'boy-and-girl affair' for a couple of years. However, in what had become the norm by that stage in his life, he feared matrimony looming, and he had no intention under any circumstances of making his life in the USA. Barbara had started to take over Hungerford's social life, which he came to resent, and he severed the relationship. Hungerford has always liked being in full control. He also had a 'loving relationship' for a short period with one of the Australian secretaries, but as she was married with four children, he was careful not to let the affair progress.

Settling into the work routine in New York initially was hard, mainly because his director, 'a nice man and good journalist', was on his way to becoming a dipsomaniac. He used to take home a bottle of rum every night, and he was frequently drunk during the day. ANIB staff had access to liquor in bond, so they did not have to pay much. One day when the director had not arrived at work, Hungerford poked around in his office and found a myriad of Coke bottles in his drawer that smelt of liquor. It was a very difficult situation, because the director had to confer with a number of senior Americans, businessmen and politicians. 'I tried to cover up for him—"Look, the boss isn't well today. Just direct anyone who comes in into my office, and I'll take care of them." Then I would sit in a cold sweat, dreading my boss's unsteady entrance.'[8]

At one stage after his wife had returned to Australia, the unfortunate man was even more under the influence than usual. He was due to stay in New York for a further eighteen months or so. He fretted for his family. Hungerford went to see Sir Joss and pleaded with him to send his director home. 'Sir Joss had four or five chins that he patted while dealing with tricky matters.' He patted away while he thought, but it was all too hard for him, and eventually he directed Hungerford to do as he thought best, which did not impress the latter, who felt strongly that when a senior staff member needed positive support, he should not be abandoned. But Hungerford has never side-stepped difficult issues. He rang Kevin Murphy, the ANIB director in Canberra. and explained the situation. 'I was worried about a possible New York headline: "AUSTRALIAN DIPLOMAT KNOCKED DOWN DRUNK AS A SKUNK." The recall was organised, and I covered both positions until a relief was sent out.'[9]

One of the most enjoyable aspects of life in the USA was the pleasure of travel outside New York. Once Hungerford stayed at the home of a diplomat friend in Washington DC, and was there on the day the local birds returned from their winter quarters.

> It was the beautiful calm of an early morning in Washington and I awoke to tumultuous birdcalls, whistling, cooing, whooping and shrieking, quite unlike even the noisy parrots, cockatoos and galahs of Australia. Later I drove up through West Virginia. It was the height of spring, when every hillside was covered with pink rhododendrons. I stopped at a run-down little hillbilly settlement, and called in at the local hardware store. It was a long, narrow little shop, about fifteen feet wide, with a path down the middle and a counter each side. I paid for my purchases down one end, and was returning to the front of the shop. There was a very old coloured man who had just walked in the door. As I approached him, the old man crouched and squeezed up against the counter, as though I was going to kick him or say, 'Get out of the bloody way!' It seemed as if it was a hangover from the slaving days.[10]

On one or two occasions when the winters got too bad in New York he would engineer a job for himself in Los Angeles. He had a good friend there whom he had met on the Great Barrier Reef in 1951. Wentworth Singleton III had been married four times and had been one of 'Chenault's Tigers', the pilots who ferried aircraft across the Himalayas and over Burma to Chungking in World War II. He had been doing some aerial filming for the Australian Government when Hungerford met him on the Reef. They became good friends, and Hungerford later received a letter from him via Canberra, which was passed on to him in New York. As ever, keen to work outside, doubtless in return for a free bed, Hungerford remodelled Went's garden for him, and they used to drive down the coast into Baha California via Tijuana. Another time he drove from New York right up to Toronto during the fall, a scenic drive through forests in full colour nearly all the way.

> Those were the unforgettable impressions of the US that I was to take away with me. I wondered how I would get used to the Australian bush again, with its prickles and starkness, but when I returned, it took one drive into the Australian countryside for me to fall in love again with the beautiful subtle shades of green, gold and brown.[11]

Together with a straightforward approach to the natural world, Hungerford was and is still renowned for a naïveté, a small-town, simple approach to his fellow beings that was notable in the sophisticated bustle of New York. Together with other staff, he was watching the annual St Patrick's Day parade down Fifth Avenue, from the balcony of the Australian consulate-general offices. On the balcony opposite he noticed a figure dressed in red. Hungerford asked loudly of those standing next to him: 'Who's the old bloke in the red dress?' It was actually the Catholic Archbishop of New York.[12] The St Patrick's Day parade was followed by a party at an Irish pub on 9th Avenue where Hungerford was dancing with a charming young woman of Irish ancestry.

As everyone did, she asked me if I was a 'Limey'. 'I'm an Australian.'

'Oh, my uncle—my mother's brother—went to Australia years ago. He wrote a few letters and then we haven't heard from him for years. Mom would love to hear from him. Do you know him?'

This too was commonplace. Americans imagined a tiny little island where everyone knew everyone else. I replied: 'I'm afraid I don't, but do you have anything on him?'

'Yes, the last letter we had from him was from a place just-down-south from Sydney.'

I had a friend, John Hetherington, a senior columnist in Sydney at the time on the *Sydney Morning Herald*. I contacted Hetherington to put a piece in his column, to ask the brother to contact his sister in the US. I then forgot about the contact until I had a telephone call from the daughter, saying that her uncle had been in touch with her mother and that he was coming to New York to see her: 'My mother says she is going to pray for you every night of her life, until she dies!'[13]

His social life mainly resulted from his ANIB position and brought him into contact with a number of celebrities of the day. He met Kirk Douglas, President Eisenhower and Prime Minister Robert Menzies. His particular joy was being introduced to the beautiful Merle Oberon, whom he had admired as Anne Boleyn in Charles Laughton's *Henry VIII*. She came to a party in a necklace of emeralds setting off a grey suit, topped off with a grey Russian cap and silver fox furs, high fashion at the time. On another occasion there was Judith Anderson, a great Australian actor, who had played Medea in Melbourne, just before Hungerford left for the USA.

The part had left me with the impression of a big, forceful woman, dressed all in black, topped with a black wig. Anderson had also played Mrs Manners in *Rebecca*, with Laurence Olivier. I was at a reception at the Australian consul-general's, standing with a glass in my hand, when someone walked up and started to talk to me. He said there was 'Poor old Judith'. I looked around and noticed this thin, mousy woman, leaning against the wall.

'Judith who?'

'Judith Anderson.'

'It can't be!'

'I'd better get her boyfriend to come and look after her,' and he returned with a languid young man.[14]

The consummate actor being an unimpressive little woman in real life reminded him not to assume that the pizzazz and glitter of New York reflected reality.

There were the other people he met from the colourful mix of the 'show-biz' crowd who were to make a lasting impression. As a professional writer based in New York, Tom Hungerford was fortunate to use his talents outside the life created by his job. He was persuaded to write the script for a musical, through a friend, Bernard Q. Paganstacker, known more familiarly as Jim Brett, who worked in advertising on Madison Avenue. To produce the musical, Bernard alias Jim, a fine musician, had teamed up with Bob Felstein, son of one of the biggest leather merchants in New York, and with Gerry George, a good-looking and charismatic Greek-American.

I had a fascination with the more unusual American names, and as Gerry's full name was Gerald R. George, I wondered whether 'George' was a shortened version of a

Greek name, and I was especially intrigued with what the 'R' stood for. The answer was 'Rangipur'. 'What a strange name! Were you born in India?'

'I just liked it, so I took it for myself.'[15]

Writing the script for a musical fascinated him, if only for the experience since he was not to be paid for this work. His reward was assured later if the musical was a success. As a novelist, he had never written a script, but at their request he drafted the first act, which they liked. The trouble was that each one of them as an investor in the business of theatre had his own idea of how the script should read. Hungerford would be working away when one of the collaborators would propose an addition. Hungerford, knowing little about theatre, would have to accept that it was a valid suggestion. Then one of the other two would ask for something to be included. As a result he finished up with something that he felt was nearly as long as *War and Peace*.

With Hungerford busy on the words, Jim Brett composed the music, in conjunction with a capable lyricist, Don Reed. 'When the whole production was ready, we took the score to a contact in RCA who enthused that he had rarely heard a more tuneful collection of songs, and from that we took great pleasure and encouragement.'[16]

Casting performances were held in the enormous Park Avenue apartment of Felstein's parents, and Hungerford enjoyed watching and listening to the professionals being auditioned. But the script was deemed to be too long and rambling, and the backers asked very nicely whether Hungerford would mind if someone else worked on it. He read of his official demise as a budding scriptwriter in the entertainment pages of the *New York Times*: 'HUNGERFORD OUT AS AUTHOR'. He smiled to himself, to think of readers asking each other who Hungerford was, but was quite happy to make way for another writer. He had no real regrets, he would not have missed the chance to write a script, and the experience was to be useful in later years when he tackled writing scripts for himself. One incidental benefit was that he had learnt how to make 'Hungarian Frankfurter Goulash', taught to him by a female relative of his show-biz colleagues.

Then the venture collapsed. None of the major Broadway producers showed interest. Perhaps it was the title, *Sure Sign of Spring*, or more likely the theme, a young girl in a fishing village up the Gaspay coast in Canada who was going to lose her sight unless she received replacement corneas. From the beginning, Hungerford had felt it was a strange subject for a musical. Although the team continued to work on the musical for months, *Sure Sign of Spring* sank without trace.

———

As previously related, Hungerford was determined to write a novel—his fourth—while he was in New York. When he was looking for a theme he was lucky to meet Tony Madigan, an impressive young man, 'a good Catholic boy' from Sydney, and became friendly with him. Madigan was a professional boxer who later nearly defeated Cassius Clay (Mohammed Ali) at the Rome Olympics in 1960.

> I was discussing writing a new novel with Madigan, and Tony suggested the theme could be the boxer's life in New York. A wealthy and prominent lawyer, who was on the US Olympic committee, had noticed Madigan in the training gym. The lawyer thought the boxer would probably win the 'Golden Gloves' competition, so he offered a contract to maintain him while he trained, paying Madigan $70 a week. It seemed to me that a fictionalised version of Tony Madigan's story would make a good read and so it proved.[17]

The scenes switch from a vivid picture of Charlie Dangerfield, the Australian boxer experiencing the colour of a New York day, to intense descriptions of the upper-crust set among whom he found himself. Hungerford pitchforks the reader into the turbulent world of New York, and the forceful introduction of the cast of characters is a jolt. Perhaps it was the character of Charlie himself who jarred: he is depicted as unpleasant and ill-mannered, a lout who leaves the reader barely caring what happened to him. Tony Madigan's reaction to the Charlie Dangerfield character was mild: he commented to Hungerford that he wished he had had half the opportunities enjoyed by Dangerfield.

In the novel Hungerford's use of colour and the impact of the settings is his writing at its very best. Charlie's casual intriguing as he made his mark on the foreign world of old money and on the Bowery types in the gym worked well. So did the story of Charlie's various promiscuities; the sexual side being handled with just enough said to leave the reader to imagine the salacious detail. The various females in the story likewise are well drawn, especially his hostess, Venetia (whose model in real life was desperately in love with Madigan, forcing him to move in with Hungerford) and the ageing actress, Deborah. The contemporary American slang—shades of Damon Runyon—makes for some tortuous reading, as do the racist references to the Australian Aborigines and the New York African Americans. It is doubtful, however, that Hungerford would change much if charged with political incorrectness and asked to rewrite the text for a modern readership. He is always quick to criticise anything he sees as having been composed to suit today's norms. By contrast, the one homosexual character in the book projects as a gentle, lovable type, quite contemporary in its handling, which at the very least suggested an empathy with homosexuals at a time when there was less than universal support for them outside the theatrical world.

Angus & Robertson published *Shake the Golden Bough* in 1963, after Hungerford had returned to Australia. It did not achieve much of a run. Douglas Stewart reviewed it, and it was suggested that Hungerford was very upset by Stewart writing that the book was full of homosexual imagery, which it must be said is hard to identify years later. However, by contrast, an admiring writer friend described *Shake the Golden Bough* as one of the most beautifully written books he had ever read.[18]

Shake the Golden Bough had been composed between social evening engagements, in sections of 200 words a time, with a bottle of rum at his side. Novel writing was a tough routine after a full day of work for the ANIB, and it was to be Hungerford's last major publication until the late 1970s.

———

> In 1960, I had a call from the ANIB director in Canberra, Kevin Murphy: 'Tom: we want you to come back. We have finally got an office in Perth, which we have been trying to open for a long while. We want you to take charge of it. Would you like to?' There had been an ANIB office in every Australian capital except Perth.
>
> 'Would I ever! I haven't been back to Perth for so long! How long will I be there, Kevin?'
>
> 'Well, we don't think for more than a couple of years, really...'[19]

With that enigmatic invitation Hungerford had to be content. He was not a confidant of Murphy—'in fact, I knew the director disliked me'—but it was someone else who later confirmed it to him: ' "They all hated your guts. Kevin Murphy hated you."

' "But why?"

' "They were jealous of you, because you had made the grade as a writer, which they all probably wanted to do, being journalists, and never made it." '[20]

John Murray, then secretary of the Commonwealth Film Board, provided this revealing insight, although it can be suggested that perhaps Hungerford's own entrenched black-and-white approach towards the people he meets perhaps contributed to this dislike of him, if the first meeting had been unpropitious. It was Murray who gave Hungerford the famous line about the distribution of books or films. He said that they had learnt at the Film Board that even if there was a film of *The Last Supper*, with the original cast but with no effective distribution, an otherwise brilliant work would never be acclaimed. It was very true. With the exception of *The Ridge and the River*, his other novels never received the full recognition that was his due, he felt, because of poor promotion and distribution by the publishers.

Tom Hungerford packed up to go back to Perth in 1961.

Tom Hungerford's parents, Arthur Hungerford and Minnie Hedley.
Photograph property of T. A. G. Hungerford

Hungerford &
Kirkpatrick's camel
team setting off
with a 14-ton boiler.
*Photograph property of
T. A. G. Hungerford*

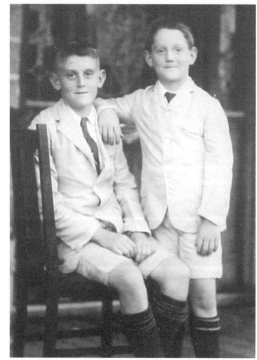

Tom Hungerford
(at right) and his
brother Mick.
*Photograph property of
T. A. G. Hungerford*

Hungerford on joining the army.
Photograph property of T. A. G. Hungerford

March past of the 2/8th Independent Company (Commando Squadron), Lae, New Guinea, 7 October 1944. Hungerford is third from left.
Australian War Memorial 076465

Tom Hungerford
relaxing with a book
between operations,
outside his hut at B
Troop HQ, Nairona
Village, Bougainville,
7 June 1945. *Australian
War Memorial 093033*

Tom Hungerford as
a sergeant. *Photograph
property of T. A. G.
Hungerford*

The 'Morotai mutiny',
December 1945:
Australian troops
assembling to march
to their protest parade.
Australian War Memorial
124201

Portrait of Tom
Hungerford; c. 1963.
Kate (Kathleen
Laetitia) O'Connor,
1876–1968. Oil on wood
panel; 69 × 54·8 cm.
Copyright © Estate of
the late K. O'Connor,
Perth. National Library
of Australia R10292 nla.
pic-an4302527

Tom Hungerford at
Wittenoom Gorge
in the Pilbara, 1960s.
*Copyright © Richard
Woldendorp 2005*

Hungerford at Mount
Tom Price. *Copyright ©
Richard Woldendorp 2005*

Climbing the Stirlings,
Toolbrunup, 1969.
*Copyright © Richard
Woldendorp 2005*

In pensive mood: Tom
Hungerford at Koolan
Island, 1969. *Copyright ©
Richard Woldendorp 2005*

Winner of the Patrick White Award, 2003. *Copyright © West Australian Newspapers Ltd 2003*

CHAPTER 12

The Back of Beyond

Hungerford returned via Canberra, where he called at a minister's office in the Prime Minister's Department, to be briefed on the priorities of his new position. 'Was there anything in particular which I was to concentrate on? "Oh no, let us know the cricket scores, and stuff like that." '[1] This was the sort of ignorant indifference he had come to expect from Canberra's higher circles, particularly towards the 'Cinderella State', as Western Australia had been known. As it was, he need not have bothered to seek advice: there was a full job awaiting him in Perth. One of the reasons he was retrieved from New York was to work on publicity for the Commonwealth Games in Perth, in 1961.

He still found time, initially at least, to work on his short stories and was gratified to start his Perth posting by being awarded the Patricia Hackett Short Story prize. His reputation as a published writer had gone before him, and Tom Hungerford was soon established in Perth literary circles as someone who had 'made it' and who was always ready to help a fellow writer. However, the demands of his job were soon to dominate most of his waking hours. As federal press officer in Perth he worked out of the old Gleddon Building on the corner of William and Hay Streets, opposite the Wesley

Church. He shared the services of a half-time secretary/switchboard operator with a federal MP. The building housed a number of federal parliamentary offices and their incumbents, one of whom was the prominent Liberal politician, the late Fred Chaney Senior, who was known to enjoy a practical joke.

> He came into my office one day and said: 'Tom, I want to introduce you to your new Minister in the Prime Minister's Department.' This was a good-looking man, apparently about nineteen years of age and plainly a set-up—the man was far too young. I said solemnly: 'Yes, how d'you do? I'm the Virgin Mary.' It was in fact the new minister.[2]

Later he was moved to the newly built Council House on the river side of St George's Terrace, a prominent example of 1960s architecture that still arouses aesthetic controversy. It suited Hungerford. He had a whole glass wall to look through at the Swan River and down towards Fremantle. He was so busy that after about a week he no longer noticed the view, but occasionally he would look up in wonder at the pristine panorama of the river across to South Perth where he had lived as a boy and where he had re-established himself.

He was living in an apartment in South Perth, not far from his sister Peg and her husband in the family home, in Jubilee Street. 'One day, she said to me: "The house next door is for sale. Why don't you buy it?"

' "What would I do with a house?" She said it would be a very good investment and she persuaded me to purchase it.'[3]

He then built a flat at the back as a base, somewhere to leave all his possessions. He paid cash for the property, and when Peg suggested he should buy another up the road, he asked what he was going to use for money. He only had about £1,200 left in the bank. That he had never thought of borrowing money, of using the rent to pay off the bank mortgage, was another example of his naïveté. The initial investment resulted in his buying other houses, all prompted by his sister, using one house to buy the next one. Eventually he owned four houses in Jubilee Street and another one in Subiaco, and sold them all over time, as property prices steadily rose, to finance his final dream purchase, a block in Canning Vale. His sister's wise advice was eventually to result in a financial independence that enabled him to visit other parts of the world and to display his generosity towards relations, friends and many aspiring writers.

Hungerford's relations were and are dear to him. From the start of the war he wrote regularly to them, initially in longhand until he had a typewriter. His sister-in-law Mollie Hungerford remains very close in spirit to him and, with her two daughters, she used to visit him in Jubilee Street. Mollie was to rely on him when her husband Mick lay dying in Royal Perth Hospital. Tom had sat by the bed of the unconscious man, holding his hand, tears streaming down his cheeks, and when his brother was gone, he took over all the funeral arrangements. On much happier occasions his favourite nephew, Rob Archdeacon, as a youngster enjoyed being taken by his Uncle Tom to the cinema in Fremantle and being accompanied on expeditions to Penguin Island. Later, there were card games at Jubilee Street and games of squash nearby.

Hungerford was now able to meet his old flame, Vivienne, without a real pang. Her husband was working for the oil refinery in Kwinana. Hungerford liked him and their four boys. Although he avoided meeting Viv as much as possible, at some stage the old crowd from the beach days would visit her, and Hungerford went with them. Later her boys sought him out. He was that sort of father figure.

In 1962 he was asked to do a story on Kathleen (Kate) O'Connor, an eccentric 86-year-old woman and a prodigious painter. She was the daughter of C. Y. O'Connor, the famous engineer who was responsible for the construction of the pipeline to Kalgoorlie, among other achievements, before World War I.[4] Miss O'Connor lived then in Mount Street, Perth, and she summoned numerous visitors there, most of them men, whom she entertained with sweet sherry and cakes. Hungerford found her impossible to interview: she was deaf and fixated on grievances against the Perth establishment. In desperation he asked whether she would do a portrait of him so that he could interview her at the easel. In the weeks of sittings that followed they developed a warm friendship, although it was always 'Mr Hungerford' and 'Miss O'Connor'. To his surprise, what eventuated was a portrait of him as a young man. 'Mister Hungerford! If you want a photograph, you go to a photographer. If you want a portrait you go to a portrait painter. I see you as a young man, and I shall paint you as a young man!'[5]

There was a problem with the mouth, however, and O'Connor said a friend of hers would 'fix it up'. The old woman died some time thereafter, and when he asked eventually for the portrait from the other painter, he was informed that the latter owned it; she offered to sell it to him. Disgusted, he forgot about it until some years later, when he was rung by the National Library in Canberra, to be informed that they had purchased it from the recalcitrant painter for $5,000. It is there today, and the mouth is still not quite right.

Hungerford's return to Perth was at a momentous time in the state's history, only shortly before the start of the great iron-ore expansion and the subsequent booms in nickel, industrial salt, gold and oil. Far from being required to provide only the latest cricket scores, his job as the federal press officer quite suddenly became the focus of every important newspaper in the world. Photographers, film producers, TV outfits, journalists, all came to examine the remarkable industrial development in a hitherto unknown far-off part of the globe. Naturally, on Canberra's recommendation, Hungerford's was the first office they approached, and he had the job of introducing them to the people they wanted to meet and often accompanying them to the places on their itineraries, such as to the new mining centres of Paraburdoo and Tom Price. This meant hours of liaising with those involved, preparing an itinerary and showing the visitors around. He also had to introduce them to the various ministers they wanted to see and present the visitors to the state's Premier, Dave (later Sir David) Brand. Ostensibly, the Premier's Department was there to handle the visitors, but as Hungerford initially received most of them, the on-going schedules nearly overwhelmed him.

He was also supposed to keep up a flow of articles and pictures for Canberra, to publicise Western Australia. This required travel all over the state, quite apart from the trips he made with overseas visitors, and to illustrate his written pieces he needed the services of a professional photographer. Hungerford had heard of Richard Woldendorp through the state Department of Industrial Development. He contacted Woldendorp and said he wanted a 'stringer' (a casual photographer) for the ANIB. Hungerford initially asked for photographs once or twice a week, and it was the start of a long relationship between the two, both professional and personal.

Woldendorp, who had started life in Western Australia as a house painter from Holland, had first visited northwestern Western Australia under contract as a painter to MacRobertson Miller Airlines. He had been impressed by the landscapes and had then decided that professional photography was his metier, focusing mainly on the dramatic landscapes of the Outback. He subsequently became one of Australia's finest landscape photographers, but in the early days he was grateful for the bread-and-butter work from the ANIB. One of his early tasks when working with Hungerford was to become attuned to exactly what the latter wanted. Woldendorp's first love was of course photographing the Australian landscape, but in the early days Hungerford required him to snap personalities arriving on aircraft, particularly the Japanese who were involved with the giant mining projects. Hungerford directed the shoots: Woldendorp being his own man, this was something to which he was unaccustomed, but he learnt quickly. Then larger jobs for the ANIB were commissioned.

Woldendorp drove with Hungerford into the wheat belt with its thousands of hectares of golden grain, and to Esperance on the southeast coast, where new farms were being imposed on the fragile soils of the area. In those days they travelled in Hungerford's old green Holden station wagon, interviewing farmers on the way and taking notes. At Esperance Art Linkletter, the American media personality, had started to develop his spread. There they also met English immigrants, and Hungerford would generally interview these modern pioneers in the freshly cleared paddocks. This was the period of headlines like 'A MILLION ACRES OF LAND A YEAR CLEARED'[6] and, only a few decades later, increasing salinity was to put paid to many such enterprises. 'We're from the ANIB. I've got a photographer with me. Would you mind if we…?' Sometimes they would linger for a few hours, because the immigrants wanted to offer hospitality to the visitors, but it was more a whistle-stop tour. From Esperance they drove via Salmon Gums to Kambalda and Kalgoorlie, where the nickel boom had started. Woldendorp photographed the old buildings and the modern miners, and then they travelled back to Perth, via Merredin.

They enjoyed a good working relationship, on the whole. There was one instance when they disagreed. When they arrived at Northam at 5.30 p.m. Hungerford drew up, saying, 'Let's find a motel.' It was only three-quarters of an hour to the outskirts of Perth, and Richard Woldendorp would have been home. But Hungerford said no, find a place, so they did. He had no welcoming wife to rush back to and, of course, he was a public servant, so for him to find a hotel and relax was much more important than to drive home, where he would have to cook for himself. But they had been up early in the morning; they had driven a long distance, so that was that.[7]

When Woldendorp was working with Hungerford, he had a year's contract with Hamersley Iron to photograph their iron ore developments. On one of those trips Hungerford joined him, and it was then that Woldendorp suggested a publication on Western Australia. He had already produced a book in conjunction with Peter Slater, the bird photographer. Woldendorp talked to Hungerford about whether he would like to write it. He agreed. Apart from accumulating pictures as they were working together, Woldendorp organised a visit by road to the majestic, rugged and iron-rich Hamersley Ranges with its gorges, which Hungerford had not previously visited. Included in the party was a couple, Bill Warnock and his soon-to-be wife, Diana.

It was a momentous occasion for them all, although neither Hungerford nor Warnock realised it at the time. Woldendorp had done some photography for Bill Warnock, who was then the premier advertising man in Perth and had given Woldendorp his first real photographic job. He was a remarkable character in his own right, a cheerful, clever, sparkling individual, passionate about any enterprise in which he was involved, particularly to do with writing or film. Hungerford, Woldendorp and Diana Warnock drove up together, in Woldendorp's Peugeot, to Wittenoom on the edge of the gorges, near the asbestos mine site where blue asbestos was silently killing the miners (the danger was not fully recognised then). They were meeting Bill Warnock there: he had an important advertising commitment in Perth at the time and had to fly up.

Warnock was to become Tom Hungerford's dearest friend after that trip, but their first meeting was inauspicious. Hungerford said to Woldendorp: 'Who's this fellow Bill Warnock, and why are we going to all this trouble to meet him?'

'Oh, he's a very interesting bloke, and he should come along on this trip with us.'[8]

Hungerford was unimpressed by advertising people, and the idea that they were making special efforts to meet one did not thrill him. Shortly after they met, he and Warnock argued with each other and then came to like each other, because Hungerford found to his surprise that Bill Warnock was a poet and a writer, and not just an advertising man. From that time onwards, he and Warnock became very good friends and, in a sense, Warnock filled the role of a surrogate younger brother. Warnock had ambitions to do film work, so he and Woldendorp had bought a camera together. They had made one film already, *A Mighty Big Paddock*, and the reason for this visit was to make *Yellow Boat Wittenoom*.

Richard Woldendorp had packed a dinghy for the gorges. After a bitterly cold night they descended Knox Gorge, down a hazardous track flanked by lowering red cliffs, to a stretch of the clearest water, alive with fish and birds, but only negotiable on the water. Hungerford carried the dinghy and Woldendorp his equipment. They paddled along the narrow stretch, and Hungerford marvelled at the rugged grandeur and the peace, lost in a reverie—'Oh Man!' "…the every-but-which-way, purple and pink and yellow and rose rock gorges and gullies…"'[9]

Hungerford and Woldendorp continued up north to the Kimberleys for their book. Although writing the book was Woldendorp's idea, Hungerford was used to directing the other as to what to do and where. He wanted to include material similar to what he had been writing on the state. By contrast, Woldendorp intended this to be a book promoting Western Australia but at the same time presenting an independent point of view. That meant including subjects of little direct interest to Hungerford, such as landscapes and other visual focuses, and there was some spirited argument before they could agree. Woldendorp had a high regard for Hungerford's professional expertise and kept this in mind when they negotiated what eventuated. Hungerford would sometimes take over and say where he wanted to go; occasionally Woldendorp insisted on something, and Hungerford would acquiesce, if reluctantly. There had to be a degree of give and take between the two men, one who was used to getting his own way and the other a quietly determined Dutchman.

Their visit to the far north was before the momentous referendum in 1967, when Australians voted to allow a change to the Constitution by recognising the original inhabitants as Australian citizens, which would lead to full voting and other rights previously denied them. Many Aborigines were still working as menials on the cattle stations, in return for their keep and nominal wages. The pair visited a mission just south of Broome, on the coast. Hungerford was keen to do a story on the mission. They accompanied a truckload of Aboriginal children, while Woldendorp photographed and Hungerford made notes for a piece about the relationship of white and Aboriginal. Other times Woldendorp would take over and insist on visiting Broome or Fitzroy Crossing. He carefully negotiated the Peugeot along Kimberley tracks, shuddering with corrugations. Nearly all of the pictures he took were black and white, because that was the only way they could be posted for newspapers and books. There was only limited colour in the book that resulted from their travels together. *A Million Square* was published in 1969, probably the first coffee-table book on Western Australia. It sold 10,000 copies in nine months, but was not reprinted because of the publisher's intransigence.[10]

Although Woldendorp remained a friend of Tom Hungerford, he was occasionally at odds with the latter's dogmatism. Once they had stopped to help a couple of people at the side of the road, who were out of petrol. As they were in Hungerford's green Holden station wagon, Hungerford gave the others petrol. Woldendorp tried to insist that Hungerford should charge them. But he was adamant he would not, and there was no further discussion. He had none of the flexibility of their mutual friend Bill Warnock, who would listen to anything. Politics brought out the same stubbornness in Hungerford. Those who did not share his views learnt not to argue with him.

He was just as cutting with those he regarded as guilty of cant or political correctness. On one occasion during dinner at the Warnocks, a male guest was sitting next to a young woman, and used the term 'bird' in conversation. She icily rebuked him for what she saw as a sexist term. The offending male began to apologise, and Hungerford, who was on the other side of the table, exploded: 'Stop there! Don't you apologise to her for that!' Poking his finger at her across the table, he began to debate the use of the word, and the unfortunate woman, after her initial rebuke, retreated.[11]

Hungerford was working most hours of the day, a punishing routine he kept up until his secretary, by now a good friend, became concerned about his workload. Thinking that he needed a thorough medical check-up, she booked an appointment with Professor Ian Saint, the top cardiac specialist in Perth at the time. Grudgingly Hungerford agreed to keep the appointment. He felt it was a waste of time and money. He was very fit; he was playing squash four times a week, swimming at Scarborough and doing some horse-riding, too. On the day of the appointment he had been very busy as usual. He ran across town, and when he arrived at the consulting rooms he was out of breath. The doctor checked him over but said nothing, other than that he wanted Hungerford back in a week. The next Friday was a less punishing routine, and Dr Saint once again examined him. He asked his patient what sort of day he had had, and Hungerford told him it had been unusually peaceful. Dr Saint commented: 'You'll have to watch yourself. Your blood pressure's fairly normal this morning. Last week it was dangerously high.'[12]

Having received such a stark warning, Hungerford contacted Canberra to inform them of the warning, and said that he wanted a change. Kevin Murphy, his director but no friend, had in fact visited Hungerford halfway through the six years to discuss another posting for the latter, as had been mooted originally on his initial appointment to Perth.

> I had introduced him to the Premier. David Brand had interrupted Murphy: 'Mr Murphy, if you had any ideas about taking Tom out of Perth, forget them. I will stop you at the highest level. He is not to be taken away from Perth.' Although I appreciated this, I did want a change, even then.[13]

Now, after six years, he was really suffering from the heavy workload arising from the Western Australian mineral boom, and he believed he had earned an overseas post. San Francisco would be ideal, and then he would be prepared to return to Perth. He knew that the current incumbent in San Francisco had been a political appointment. The man had been there for ten years doing very little, since most of the work was done in New York. Hungerford asked to be posted to San Francisco for three years. Murphy flew to Perth to try to talk Hungerford out of his idea of moving overseas. He suggested Canberra, but Hungerford was adamant he did not want to go to Canberra. He felt he had earned San Francisco.

The discussion became heated. Murphy was in Hungerford's office, and Hungerford's secretary was next door in tears as the voices rose. She fancied herself in love with her good-looking boss. 'Finally I said: "Kevin! For Christ's sake go away! You're boring me stiff and I'm boring you stiff—now go away!" I virtually threw Murphy out of the office and then put in my resignation.'[14]

What irritated him more than anything else was that he had made several attempts to persuade the ANIB to recruit another journalist to do the extra work that Hungerford had no time for. He would sometimes return from three or four weeks up north, to correspondence piled on his desk and myriad phone calls. It was an impossible situation, and he had finally had enough. But before he left, a telephone call from the editor of the ANIB in Canberra requested Hungerford immediately to press the local Public Service Board for another journalist position in the Perth office. Hungerford said bitterly: 'You bastard! I've been trying my head off to get another man in here and the moment I turn around and say I'm leaving, you say get a second man.'[15]

It was too late. True to the stubbornness of someone who always followed through on any firm decision made, he resigned from the ANIB in 1967, at the age of 52. He had leave owing, including long service for which he was paid out, and he had put money aside. He felt he relaxed sufficiently after work, so he did not need to go on holiday. In an interview with the *Canberra Times* on 18 July 1967 he talked of working on the Nullarbor as a surveyor's assistant, before he resumed writing. But as soon as it was learnt that he had resigned from the ANIB he was offered comparable positions with the State Government, which had always been interested in having Tom Hungerford work for them. Bill Mitchell was a significant figure behind the Liberals then.

> He had tried to entice me away from the Federal Government: 'Come on! Don't work for the Feds—come across the road.' Mitchell was based in the old Treasury buildings on the corner of St George's Terrace and Barrack Street when I was in Council House, across the road. My response was: 'One of these days maybe.' I wanted to keep my options open.[16]

At some stage he was also approached both by Ray O'Connor on behalf of the Liberal Party and Crawford Nalder on behalf of the Country Party asking him to take on pubic relations for the respective parties. Hungerford with his experience and contacts was ideally placed to work for either party. Bill Mitchell in fact enticed Hungerford to do some writing for the Liberal and Country

Party government, and he was happy to freelance for a while. He was doing the same for Canberra, and for two years this suited him. He did not want to do a great deal, but just to keep himself reasonably busy.

He had also been doing some travel: a few short visits to Hong Kong where he had a friend from his Sydney days. He was developing an affection for Hong Kong and thought of spending more time there and started to plan to that end. Moreover, his love life had become patchy and unsatisfactory. First, there was someone who was already married, whom he had known in the old days at Scarborough and of whom he was very fond. That would have been messy. Then there was his secretary, and that was a great worry to him at the time. He felt she was determined, as he saw it, to entrap him into marriage. It was time to leave Perth again for a while.

CHAPTER 13

From Oriental Interlude to Premier's Voice

I was talking to Frank Devine, the [then] editor of the *Daily News*, who enquired: 'You're going to Hong Kong? Why don't you go to Macau?'

'Why?'

'It's a wonderful place.' Frank Devine himself had stayed there and suggested that I could always live in Macau, freelance from there, or write a book. I had thought of Macau as being a tiny little island off the coast of Hong Kong, and I knew nothing about it.[1]

In his straightforward if uninformed way, Hungerford saw Hong Kong as being connected to Macau by one of the little bridges, as depicted on the 'Willow Pattern' crockery.

In late 1969 he made up his mind. He would base himself in Macau, but first he stayed with an old eastern states friend for about three to four months, at a big house in the New Territories. There he helped his host lay out a large garden and all appeared to be going well, but the friend's wife thought he had outstayed his welcome. Their relationship lacked something—his friend thought that Hungerford's mind tended to be full of poetry, perhaps to the exclusion of others around—and, rather upset at being unwanted, he moved to Macau. It was quite unlike the sophisticated bustle he was used to across the water. He was entranced by Macau.

'The smell of Macau was of the sea and of cooking, and raw fish and frangipanis, and ripe fruit and wood smoke, and incense from the temples.'[2] Its ambience was still part of the nineteenth century, the local people oblivious to the modern world as they scurried about in what was for all the world like an exotic ants' nest. In those days the settlement was an attractive, little old entrepôt centre, with just a few Portuguese soldiers wandering around. It was very quiet then, with its air of faded decadence. The crouched three-storey buildings, which had laced colonnades, were festooned with bougainvillea. The walls were a beautiful Mediterranean pink. The houses perched on winding cobblestone streets, with very few cars, just rickshaws and bicycles.[3] Hungerford started searching for lodgings, which he finally located on the second floor of a house owned by a Macanese woman. The only disadvantage of his new home was that when it rained heavily the floor was flooded. He had two rooms, one with views overlooking the harbour and fine teak floorboards. Now he needed to make it a home:

> I found my way to the market and bought lengths of green material which I tore up and pinned on the walls above the windows, to make curtains. I bought the furniture I required—a comfortable chair, a coffee table, and a mat for the floor—from a local dealer.[4]

The dealer ingenuously offered him a second-hand mattress, which had suffered from someone being sick on it. Hungerford purchased a new straw mattress. He had a small fly-wire cabinet made to store his food, not unlike a Coolgardie safe.

He was in his element, down on his hands and knees polishing those teak floorboards until he could see his face in them. Sitting on the balcony at the front, Hungerford revelled in the view of the harbour and the busy life below him, an entire population living off junks with their coloured lugsails. One old woman was washing up in the turgid water swirling below, while another relieved herself unconcernedly off the prominent stern, just a few metres away. It was colourful, vivid and, in those days, reasonably safe for a solitary *gwelo* (European) to live among the locals.

Of course, he had brought his typewriter with him, but he did not discipline himself to write and just used it when the mood took him, although his new lifestyle did result in some feature pieces for the *South China Morning Post*. He also wrote an (unpublished) guide to Macau, 'Stopover in Macau', which would now be a good historical record of the place at that time. Now Macau has changed. The Hong Kong money-men moved in with their casinos and racketeering, and the age-old history of Macau has been absorbed by modern Chinese culture with just a veneer of Portuguese architecture remaining. Chinese temples and shrines coexist with restored villas from the colonial period. 'Canto-pop', a popular form of music, throbs in the background.[5]

Although he was lonely at times, knowing no one and not speaking the language, it was a halcyon period.

> I spent much of the time hiking around the two little islands off the south of Macau, Taipa and Coloaine. I was told the latter was really called 'Lowan', acquiring its Europeanised name from one of the first Europeans there, who allegedly asked a Chinese, 'Where're you going?' and heard, 'Go Lowan [Coloaine].' I would catch a ferry to Taipa early in the morning and walk all day through the hills, crossing by the old causeway between Taipa and Coloaine. There I restored my fitness by swimming off the Hak Sa [Black Sands] Beach.[6]

Every fortnight or so, if only to raise his social tone, Hungerford made a quick trip by hydrofoil to Hong Kong and visited his friends there, on Tolo Harbour, beyond Kowloon. It was beautiful; certainly by contrast to what he discovered when he visited the South Perth Chinese market gardener, Wong Chu. The old man had retired to his homeland and lived in an overcrowded and rundown area of Kowloon, situated on the Chinese mainland north of Hong Kong Island. Wong Chu resided on Taipo Road, in Hung Lo Mansions, which sounded grander than they actually were. With his tiny wife and his two sons, he existed in the smallest of flats, no bigger than a medium-sized kitchen, with a minute kitchen and toilet and a bedroom space that just accommodated a double bed. He told his Australian friend that the family farmed at Mong Kok (one of the most densely populated areas on earth), which sounded promising, but he and his sons were just labourers working on a farm. Tom Hungerford's heart bled for the old man who had been such an important part of his earlier life.

He was in Macau for a year, but the time came when he had enough of his solitary and exotic existence and began to long for the familiar background of South Perth. He had earned very little during his time in Macau, and it would be good to start being paid again. It was time to return to Western Australia. He flew into Perth airport in early 1971 'rarin' to go'. He had it all worked out: he would write in the afternoon and work in the morning on any job he could find. He was driving home from town one day when he passed a pleasant block of flats. He noticed the block's appalling garden, with weeds everywhere. Hungerford has always been a gardener, and he could not bear to see a garden go to ruin. He used to maintain the gardens of two of the houses he owned. He had the mower, the edger and all the tools needed for a garden, in the back of his utility (which was his hallmark. He never owned a saloon car, the closest to one being the green station wagon of his ANIB days). 'I walked in and asked the owner: "Who does your gardening?"

' "Oh, some bloke comes. He's terrible, he never does anything, really."

' "I'll take it over, if you'd like." I started work at once on the neglected garden, transformed it and thoroughly enjoyed what I was doing.'[7]

The owner was impressed and asked if she could pass on his name to one of her friends. Hungerford was happy to do the friend's place, too, and before long he could have started a business with others ringing him to maintain their gardens also. But much as he enjoyed gardening as a pastime, he did not want to do it for a living, and he looked elsewhere for a livelihood.

In 1971, he walked into the Premier's Department, to catch up with Bill Mitchell, but Mitchell had left on the retirement of Sir David Brand as premier of the out-going Coalition government. Labor had just been returned to government in Western Australia under the leadership of John Tonkin, who was to be premier only until 1974, when Labor lost the state election. 'Derrick Flynn, who had been Mitchell's second-in-charge, had taken over the Premier's Public Affairs Office. "How about that job you've been offering me over here?"

' "There's your desk," and I sat down and started to work, there and then.'[8]

The steady flood of tasks landing on his desk kept him busy until 1975, under two premiers.[9] In neither case were the relationships particularly close, although he admired both men. His role included making the tour arrangements in 1972 for the visit to Western Australia of Princess Margaret and her then husband, Lord Snowdon. Piers Akerman remembered the tour:

> The government was feigning disinterest in the visit. Curiously, a number of ministers' wives were most interested in their brush with minor royals. The WA Government didn't make it easy for the media to cover

the tour, but I chartered aircraft to enable our people to be in situ around the state. I think Tom wasn't happy with that. He was also displeased when I wrote that he had not turned up at a scheduled press briefing because he had chosen to have a haircut.

The Snowdon marriage was disintegrating. Tony used to slip out and join the press at night, Margaret was drinking with her ladies-in-waiting. A lot of drinking was taking place.

I believe the News [Ltd] team consisted of David McNicoll Snr, Janet Hawley (*The Australian*), Sally Macmillan (*The Telegraph*) and James Oram (*The Mirror*).[10]

Hungerford would have been unhappy because the coverage of the tour alluded to the marital break-up, because it did not serve his government in any particular way, and because Akerman's chartered plane enabled journalists to attend functions from which the government had attempted to keep them away. One such function in particular took place at GoGo Station in the Kimberleys. It had been intended as a private lunch for the royal pair. A bored Snowdon clowned around on a motorbike for the amusement of the uninvited press party, and Hungerford would have glowered in the background.[11]

In addition to publicity material generated for the State Government, Hungerford drafted speeches for the premier. The writing side of his job was an excellent reintroduction to the role in which he had excelled with the ANIB. Working with John Tonkin was the sort of experience he claims he would almost have undertaken for no pay because he particularly respected the man. He saw Tonkin as being principled, intelligent, compassionate and very knowledgeable. As Hungerford saw it, Tonkin was able to demonstrate that as a politician he was swayed by more than political expediency. He was not motivated solely by mega-projects that would generate jobs and big revenues for government.

Before he went to work for John Tonkin, a proposal had been put to the State Government for an aluminium smelter to be constructed in the Swan Valley, northeast of Perth. The Brand government had welcomed the potentially huge investment in jobs and income with enthusiasm, and indeed the cabinet of the incoming Labor government was very keen; except, that is, for Premier Tonkin. 'The day the decision was made to accept or reject the plans, John Tonkin came out of the cabinet room, white-faced after confronting his ministerial colleagues.'[12] He had vetoed the proposal absolutely: the valley was not going to be defaced.[13] Subsequent generations are still grateful to the man, and the Swan Valley remains one of the premier grape-growing areas of the state.

Hungerford had never forgiven the Brand government for demolishing the Barracks, a two-storey building in much the same style as the adjacent Town Hall constructed in colonial times, which gave Perth's Barrack Street its name.[14] It had been part of a square of colonial buildings that incorporated the Town Hall and the old Treasury building, both of which, thankfully, are still standing. In its place, the government allowed construction of the hideous Rural and Industries Bank head office, now demolished, followed by the Law Chambers, which today must rank as the ugliest excrescence in the fair city of Perth. The same fate was due for His Majesty's Theatre, which was to be replaced by a car park, but by then outraged public opinion saved the theatre.

Perhaps unfairly, because he was not the premier at the time, the remarkable Sir Charles Court is associated in Hungerford's mind with demolition of the Barracks, although Court should be acclaimed for actually saving His Majesty's.[15] He was the formidable character with whom Hungerford worked for the reminder of his time with government. More properly, Court is credited with engineering huge contracts with overseas conglomerates for much of the iron ore extraction and shipping, which he negotiated with some of the best business and legal brains in the world. The fact that each of those contracts also stipulated that a secondary treatment process would be established in twenty-five years time—which in the main has not happened—must not detract from the practical achievements of the man.

When the ALP lost office, Tom Hungerford had no intention of working with Court, whom he regarded as representing a side of politics that was at odds with the Tonkin regime he had come to admire. Hungerford had originally signed a contract for three years but, on the new premier's taking office, had his office cleaned out, preparatory to moving. The first day the incumbent came into the office, Hungerford thought he would walk down, welcome Court and wish him good luck.

> But there was a summons from the premier's office below. 'Tom, could you come down and see me?' I stood at the doorway. 'I didn't think you'd walk out on me, Tom.'
>
> 'Mr Premier, I'm not walking out; I just want out. I only joined this place for three years. I have got so much I want to do off my own bat. I've got writing I want to do.'
>
> 'Will you just stick around until I get into the job?'
>
> So I agreed, restored my desk to its organised confusion and settled into the job. I stayed for the next three years.[16]

Charles Court had been impressed by Hungerford's skills as a writer ever since he had read *The Ridge and the River* and recommended it to his colleagues. The book was also of particular interest to the premier because of his war-time service, which included a posting to Bougainville as a staff officer in charge of supplying troops in the field. When Hungerford joined the premier's staff, Court bore in mind that the writer and journalist had previously worked for John Tonkin. He thought he knew, of course, of Hungerford's leftist philosophy in this regard, but he assessed Hungerford on the quality of what he could do. This progressive attitude was contrary to the natural tendency on the part of most incoming governments to regard with suspicion those public servants, or previously engaged specialists with political views, who might be opposed to the incoming government. Hungerford for his part saw Court as a man of tremendous vision and capability, if apparently uncaring about people as such. He had seen Brand as

> the baby kisser, Court as the engine. Court was a strange man in this respect: that while he appeared as a hard—even vindictive—man in many ways, he longed for appreciation and love. He used to stop me and talk about what he had done, where he'd been in the war.[17]

The only clashes that occurred between them were on those occasions when Hungerford came to the premier with what he plainly regarded as the ultimate in speeches. He would plant the document on the table, with a defiant air of challenging the premier to alter even one word. But the premier knew that some changes in the text were inevitable. Most of Court's speechwriters would accept changes in good heart, but not necessarily Hungerford. Invariably, it would have to be spelt out: 'Tom, I've got to give this speech—not Tom Hungerford! I've got to get re-elected, not Tom Hungerford! Have you got the message?'[18] Because he always regards what he has written as the ultimate, Hungerford still protested stubbornly—as he has done with editors of his short stories over the years. Standing in the premier's office, however, he had met his match. The premier was adamant, although he never once challenged Hungerford's professional ability. He knew the other man had an instinct for good writing, but whether Hungerford could carry that through to draft what had to be interpreted in the Liberal mode was of course quite another matter.

In retrospect it was all quite amusing, and the exchanges were conducted in a good-hearted way. Hungerford's abilities were widely admired, both within the premier's office and among his fellow journalists, who had come to regard him with a certain awe as a professional writer and competent journalist, certainly not someone who was to be lightly crossed.

The time came when Hungerford had simply had enough, both of churning out media releases and of writing the premier's speeches. 'I had great trouble in extracting myself from the Premier's Department, but finally I said: "I'm going at the end of June [1975]. The sky won't fall on your bloody heads." '[19]

Chapter 14

Living the Life

While Tom Hungerford had been busy trying to give what he considered was just the right slant to the speeches he drafted for his political bosses, he had become—like Mole in *The Wind in the Willows*—increasingly drawn to a settled rural lifestyle. The anthropomorphic *Swagbelly and the King of Siam* (published in 1989) might even have suggested that he saw himself as just another of the Australian bush creatures he described with such feeling. Reality was a beautiful 1.2-hectare block of that sand-plain bush that glows with spring colour. It was in Canning Vale and looked east towards the rounded slopes of the Darling Range, which parallels the coastline west of Perth. He had purchased the land in the early 1970s, when he was still based in his Jubilee Street flat.

His longing for the serenity of a rural lifestyle had increased with what he regarded as the urban vandalism of his beloved South Perth, with its modern high-rise buildings and increasing traffic. Now he was progressively divesting himself of the various houses he had bought in Perth, which he had personally managed, having developed a jaundiced view of estate agents who had acted on his behalf. The first time he went overseas for a holiday, the agent just ignored the problems that had arisen in his absence, and 'when

I returned it was I who caught a poultice from the tenant. Agents are the bloody end, mate.' Now he intended to focus on his writing in idyllic surrounds.

Although there are still some large properties there, Canning Vale is now a mass of new housing, interspersed with factory complexes, the principal wholesale fruit and vegetable market and one of the state's main prisons. But Hungerford discovered it as an expanse of pristine bush, the grey-green of the coastal banksias, ti-trees and peppermints, broken only by majestic stands of tuarts, red-gums and the startling orange of the Western Australian 'Christmas trees', the *Nuytsia*. There was just one house below the hills from his home site, a couple of hundred metres away, and another dwelling some way down the road.

He had come across Canning Vale quite by accident while visiting Kwinana to research the steel industry. He decided to return through Mandogolup and was heading towards Albany Highway, out of Cannington, and passed a side street, Amherst Road. It was all bushland then. He saw a sign, 'Ranch Lands', which at the time struck him as pretentious but, as he knew the man behind the project, he was encouraged to contact the developer. Although it was summer, dry and hot, a block on the side of the hill immediately entranced him. He asked for it to be kept for a week; he would make a decision after he had talked to his favourite younger nephew, Rob Archdeacon, who had recently become engaged. This was the period of the land boom, and Hungerford had urged the young man to 'hop in now and get yourself a block, because otherwise it will clean you out to get even a block of land, if you want to be anywhere close to Perth'.

Hungerford suggested that they should split the cost of one block of land and erect two houses, with plenty of space around each. When Hungerford died, Rob Archdeacon would take over the whole property. This was enticing. His nephew warmed to the proposal, so Hungerford put down the $1,000 deposit, and they arranged to pay it off between them. Not long after that, they met up at Mollie Hungerford's. Rob Archdeacon was looking very glum.

'I said: "What's the matter, Rob?"

' "Nothing."

' "Don't give me that—something is wrong! What is it?"

'He admitted that Diana, his fiancée, did not want to live out at Canning Vale.'[1]

Hungerford commented that she had had a chance to say so when they first discussed it, but he could see her point. There would be no network of neighbours around. Diana was also worried about snakes. She had met another woman living near the block who told her that snakes used to congregate on her sundeck, up to twenty of them at a time. He reassured his nephew. He would compensate him for what he had paid on the block and would take it over. Because of his work commitments, however, he delayed building the house. Then he heard that the government was going to resite the Claremont Speedway at Canning Vale, on a big paddock about two kilometres from his precious block. There would be the continual noise of revving motors and undesirable characters attracted to the area at night. His plan to write in that tranquil bush setting evaporated. He put the property on the market and bought another beautiful block in the hills, off Great Eastern Highway at Greenmount, adjacent to the John Forrest National Park.

He was occupying himself with plans for his dream house there when it was announced there had been so much public agitation against locating the motor circuit at Canning Vale that the government's plan had been cancelled. Luckily, no one had bought the block at Canning Vale, so Hungerford sold the block in the hills, resumed the original property and commenced building the house in 1974. He laid out for the architect a general ground plan of what he wanted: one large room to include the dining area and living room, five metres high at one end and more than three metres at the other. Originally the house had only one bedroom and later, on what he called the 'bush side' of the house, he built two more bedrooms, another bathroom and a lobby. He had in mind his overseas friends, who could be separate from his part of the house. He created an atmosphere of warm and functional spaciousness in a home that sat comfortably with its surrounds. He then laid out his garden, which turned into one of the most spectacular displays in the area, the traditional 'riot of colour', and an orchard that provided the makings for his much-appreciated jams and chutneys, ripe figs and vegetables.

The large kitchen was filled with the appetising aromas of traditional Hungerford cooking, stews and soups. However disordered the first impressions on entering the property, it was revealed as a garden of abundance. There was a steady stream of family and friends to his home, for card games, for meals or just for long conversations with one or other of his close friends, sitting comfortably in the chairs on either side of the fireplace.

Hungerford enjoyed cooking for his friends, with the best silver and china on the table, handed down by his parents or bought over the years. He had always taken pleasure in entertaining, and these social gatherings had commenced in his old home in South Perth. His dinners were stimulating, with a range of guests: writers and artists, the Perth cognoscenti—Randolph Stow, Robert Drewe, Hal Porter, Bill and Diana Warnock, Ian Templeman, Terry Owen—to list just a few. Although his guests saw eye-to-eye on the topics of the day, such as what was happening to the skyline of Perth and the demolition of favourite landmarks in favour of giant office towers, there were arguments about authors, about the latest stage productions. Because the host always liked to be in the kitchen, irrespective of whether there were guests to be entertained, he would suddenly leave the dinner table, abandoning his guests, and do the washing up in the middle of the dinner. His guests would protest. Hungerford would continue resolutely rattling away with the pots and pans. On more than one occasion some of the guests wished they could join him in the kitchen, because in Hungerford's absence some of the arguments became stressful, requiring his return to weigh in with a forceful opinion that redirected the conversation to a more harmonious level.[2]

Usually, however, the house radiated tranquillity, with just his devoted companions—the two dogs and two cats—stretched out together in front of the crackling fire in the kitchen on a winter's evening, the only human present deep in a book. Sam, the 'seigneur of the pack', and Bill were complemented by Bud and Mr Black Cat, the latter a feral cat that took an age to accept—and be accepted by—his domesticated companions. Sometimes they became part of the dinner parties. One night, Bud strolled into the gathering, with guests seated around the table with its gleaming silver and attractive dinner service. Conversation dwindled and guests stared at Bud, who had entered proudly with a half-eaten dead rat. He made himself comfortable on the smooth carpet and finished it off, the guests averted their eyes, and conversation resumed on Life and the Arts.[3]

Hungerford has always enjoyed female company, and women are very fond of him. Mutual affection continues to provide warm companionship. They accompany him to the cinema, to theatre and to the many social events to which he is still invited. The lack of one particular woman in his life has not worried him. His urge for any physical relationship dwindled in the 1970s, as the other pleasures of living a full life—of which his writing was the major part—predominated. Twenty years later he had a prostate operation, to be followed years later, when he was well into his eighties, by the removal of a cancerous testicle. Perhaps, however, he is still most comfortable in the company of just a few men or even just his own company, although he is very much at ease in groups in which he has a role to play as 'Tom Hungerford the Writer'. But he does not seek out these occasions and never has. It could be that he prefers the company of men because one part of him has an old-fashioned view of who women are and, relatively speaking, their place. He is typical of many single men of his generation who were to be found—particularly after war service—in positions that had often deprived them of regular female company.

It is an intriguing question: how and why do people live contentedly by themselves into old age? Generally they are not believed to be homosexually inclined. Rather, it is probably force of circumstances. In the Australian context, it was also growing up in the bush, the isolation of living on stations or at remote mine sites. The British experience was of the 'old sweats' who had been away from the Home Country and who served in various remote British dependencies for years, again often in distant locations. When they returned on leave to the UK, women adored them, liked the image of the bronzed Empire Builder and eagerly accompanied them to dinner and the theatre—and frequently fell in love with them—but these solitary characters were seldom inclined to seek wives. They had actually come to enjoy their own company.

In Hungerford's case, forced deprivation of female company applied only during his war service before his time in Japan but, post-war, he was so involved in his working life that it appears he was not prepared to make space for another person. Whether he would have done so if that special person had come along is open to speculation. The probability is that most healthy single males would have, once the chemistry created that special spark. The adored one usually becomes the priority—above work, above everything else. Women have certainly been attracted to Tom Hungerford; they have been in love with him. None has been the one for him. It is clear that he would have revelled in his own children and especially grandchildren. However, after a lifetime of a solitary existence, he has come to enjoy his own company, compensating for his single status by being thoroughly and generously involved in the lives of a wide circle of family and friends but, it must be said, being prepared to drop such friends abruptly if they displeased him.

It was natural that women found in Tom Hungerford someone special, and he for his part has particularly appreciated women who are free spirits—self-reliant women who take care of themselves. Of the many names associated with him over the years, one was Cécile Dorward, an eccentric writer and traveller who had been asked to look him up in South Perth and who by sheer chance had called at his door in Jubilee Street one evening. She was often out at Canning Vale, where they enjoyed each other's company. Another was Mollie Taylor, personable and humorous, one of his real favourites. A staunch Catholic, she had never married. Another Mollie, widow of his elder brother Mick, remains his closest female friend from those and earlier days. There is the manager of the Curtin University Fitness Centre, Shelagh Pascoe, who counts him as one of her dearest friends, as do Terry Owen and Diana Warnock. Many women, married to male friends of Hungerford, feel strongly for him and relish his company.

Hungerford himself has admitted in the evening of his life to a rush of warm affection, of love even, for one of his current companions. A few years back they were dining with two others in Subiaco, before the theatre. He confessed to the other man present that had he been twenty years younger, his companion might well have been the one he would have asked to marry him.[4] Wishful thinking, of course. He would be the first to agree that he has grown to be too set, selfish even, in his ways, and he is many years the senior of the woman concerned.

—·—

By the 1970s, Hungerford had become one of the doyens of the local writing scene, and he was appointed to the Western Australian Literature Committee when it was formed by the Court government.

The fact that this coincided with Hungerford working personally for Sir Charles Court was doubtless a factor in the Literature Committee being established in the first place, although Hungerford claims it was entirely Court's idea. The Literature Committee's brief to fund Western Australian publishing houses with $25,000 towards the cost of publishing each book was a promising development. Hitherto a lack of publishing houses meant that many Western Australian writers went unpublished, including Tom Hungerford (who had been bitterly disappointed that his novel *Code Word Macau* was turned down by Angus & Robertson).

Partly as a result of the Literature Committee's inception, Fremantle Arts Centre Press (FACP) came into being in 1975, under the management of Ian Templeman, the director of the Arts Centre, and Terry Owen, the inaugural manager of the Press. They had assurances from Tom Hungerford that he would use the Press. One of them had telephoned him: ' "What are you doing?"

' "I've got me bum on a chair here; I'm just finishing off a book of short stories."

' "What are you going to do with it? Who is going to publish it?"

' "Oh, I suppose Angus & Robertson."

' "Why don't you give us a go?" ' [5]

Other local writers ridiculed him for considering FACP and suggested he would lose out—FACP had no distribution. They were wrong. Terry Owen travelled to meet distributors in the eastern states and mentioned that FACP had the support of the redoubtable T. A. G. Hungerford. This was a valuable marketing tool: middle-aged literary editors all remembered *The Ridge and the River*. The Press specialises in regional and literary works and is now acknowledged as one of the finest publishers in Australia. In 1976 FACP published *New Country*, a selection of Western Australian short stories edited by Bruce Bennett, which contained three of Hungerford's stories, including 'O Moon of Mullamulla' and 'The

Lady in the Box'. Then his *Wong Chu and the Queen's Letterbox* turned out to be a modest triumph for both him and FACP. It was the third of the Press's titles, being published in 1977 and reprinted in November, and it was reviewed favourably.[6] In the meantime, Hungerford was keeping himself busy, writing on commission. Part of this output was contributing to the *Daily News* whose editor, Frank Devine, was enthusiastic about 'Wong Chu and the Queen's Letterbox', which he said was the best short story he had read.[7]

In 1979, at Ian Templeman's request, Hungerford wrote the text for *Fremantle: Landscapes and People*. He prepared a similar manuscript on Broome, but it was not published. By 1978 Hungerford had moved from South Perth to live in Canning Vale, relieved to be free from working for government and able to concentrate on a stream of commissioned pieces for newspapers and magazines. This proved to be the next significant period of his life as a short-story writer, with FACP publishing the famous *Stories from Suburban Road: An Autobiographical Collection 1920–1939*, the first volume of his autobiographical trilogy.

The trilogy actually started with his idea of writing up his early life as a series of short stories. He contacted Ian Templeman and told him what he had in mind. Templeman was interested, and Hungerford thought further about it, how he would structure it. He wanted to recall salient features of his boyhood in South Perth, then write them from the boy's point of view, what the place looked like, what the social mores were, who the different people were. He remembered all sorts of funny people in South Perth then. Templeman had suggested that the autobiographical *Stories from Suburban Road* be rewritten in the first person, in short story format, and include further stories that would round off the period of his youth, leading up to World War II. A further five stories were added. *Stories from Suburban Road* took him some years to complete, but the delay was worth it. The book was finally published in 1983 and received the Western Australia Week Literary Award in 1984.

It was very well received. The *West Australian* of 10 December 1983 carried a review by Athol Thomas, typical of others of the time. He wrote of the profundity of the feeling of nostalgia, the lack of pretension, the realism, honesty and whimsy. Hungerford's ear for dialogue and depth of observation provided a classic example of how a good writer makes the most of experience and observation. In fact it was impossible to tell where fact ended and fiction began. In an interview recorded by Gail O'Hanlon in 1998, Hungerford noted that his principal interest in writing what was in effect his autobiography was that the 'Australian character' had suffered a severe regression.[8] This was a constant theme of his, dating back to the 1960s when he was interviewed on leaving the Australian News and Information Bureau. There was a loss of his beloved 'mateship'. He foresaw the modern country of Australia as being increasingly populated by immigrants from many countries who inevitably diluted the character of the Australians of his youth. (This is perhaps inevitably at odds with Hungerford's sympathy for the 'New Australians' in the post-war period.) These were the rawbone stalwarts among whom he had grown up, his mates in the army, people who could be relied on and who displayed old-fashioned virtues of sincerity and reliability, for all their faults and failures.

Andrew Sant wrote of *Stories from Suburban Road* that it created an impression of innocence and delight, an orderly, accepted world, complemented by the selectiveness of the author's imagination. A sense of wonder was projected, and the style of writing was clear and colloquial. There was a suitable sense of variety and engagement, which seemed limitless. This was about a child free of adult prejudice. Even some of the terms used were appropriate to the times: Sant noted, for example, the old-fashioned use of 'subsistence' rather than a 'benefit'.[9]

Stories from Suburban Road became a standard text for schools and was also dramatised in 1991, with a cast of six characters, presented originally at the Swy Theatre by Perth Theatre

Company. In 2002 the production toured New South Wales after a sell-out season in Sydney, then Victoria and the Northern Territory. In Perth it also played to full audiences. In 2004 it was staged by the Old Mill Theatre Company in South Perth.

Ian Templeman had suggested Hungerford continue with the war-time period of his life and how he returned to being a civilian. The result, published in 1985, was *A Knockabout with a Slouch Hat: An Autobiographical Collection 1942–1951*, a title Templeman chose, which the author did not like at first. As Hungerford wrote in the preface, the context was that a civilian does not become a soldier merely by putting on a slouch hat. Correspondingly, a soldier does not become a civilian merely by taking it off. It took him time after taking off his slouch hat to stop thinking of himself as a soldier, being tied up with memories and thoughts of the army and meeting his old mates. Of necessity perhaps, the content was highly selective but, given the importance of that period in Hungerford's life, there was much material that regrettably had to be omitted. There were relatively brief references to his time on Bougainville, and the book dwelt in some detail on the second 'jack-up' en route to Japan. It was excellent on the Australians' relations with the Kanakas. The occupation of Japan is similarly highlighted. Back in Australia, immediately before his discharge from the army, what he did in Melbourne and Adelaide is muddled compared with his later taped reminiscences. Perhaps this is just poetic licence. His time in Canberra provided some enjoyable material on the inimitable Miss Cassie Thompson, his work at the Australian War Memorial and his meeting at Eastlake camp with Mr Ferrier, 'the Bastard'. The brief time with Billy Hughes is amusingly related.[10]

In a review of *A Knockabout with a Slouch Hat*, Laurie Clancy wrote that Hungerford was a neglected writer who had abandoned any pretence of fiction with his witty and compassionate stories.[11] He felt though that *A Knockabout with a Slouch Hat* lacked the poignancy of *Stories from Suburban Road* and that its interest was more historical than autobiographical. When interviewed, Hungerford had referred to the importance of *The Bulletin* to writers of his generation. There was a rare note of bitterness when he spoke of his own lack of recognition at the time, of the first three novels he had had accepted by Angus & Robertson but none published immediately. Clancy concluded that this was a sensitive, humane man.

Then Templeman asked Hungerford to bring the story right up to date. The result was *Red Rover All Over: An Autobiographical Collection 1952–1986*, published in that last year by FACP, and dedicated to Beatrice Davis. The title seemed very apt title to the author at the time. Hungerford was once red-haired and, moreover, he thought his 'roving days'—of travelling all over the world—were over, which of course they were not. Alex Harris reviewed *Red Rover All Over* positively in 1987.[12] The review was as sensitive as is the book's content: there was plenty to share with readers, without giving away too much of the essential man. The first part of the book is in effect an extension of *Stories from Suburban Road*, containing other delightful stories of Hungerford's youth. It was a journey of self-discovery that also gave expression to the author's humour and sensibility, his belief in the basic goodness of people and their qualities, which never led him into the trap of presenting individuals as stereotypes. There was more on the all-important relationship with his mother and the use he made of the river.

In 1989 FACP published *Hungerford: Short Fiction* (edited by Peter Cowan), which was extensively reviewed favourably in the *West Australian*, the *Canberra Times* and *The Australian*.[13] Now there are three autobiographical volumes, which were reissued as a trilogy entitled *Straightshooter* by Fremantle Arts Centre Press in September 2003. This nice acknowledgement to a lasting if limited popularity followed on a similar initiative by Penguin, which had brought out an omnibus of four books from the war, including *The Ridge and the River*. A large number of his stories were to be published in various anthologies, not only in Australia but also in the then USSR (for which of course he received no royalties), the UK and the USA. Belated national recognition of his status as one of the few remaining writers of his generation came in 1988 when he was made a member of the Order of Australia for his services to literature.

———

From his base at Canning Vale, over the next twenty-five years, Tom Hungerford travelled frequently, returning to regale his friends with some of his adventures and the extraordinary people whom he had met. He returned to the USA a couple of times and visited Japan twice. He toured South Africa, Europe and, in 1995, in his eightieth year, Yemen. He made several trips to Britain and into China, and he crossed the USSR twice by train and aircraft. After his first journey to the USSR in the 1980s, he commented that outside his war-time experiences, he had seldom previously encountered anything as tough on the body and spirit.

> It was not as if I had not tried in Perth to anticipate the experience, but it could not have prepared me for the utter contempt with which the Russians treated foreign visitors to their country, then. It was long railway journeys that first lured me: I love railways, mate! I had always wanted to travel by the Siberian railway.[14]

A detailed and amusing account of some of his many journeys is given in *Red Rover All Over*.[15]

It was amazing to his friends that in his eightieth year, he agreed to accompany his old friend Bill Warnock on a journey to the Yemen, led by the author. 'I found it to be the crowning journey of my life. I thought I had walked into the *Arabian Nights*.' Yemen, in the southwest corner of the Arabian Peninsula, had emerged as one country in 1990, when the USSR collapsed and withdrew its support from what was termed the People's Democratic Republic of South Yemen, the terrorist state that succeeded the British withdrawal from Aden in the late 1960s. The northern half seized effective control of the whole country after a brief civil war in 1994 and was open for tourists, who had to be prepared to 'rough it'—or so Hungerford understood. His first great surprise was the luxury of the hotel in Sana'a, the capital. His second surprise was the people: generous and kind. They travelled in Toyotas, and the further they got into the High Yemen, the more exotic it became, with medieval villages perched on mountaintops and roads that snaked around ravines and traversed dune desert. Both the look and feel of the place were unlike any country he had ever been in.

On one occasion, the party was invited to stay in a shaikh's residence, a many-storeyed citadel that towered over the massifs of a part of the world that traced its roots back to the Old Testament. It was a magical night, because the shaikh's niece was to be married the next day and the small group of foreigners was invited to share in the festivities. As is the custom, the men were being entertained separately, in a big marquee, and the European female travellers were taken to the harem where they were invited to participate in the dancing and celebrations. Hungerford and Warnock with the other male visitors were escorted to meet the Yemeni men. As they were standing there in a row, looking down into the marquee, one of the welcoming party discharged in their honour a full magazine from a Kalashnikov firearm, just over the visitors' heads.

It was the first time Hungerford had heard live rounds fired since the war, and he was immediately back in the jungles of Bougainville. Instinctively he dived for the ground and slowly got to his feet, feeling somewhat foolish. The grave men surrounding him had to be told why there was this reaction from an old ex-soldier, and there were understanding smiles all round.

Yemen had been the centre of the frankincense and myrrh trade more than 2000 years ago, and the party visited one of the great citadels of the Queen of Sheba, where Hungerford particularly admired the artisanship that had shaped the huge blocks of stone, held together without cement. He closed his eyes as he imagined the camels loaded with frankincense and myrrh passing through to Petra and Jerusalem, on the very spot he was standing, an eon ago. After a long, hard day driving across the dune desert from the Hadhramaut valley, the party checked in at a hotel that was only half-built when the money ran out. Otherwise it was a welcome break for weary travellers. The air-conditioning did not function, it was hot inside the building, and the shower produced the merest trickle of water. Hungerford's usually sunny mood was frayed, and he thought to recover his composure by dozing for a while. There were lights by the bed, but he could see no switch anywhere. He searched the room without success, and he rang the reception desk, thinking that one of the lads hanging around the foyer could show him where the light switch was: 'Would you please send a boy up?'

The manager was aghast. He said: 'Oh, no, no! We are not allowed to do that! This is against the law! Oh no, we never do that here! It is the Government Order No. [xx]. We may not do this!'

Hungerford put the receiver down, totally confused, and was just getting dressed when a small youth walked past the door. Hungerford seized the chance to be shown the light switch. Urgently he said: 'Hey! Come in here!' The boy cringed against the far wall. 'Come in here!' The boy entered, still standing with his back against the furthest wall. Hungerford pointed at the lights: the boy understood. Relief followed by amusement chased across his thin features. The light switch had been behind the television set. His friends much enjoyed hearing about the incident that again demonstrated Tom Hungerford's sometimes child-like innocence in the way of the world.

His intense enjoyment of what was the climax of his extensive foreign travel is summed up in the letter he wrote afterwards:

> Thank you for making the Yemen trip such an unforgettable experience for me. Since then, it's been a bit of a mish-mash—a severe cold in London and bronchitis in Seattle and a general stuffing of the mood and morale. Well…getting over it, but feeling once more I'd battled up those fucking 98 steps at that last-night dinner at that sky-top restaurant. Also I twisted my ankle on a bit of inferior Pommie paving—as well as losing my reading glasses somewhere in Kent: but on one of the most beautiful, halcyon Spring days I've ever experienced.[16]

Chapter 15

Epilogue

~~~~~

ANZAC DAY

This spot at the corner of Pier Street and the Terrace
between two churches—Presbyterian one side
C of E on the other—is just made to order
for us Second Eighth blokes to form up for the March
this mild April morning. Wild men we were, all of us.
Brawlers and—when the chance bobbed up—fornicators.
Nick the eye from your head and the wife from your kitchen.
Well…fifty years ago, anyway. And each one a killer
with the old blood of other men rank on his hands.
These smiling grandfathers, members of committees,
Councillors, shopkeepers. Even one vestryman.
Work in their gardens, go driving Sundays
to visit the rellies. Wash the dog, pay the bills,
remember the birthdays, donate to charities.
Snooze after dinner in front of the telly.
Sometimes I'm with them at Pier and the Terrace,
engulfed in the bullshit but putting my spoke in—
as one does—I wonder if ever they think of

the jungle? Those green rushing rivers we forded,
creeping up in the dawn-light on Japs, sleeping, dreaming,
in huts in a clearing? The snarl of the Bren-gun,
the Owens, the hand-bombs. The blue wreath of cordite,
the birds' cries. And after, that terrible silence?
I reckon they do—in fact bet my house on it.
I remember one time with the boys in the boozer,
after the March. We're listening to Rusty
retelling—again—how he shot this Jap's head off.
One burst and a lovely red fountain! he reckons.
I swear to sweet Jesus his pupils grow crimson
as he says it. For a moment. Then—same old Macka.
Mild as a milkshake, never hurt anyone.
I think of one day when I'm at the Zoo, years ago,
standing there watching this tiger sun-baking.
Slack as a sack of shit. Big pussy-cat purring.
He rolls over and his eyes glare topaz hate at me.
Suddenly, like looking through parted fence pickets,
I sense a green jungle. Those yellow fangs, snarling.
Red on the grass some mangled thing, jerking.
He stretches and yawns, and douses the fire
some memory had lit in his eyes. And blinks at me.

After the March, formed up on the Esplanade,
still in our own groups, Stand at ease! Stand easy!
Flop on the grass and break out the lung-busters.
Look around. Nothing's changed—just like last year
and all of the Marches and years you remember.
The Navy in white, the fly-boys in blue,
the Army in camouflage, khaki-and-green.
The Scotties in kilts. But…more women than ever.
'They're creepin' up on us!' says Wally. 'Some army!
'Bloody birds givin' orders to blokes! Holy Jesus!'

I look at the river, a bolt of blue satin
rolled out, not a wrinkle from here to Fremantle.
High up, an aircraft roars westwards. To somewhere.
Behind us the city is talking in tongues.
'Here come the jeeps with the Old Diggers!' shouts someone.
The Old Diggers. Icons as fragile as cobwebs
encased in this reliquary of sunshine and cheering.
Holiest relics of a national religion
called Anzac. Each April brought out and paraded
in this, our own auto-da-fé. To remind us
that we have been great, one day might be greater.
Or so someone tells us.
I have a suspicion
that here in this crowd with everything happening
around them; flags flying, kids waving, bands playing,
the media mob with cameras trained on them...
the old Diggers are thinking about other days. Other men
none will recall when death claims the last of these.

Blue's watching some old blokes propped up in the transport.
He's nutting out something—I know all the portents.
'Holy Jesus!' he says, at last. 'You know what I reckon?
That's us in a few years! Medals and ribbons,
hair brushed, bums wiped, shoes shined, our teeth in.
Wheeled out once a year for the Anzac Day shindig
And then carted home!'
And for once, Macka says nothing.

It was 2003. T. A. G. (Tom) Hungerford AM, MID, stood outside his back door, waiting to leave for the Anzac Day Parade where he would be marching with the few survivors of the Independent Companies, those commando squadrons now alas represented by a mere handful of old Diggers. He is a handsome man, with the remnant good looks of an archetypical Aussie drover of the 1950s. In his late eighties, he looks in great shape—his shock of white hair neatly in place, casually yet neatly dressed, alert and upright—self-assured, ready with a quip or a sharp comment. Where he lives, in a small retirement unit at Bentley in Perth, he maintains the lifelong home routine of reading and writing, gardening, cooking, making marmalade, bottling fruit (his marmalades and pickles are still relished by his friends) and socialising (somewhat reduced from earlier years). In his spare time he lends a hand to his less active neighbours.

His present home still shows off some of his favourite artefacts. Each painting, each photograph is significant, a scene, an old friend. Hungerford has been a collector of valuable and interesting items from abroad, including Chinese carvings and antiques. Frequently he has made surprise presents of them to his relatives and friends. His dining table is piled with manuscripts competing for space with the elderly typewriter that has produced the stories that continue to flow from his store of reminiscences and experiences. In the sleep-out his narrow bed is stripped but not made (a practice inherited from his mother who saw airing the bed as more important than daily bed-making). Outside, the flowerbeds are glowing with bright colours. Hungerford continues to live a simple life to the full. With the aid of a stick, he is forced to move more slowly than he would like, because of that ankle broken at the start of his war service and walked on for the next fifty years.

He comes across as genuinely friendly with everybody he meets and is never perfunctory in his greetings. He has one of the firmest handshakes in town; he looks the other person in the eye, seems genuinely interested in the other person, to whom he gives his full attention. Everybody says, 'How are you, mate?' but Hungerford actually seems to mean it. He seizes hold of anything that could lead to an anecdote or a story. Naturally, he is a very good storyteller himself, even if this sometimes leads to a monologue, rather than open conversation.

He keeps himself in relatively good shape and has been a member of the Curtin University Health and Fitness Centre since the late 1980s. His exercise routine used to be energetic for a man of his age, peddling on the cycling machine and lifting weights, but this was interrupted by travel and later by bouts of illness. His routine at the gym has therefore been spasmodic for the past few years, but he occasionally walks down and back to his unit on his stick, just to visit the centre. He likes the Curtin campus and has become a familiar figure, making his way to the bookshop and stopping to talk with the youngsters. He intends to return to a proper exercise routine but, with the walk, five minutes on the exercise bike tends to exhaust him. He formed close social relationships with the staff there and with some of the other members, most of whom are a fraction of his age, and some of whom are disabled. He remains an icon to those who recognise that growing old is not necessarily the end of life, and the centre has used him as a model in promoting its facilities.

Hungerford's generosity is also well known there. He wanted to pay for a party at the gym and bought a large ham, and more than seventy guests attended. He once came over to the fitness centre with his home-made scones, cream and jam for the staff, but many of the latter, although grateful for the attention, were painfully fanatical about their diet, leaving the delicacies to the less fastidious.

His mind has slowed not at all; the direct, opinionated but witty style of his delivery is still the Hungerford trademark. It is entertaining to his friends, and perhaps confrontational to those who do not know him. He is still described as being larger than life. He is gregarious and outgoing, with his friends and, over the years, with his publishers. He is encouraging to aspiring writers who he feels have promise. At the 2003 Hungerford Award at the

Perth Writers' Festival, it was he who produced a surprise cheque for $1,000 for the runner-up, in addition to the established prize for the winner. When he was younger, he regularly attended writers' events, launchings and workshops.

The other side of this very human person is that he can also be irascible, even unfair, in some of the things he says to or about people who might not deserve it, although he does not necessarily come over as vindictive. Hungerford is never backward in coming forward when he has a strong feeling about someone. If he considers someone has let him down he is inclined to go off that person, writing him or her off entirely, showing an impatience with or memory of an event that has hurt or displeased him in the past. It is even a kind of bravado, or a tone he can adopt when he is throwing out comments that are negative or critical of somebody, but it is often done almost on an impulse, rather than because of a deep-seated dislike. This can cause umbrage, although his ranting does not necessarily get back to the 'offender'. Years later someone's name comes up and, as though the alleged offence happened yesterday, a stream of invective demonstrates that the Hungerford mind has stored up that particular slight or omission.

One example of this arose because a friend of his, knowing Hungerford does not find time to read daily newspapers, thought he would like to learn of certain local news events that might otherwise pass him by. One day he received a call from this friend, to tell him that a certain writer had died. Hungerford might have wanted to attend the funeral.

'Oh, Tom—I know you don't read the paper, I thought you ought to know that [X] has died.'

'Oh God! That boring bastard! The only reason I'd go to his funeral is to make sure he's dead.'[1]

He is very direct, not to say hurtful, with those he considers indifferent writers. One person with writing experience asked him to read something and to give his opinion: 'What did you think of it?'

217

'Sell your typewriter.'[2]

Again, there was no real malice in it, just an instinctive reaction to what he saw as poor writing, with apparently no thought of the hurt that might be caused by such an abrupt rejection.

His strong sense of self-worth comes through in the narration that his stories sometimes adopt. There is a bluster or an over-confidence often in that voice, which is sometimes a strength—but other times perhaps not, in that the bravado does not always do the best by his stories. The villains are blacker-than-black. As noted earlier, the accounts can read as being overwritten, because of Hungerford's insistence on depicting someone so forcibly that the reader, in attempting to relate to the character, cannot make an independent judgement.

On the other hand, to choose just one from the many positive examples of Hungerford's confidence at work, there is the account of his mother's possible marital indiscretion. The American adventurer Rudolph, a larger-than-life 'Wild West' character, fascinated the boy Tom as they exercised the horses together. The other side of this story was the tension in the Hungerfords' home when Rudolph came to play cribbage. Hungerford handles quite wonderfully his sister's attempt to raise the matter of their mother's transgression by reciting some doggerel, being sent to her room and the adults left staring at their cards. 'This is how I'll always remember them, sitting like painted people in the room behind the mirror.'[3] As depicted by someone less self-confident than Hungerford, the scene might otherwise have been mawkish.

So his writing works where he has been able to recreate the feel, the voice and the sense of uncertainty of the era he is handling—when he is in effect talking about himself at that time. Hungerford's technical ability as a writer is his greatest strength, and because he used to make his living as a press officer and as a journalist, this has given rise to problems of outside editing. Hungerford hates being edited himself, although he claims otherwise, perhaps because he sees his whole identity and his character tied up in being a writer. He might view constructive criticism of one of his pieces as being a direct reproach of himself as a person—unless he has the highest personal regard for his critic as a fellow writer. There was the occasion when a friend innocently altered a misplaced word in a manuscript Hungerford proffered him. There was outrage: 'Did you alter that? That's what I wrote!'[4]

Of course, all artists need to have egos to continue with their craft, but apparent healthy self-esteem is a cover as well for areas of insecurity, and Hungerford, like everyone, certainly has his. The dark, deeply buried, self-doubting side of the man, his inability to accept the possibility of criticism, shows. The other likely insecurity is in the face of intellectuals and academics. He has been scathing about such people he has met during his lifetime.[5] Perhaps it is because he does not necessarily share their cultural language. They might be discussing writing but using a different idiom, and he, like many people, might suppose there is a kind of assumed snobbishness. This can make for a perceived anti-intellectual and anti-academic attitude in him, perhaps because unconsciously he might feel it is a put-down of someone from a parochial background, or even because of his lack of tertiary education. Maybe it is this attitude that has contributed to his well-known obstinacy.

Tom Hungerford can also be quite mischievous: he once attended the Adelaide Writers Week, in company with Elizabeth Jolley before she became famous, and other Western Australian literary luminaries. They were in a tent for an evening performance, listening to Geoffrey Dutton reading his poetry. Hungerford was bored and suddenly enquired in a penetrating voice: 'Who's this old fart?' The visitors quietly decided to leave. Hungerford was being difficult.[6]

On another occasion he was attending a conference at Pisa in Italy on Australian writers, who were asked to read something from their works. The venue was an L-shaped room with glass doors down one end and the audience facing the readers on a small stage, with an inset around the corner with three or four people seated there, including the professor in charge of the proceedings and the Australian ambassador. It happened to be the period of the Red Army scares in Italy. The Australian security staff did not realise that the ambassador was out of their sight, around the corner, and they panicked. There was increasing agitation outside with sirens as the police searched for the Australian ambassador, whom they feared might have been kidnapped. In the meantime readings were under way in the L-shaped room.

Dorothy Hewett and a couple of other Australian writers had presented their pieces, to be followed by Tom Hungerford, who was known for reading too much. Twenty minutes had been stipulated, but he ignored this: 'Who the fuck are they to tell me only twenty minutes?' He had chosen something that would take thirty minutes to read. He realised about halfway through that he was going to exceed the allotted time, but there was no way he would cut his presentation. Instead, he accelerated the pace of his reading, accompanied by the wail of sirens and of police searching for the missing diplomat. It was a surreal scene: against the background hubbub Hungerford was racing through an extract from *The Ridge and the River*, incidentally something from the period when the Japanese enemies the Australians were slaughtering were allies of the Italians. Fortunately this possible diplomatic 'blue' was avoided: the fast pace of his reading and the plethora of Australian slang guaranteed that hardly any of the Italians present could have understood what he was saying.[7]

More recently, Hungerford had been invited to attend a book club, consisting of about ten middle-class women, all in their sixties or seventies. They had read *Stories from Suburban Road* and were eager to discuss it, with the author present. He was invited to read something from his writings. To their surprise and embarrassment, Hungerford proceeded to read a story that was based in a brothel.[8]

Why he should have chosen it, given the circumstances and the audience, is unclear. Perhaps it was a deliberate reminder of his masculinity, or could it be that for some obscure reason he just wanted to shock or discomfit those present? It certainly caused a buzz in Nedlands–Claremont circles. Whatever the motive, it was at the very least poor judgement on his part, demonstrating that an elderly bachelor can lose touch with the realities of what is socially appropriate.

This aside, as a writer, Hungerford is always going to be seen as an interesting figure on a number of levels. One is that, technically and imaginatively, he is a product of a much earlier era—the 1950s—than he himself is writing in. Not only his novels but also much of his output of short stories are based on his life as a young man. But there is always the deep and, at times, stark humanity in his work. Throughout his writing life, Hungerford has sought to enunciate an intimate level of feeling and emotions of the many people he has come across. *Riverslake* is a prime example, in that it deals in a humane way with a subject that no one else appeared to have tackled at the time. The mainly indifferent attitudes of Australians in the late 1940s to the influx of desperate foreigners seeking sanctuary can be contrasted with attitudes of Australians today. In 2003, by contrast with 1949, many writers who are uneasy about the official refugee policy vent their disquiet via the media, notable among them the South Australian academic Eva Sallis, the journalist David Marr and ex-Prime Minister Malcolm Fraser. Post–World War II, Hungerford seems to have been almost a lone voice. Here was a writer from a certain background who, in his persona and manner, represented the 'rugged Australian': here also was a deep humanity and sensitivity.

There was also a multifaceted comprehension on Hungerford's part, not perhaps fully articulated by him, of the political, economic and social reality of the times. This was not intellectualised but is given colourful expression that emerges throughout his writings, whether it concerns the children of his South Perth boyhood, the people he met in the USSR or the 'new Australians' in those grim post-war displaced persons' camps. This empathy for unfortunates is a hallmark of the man together with a nostalgic longing for the past. When he spoke to the *Canberra Times* in 1967 he said:

> I am deeply concerned with the collapse of mateship, if it ever existed. All around us the great Australian Jack rule—I'm alright Jack, how are you?—is getting stronger. The days of giving another bloke a hand seem to have gone. I know I sound like a preacher, and that this is small town talk, but the fellow next to you is very important, whether he is a Vietnamese or a Negro.

In this context he can be compared with the American writer John Steinbeck, himself a recorder of social history, with deep feeling for the people with whom he mixed, the 'Okies', and the drifters on Cannery Row. Steinbeck of course was an American and international icon. It is always a surprise that Hungerford as a social commentator is so little known outside Western Australia, except by other writers.

Hungerford himself has a real regret about a public lack of recognition that, briefly at least, was redressed by being presented with the Patrick White Award in 2003. Deep down also, the fact he was never commissioned during the war, something due entirely to the circumstances of the time, probably left a mark, which of course he denies: 'I never wanted to be an officer, mate.' In his generous speech of acceptance of the Patrick White Award, he referred to the fact that he feels he has not been recognised as widely as he might have been.

It is probably true that historically, as an Australian writer, the 'Grandfather of Western Australian writing' will not be seen elsewhere as a particularly major figure. Even *The Ridge and the*

River is now known by relatively few readers. Now it is his auto-biographical works for which he is recognised. As with Steinbeck, it is the charming insouciance of his characters and the detail he is able to create that interest the current generation. Some of the more explicit autobiographical short stories, the best of them, particularly 'Wong Chu and the Queen's Letterbox', redolent with reminiscent nostalgia, will live on, although there has been professional criticism that some of the stories are too long. It is also undeniable that Hungerford as a writer of his age has not stayed abreast of current tastes and interests.

The fact is, however, that he is one of the most competent wordsmiths still writing, and the endless time he takes to shape sentences maintains the quality of his output. 'Mate, I've got so many stories in me.' He certainly still has many ideas, many anecdotes, but it must be seen whether they will still translate into publishable stories. Understandably, he is slowing down physically. His back now causes him problems, aggravated by that untreated ankle from the war, and perhaps his short-term memory is not what it was.

He remains positive about his lifestyle, claiming to be very seldom lonely and enjoying his own company. He has a collection of original records and his old typewriter; he reads, listens to music, does the garden and cooks. He walks a lot, albeit supported by his stick, and he has an affectionate circle of friends and close family. He has not married, but he has good friends; he has not had children, but he has loved those of others; he has been in love, and he has been loved and been thwarted in love. He is completely at home with family members and his friends, who he knows enjoy his company.[9] 'If we never see each other for ten years, it would be as though we have seen each other yesterday. That's a tremendous thing in a life.' There is always someone around to view a film or to sit and chat with. His remaining family members remain the dearest to him, in particular his sister-in-law, Mollie Hungerford, and his nephew, Rob Archdeacon. It is said that intrinsically he is not a sentimental man, although he can melt at the sight of a beautiful tree or view, or shed tears when a tender war-time memory or the loss of a family friend looms from the past.

Much of Tom Hungerford's continuing vitality derives from the energy he gains from reading and from not watching television. His use of radio is sufficient for him to be kept aware of current affairs. What has kept him so energised is that he has not put his being into anybody else's hands. Throughout, there is an essential part of him that has never been given to anyone else. He has lived entirely as an individual all his life. Part of him is inviolate to others, and with that comes the private reticence that has been his personal strength and which essentially preserves him as a young man, if not as a child. Some of this life-strength can be read in some of the stories of his childhood. This was the quality that the painter Kate O'Connor captured in her portrait of him, created when he was already moving into middle age. She saw him as a perennial 23-year-old.

I asked him once, if he was in a position where he knew that his words would be printed, what message he would have for people following on after him.

'I would say two things: perhaps do them concurrently, but get the border situation under control, and bring the Aborigines into proper participation of the life of the country. Bring them in. I don't know what it would bloody cost. They would be the two main things.'

'Finally, Tom: on your headstone, what would you ideally like to see, apart from your name and the years that you lived?'

'Nothing. Nothing.'

'Just a few words—people get a great kick out of looking at headstones. How would you like people to remember you, Tom?'

'As a good bloke, I suppose.' Then: ' "He was a good bloke." '

Tom Hungerford has no fear of death. He saw too much of it. Picture him, then, being escorted to his Elysian fields:

Dark Stranger

Do children think about death?
I don't remember. It's all too long ago.

Nevertheless—
I do recall that in my teens I was
A fully paid-up, card-carrying member
of the Young Folks' Eternity Fraternity.
What?
To die? Me?
To become simply... dead meat?
This amiable, able body of mine,
ticking along like a well-oiled clock—
quite often chiming, too!—
no longer able to run, read a book, go to a dance?
To Make Love?
No more summer-time sickies at the cricket?
Windy winter weekend afternoons at the footie?
Smoky, half-pissed, rowdy evenings at the pub?
You've got to be joking!

Nevertheless...
all in good time—
well, somebody's good time—
that lovely blue sky, strung-out, spun-glass dream
of always summer
copped the Sunday Punch.
I was on my way to meet the dark stranger.
Perhaps.
Young men were given a good talking to
(involving the flag, and courage, and so on,
and were despatched, licensed to kill or maim,

to various locations here-and-there.
No return tickets handed out, naturally.

I drew what the papers so often dubbed
the 'foetid, fever-stricken jungle hell'.
And there amongst the tropical greenery
played some weird version of cops-and-robbers
with other young blokes much the same in age—
the Yellow Peril of our national fears.
Treacherous, vicious, dirty little brutes,
we'd resolutely trained ourselves to think.
Or, perhaps, had been trained to think.
We'd called them Shintos, Pongos, Chinamen.
The fucking Japs:
could only guess what they, in turn, called us.
Or thought of us—
With fear perhaps? Derision? Hate, of course.
I never did find out.
And there I first became acquainted with—
became aware of,
began to understand,
the dark stranger.
From daily contact then,
you grew accustomed to his being there.
To know that he kept an eye on you
from that thick clump of fragrant wild ginger,
that stand of limpom palm beside the track.
Always checking to learn if you were... Available.
You tended to be a bit laid-back.
Fatally so, maybe? Perhaps. Sometimes.
Remember he had a job to do,
the dark stranger.
A state of mind fostered, I rather think,

by the comforting, ever-present certainty
every soldier hugs to his secret heart—
that while he might take Jack on your right hand,
or Mack on your left,
He never would take you.
Not you. Not you.

I speak of things half of my years ago,
of me, and men I knew, but now don't know.

These days I watch him walk towards me,
the dark stranger.
Always between broad paddocks,
green trees, cool and shadowy.
Behind him
the red foothills.
The sky.
The miles and years, the miles and years we've walked
since first he noticed me, aged about two,
floating face-down in my old man's horse-trough;
although—for him—discovered just too soon.
That he's so close now doesn't worry me.
Long ago I made it plain to someone—
or something, I don't remember which—
that all I want for that final raree-show
is simply some prior notice of the event.
And dignity.
At least a little dignity.
I wait now for him to walk up to me.
'Hello!' he'll say.
'It's quite a long time since I first met you!
Remember the horse-trough?'

Yes. I remember.
'Let's walk away together, then?' he'll say.
'And get to know each other?'
I'll go with him,
The dark stranger.
I guess we've got a lot to talk about.

T. A. G. Hungerford
2003

A MEASURE OF THE MAN

RADIO ADDRESS BY T. A. G. HUNGERFORD, STATION 2CA, CANBERRA, 19 JUNE 1954

The following transcript was forwarded to ASIO, Canberra, on 24 November 1955, as conclusive proof that Hungerford was not a communist, with the following covering note: '...it may be that this type of broadcast by Mr Hungerford would possibly have made him a person of interest to the Russian Counter Intelligence Service when he proceeds overseas.' (W. M. Phillips, Regional Director, ACT) Hungerford was certain on his first visit to the USSR that he was under surveillance. His notebook was seized, and he was cross-examined by an Intourist official on leaving the USSR to enter Yugoslavia. Perhaps his anti-USSR tirade, as recounted in 'And Now...' (in *Red Rover All Over*), might also have accounted for a jaundiced view being taken of him at the time he was in the USSR.

Good evening, Ladies and Gentlemen.

Tomorrow has been set aside by the United Council of Migrants from Communist Dominated Europe to commemorate the suffering of their countries in those lands of Europe now garrotted by Russia.

It has been suggested in some quarters that this commemoration will serve no purpose but to perpetuate hatred and through it, the likelihood of war.

This is quite wrong...and if it were not, I should not be here.

And anybody with no axe to grind, or who has an ounce of nous between his ears, can be in no doubt as to the direction from which the red wind of international conflict is blowing—and will continue to blow until it meets a barrier sufficiently strong to halt or divert it.

Even if that were the case, that this commemoration were nothing more than a perpetuation of the hatred of tyranny imposed by force and cunning on behalf of Europe, who are we to quibble?

We in Australia, who allow ourselves the rather expensive luxury of hating the Japanese for what they did to Australians during the war, should think twice before denying the same prerogative to the victims of a cruelty just as dastardly and far more calculated, which has continued and even been augmented when one wish of the rest of the world is for peace, peace, peace.

I am inclined to think that this occasion could awaken in many Australians and sharpen in those already awake, the awareness that we hold no divine charter to immunity from the fate which has befallen so many small and defenceless countries in the last fifteen years.

Poland, Hungary, Czechoslovakia, Roumania [*sic*], Bulgaria, Estonia, Latvia, Lithuania...how long must it grow, this tragic toll? This roster of democratic people cynically liberated by Russia from their rights, their freedom, their families and homes, even from life itself?

How *does* a nation perish, and how does a thousand years of culture disappear almost overnight? Each of these nations has placed its pieces in the mosaic of human advancement...their thinkers, musicians and scientists have made untold contributions to the world's story. And yet now their voices are stilled—or are at most, the thin and shameful echo of the Kremlin's directives.

Is there anyone so blind as to believe or hope what has happened in middle Europe cannot happen here? Is there anyone so blind who cannot see the pattern of conquest now tentatively being imposed on this country by the members of the Australian

Communist Party…the cynical traitors who don't care who knows what they do, the parlour-pink intellectuals who think it is fashionable to go slightly red, but haven't the guts to declare themselves one way or the other…the poor deluded clods who just don't think, don't read, don't listen to the million tongues of misery which tell the story of life under Communist rule the world over.

If this commemoration does nothing more than pierce the armour of complacency of most happy, well fed, free, forthright Australians, it will have served a mighty purpose.

The New Australians in our midst cannot forget the suppression of their homelands. The extent of their personal tragedy is shocking to anyone game to look at it, and believe me, once you *do*, you can throw away your rose-coloured glasses.

Terror and loneliness, grief and torture and starvation are the things you'll see there, and they're not pretty to look at. The stories they tell are of families murdered and scattered and enslaved, of that cynical disregard of elementary human values which have become the recognised hall mark of Russian behaviour wherever its inhuman shadow has fallen.

And yet those migrants do not sue for our pity. Surely they want our helpful understanding…just as you or I would want help or understanding in similar circumstances…if we had been uprooted, brutalised, transported half way round the world and set down, perhaps quite alone, in the midst of strange customs and language.

If we deny them, we deny our own destiny. If we withhold from them the simply neighbourly graciousness in which decent communities are founded, we should forego any voice in the conclave of nations and soft-pedal our concern for the under-privileged people of the world. Nor [*sic*] our charity, but our open-hearted understanding should begin right here, at home.

As much as we can give our new citizens, they can return it in full. We can give them freedom of speech and work and workship [*sic*], of assembly and of movement; things that cost nothing to give, the things of which because they have never been effectively challenged in Australia, many of us do not realise the full value.

We can give them ample food, and warmth of the sun, the blessing of land wide and free and glorious; we can give them the chance to overcome the past and to look to the future with hope and some assurance.

They bring us new cultures and handicrafts, new ideas and techniques, the comfort of increasing numbers in a land desperately in need of population.

Surely the ultimate reward of a full collaboration between Old and New Australians is great enough to make the effort worthwhile?

Tomorrow is Sunday—a free day. You will be free to do what you like…to read your newspaper, to attend your free churches, to ride, walk and drive through the countryside of your free land. Free.

In the afternoon, New Australians will lay a wreath at our own National War Memorial.

Remember that they do it not in hatred or bitterness, although that would be understandable. They do it to signify their one-ness with us and to commemorate homelands submerged in a tide of anarchy, which even now washes perilously close to our northern shores.

T. A. G. HUNGERFORD'S BOOKS, SHORT STORIES AND POETRY

NOVELS

T. A. G. Hungerford's novels, in order of composition, are:

Sowers of the Wind, Angus & Robertson, Sydney 1954.

The Ridge and the River, first published by Angus & Robertson, Sydney 1952. Reprinted 1952 (twice). New edition published 1966. Reprinted 1971. New edition published 1979. Republished by Penguin Books Australia, 1992.

Riverslake, Angus & Robertson, Sydney 1953. Reprinted 1953.

Shake the Golden Bough, Angus & Robertson, Sydney 1963.

Swagbelly and the Prince of Siam, Veritas Publishing, Perth 1989.

Code Word Macao, published by Platypus Press, Perth 1993.

SHORT STORIES

In addition to the stories listed below, 'Dear Ellie' was published in 1942 in an army magazine (title unknown).

PUBLISHED IN *THE BULLETIN*

Some other short stories published in *The Bulletin* have been lost to sight.

'Visit to the Lutts', 1942. Also in *Hungerford: Short Fiction*

'Lesson by Firelight'

'Station Homestead with Boating', 1950

PUBLISHED IN *AS YOU WERE*

'Splash of Scarlet'—based on Geoffrey Mainwaring's portrait, *Cavalry Commando with Owen Gun*, of Bruce 'Slugger' L'Estrange, and included in *A Knockabout with a Slouch Hat*. Hungerford called his character 'Plugger' in that story and 'Ham' in *A Knockabout with a Slouch Hat*.

PUBLISHED IN *STAND-TO*, 1949–50

These stories appear in volumes held by the Australian War Memorial:

'Hair & There in Japan'

'The Letter'

'To the Beach at Dawn'

'Last Entry in Red'

PUBLISHED IN VOLUMES AND JOURNALS

T. A. G. Hungerford's stories are now classified under 'Biography' rather than 'Fiction' in libraries. They have been published in the volumes and journals indicated below. Publication details are given in 'References' at the end of this appendix. A new collection of Tom Hungerford's latest short stories and poems is to be published by Jacobyte Press (Adelaide) in 2005.

'And Gertie Dances in the Moonlight', *Hungerford: Short Fiction*

'And Now…', (1) *Red Rover All Over*; (2) *Straightshooter*

'A Sort of Boswell', (1) *A Knockabout with a Slouch Hat*; (2) *Straightshooter*

'A Sort of Grocer', (1) *A Knockabout with a Slouch Hat*; (2) *Straightshooter*

'Balcony of Dreams', (1) *Portrait*; (2) *Hungerford: Short Fiction*

'Big Day at Ah Mah's', the *Daily News* Weekend Magazine (Perth)

'Boots, Boots, Boots', (1) *A Knockabout with a Slouch Hat*;
>   (2) *Straightshooter*
'Bushranger's Gold', (1) *Meanjin*; (2) to be reprinted as 'The Black
>   Mountain' in Jacobyte Press collection, 2005.
'Chinamen on the Footpath', (1) *Stories from Suburban Road*;
>   (2) *Straightshooter*
'Dad, I've Lost the Car', *Wong Chu and the Queen's Letterbox*
'Down Como', (1) *Stories from Suburban Road*; (2) *Straightshooter*;
>   (3) *Impressions*
'Final Round', (1) *Westerly* 4, 1968; (2) *Westerly* 21, 1978
'Give My Regards to Broadway', (1) *Red Rover All Over*;
>   (2) *Straightshooter*
' "Going Back" Say the Wheels', (1) *Hungerford: Short Fiction*;
>   (2) *A Knockabout with a Slouch Hat*; (3) *Straightshooter*
'Gracie O'Malley and the Rope of Gold', *Summerland*
'Green Grow the Rushes',[1] (1) *Westerly* 2, June 1976; (2) *Decade*;
>   (3) *The Australian Short Story*; (4) *Hungerford: Short Fiction*
'Happy Summer Days', in *Hungerford: Short Fiction*
'Incident in Morotai', (1) *A Knockabout with a Slouch Hat*;
>   (2) *Straightshooter*
'It Always Takes Two', *Hungerford: Short Fiction*
'King Bantam', (1) *Stories from Suburban Road*; (2) *Straightshooter*
'Lady in the Box'. Hungerford was interviewed about this short
>   story by Brian Dibble on radio 6NR in 1978.
'Last Entry in Red', *Hungerford: Short Fiction*
'Leaders and Breeders, the Man Said', *Westerly* 4, 1971
'Lesson by Firelight', *Hungerford: Short Fiction*
'Long Before Now', (1) *A Knockabout with a Slouch Hat*;
>   (2) *Straightshooter*
'Looking After Bert', (1) *Modern Australian Writing*;
>   (2) *Hungerford: Short Fiction*
'Look Out for the Pink Wagon'. To be published in the Jacobyte
>   Press collection in 2005.

'No More Than You Can Afford',[1,2] *Wong Chu and the Queen's Letterbox*

'Me and the National Capital', (1) *A Knockabout with a Slouch Hat*; (2) *Straightshooter*

'Millie, Mollie and Mae', (1) *Westerly* 28(3), 1983; (2) *Daughters of the Sun*; (3) *Stories from Suburban Road*; (4) *Straightshooter*

'My Time in the Barrel', (1) *A Knockabout with a Slouch Hat*; (2) *Straightshooter*

'No More Than You Can Afford', *Westerly* 1, 1971

'Of Biddy and My Dad', (1) *Stories from Suburban Road*; (2) *Straightshooter*

'Oh Mr Gallagher, Oh Mr Shean', (1) *Stories from Suburban Road*; (2) *Straightshooter*; (3) *Western Australian Writing*

'Old Ally Been Went to See the Queen', (1) *Stories from Suburban Road*; (2) *Straightshooter*

'Old Waterfront Macao', (1) *Westerly* 21, 1978; (2) *Hungerford: Short Fiction*; (3) *Westerly Looks to Asia*, 1993

'O Moon of Mullamulla',[2] (1) *New Country*; (2) *Hungerford: Short Fiction*

'Over the Garden Wall', *Westerly* 4, 1969

'Professor Murdoch and the Old White Road', (1) *Stories from Suburban Road*; (2) *Straightshooter*

'Rain at Daybreak', *Wong Chu and the Queen's Letterbox*

'Remora', *Sandgropers*

'See Y'Later, Alligator', *WA Short Stories*

'So Long, Rudolph', (1) *Stories from Suburban Road*; (2) *Straightshooter*

'Stopover in Macau', (1) *Red Rover All Over*; (2) *Straightshooter*

'That Time of Life', *Sunburnt Country*

'The Battle of Barney's Hill', (1) *Stories from Suburban Road*; (2) *Straightshooter*

'The Budgerigar', *Westerly* 1, 1965

'(The) Coodie Crab Company', (1) *Stories from Suburban Road*;
(2) *Straightshooter*

'The Darwin Jack-up', (1) *A Knockabout with a Slouch Hat*;
(2) *Straightshooter*

'The Day It All Ended', (1) *Stories from Suburban Road*;
(2) *Straightshooter*

'The Day of the Wonderful Eggs', (1) *Stories from Suburban Road*;
(2) *Straightshooter*

'The Day We Planted the Old Girl', unpublished (?).

'The Great Iron Ore Caper', (1) *A Knockabout with a Slouch Hat*;
(2) *Straightshooter*

'The Lady in the Box'

'The Lady Who was Diddled by the Judge', (1) *Stories from
Suburban Road*; (2) *Straightshooter*

'The Land beyond the Ice', (1) *Red Rover All Over*;
(2) *Straightshooter*

'The Last Camp', (1) *A Knockabout with a Slouch Hat*;
(2) *Straightshooter*

'The Letter', *Hungerford: Short Fiction*

'The Lucky Spinner', (1) *Stories from Suburban Road*;
(2) *Straightshooter*

'The Magnolia Tree', (1) *Australian Signpost*; (2) *Hungerford: Short
Fiction*

'The National Game', *Hungerford: Short Fiction*

'The Nun's Patrol'—a vivid account of the rescue of two French
nuns and three priests on Bougainville; published in *Stand-
To*, August–September 1950, and in *Coast to Coast*, 1962.

'The Only One Who Forgot', *Hungerford: Short Fiction*

'The New Kid and the Racehorse Goanna', (1) *Stories from
Suburban Road*; (2) *Straightshooter*

'The Rosary', (1) *A Knockabout with a Slouch Hat*;
(2) *Straightshooter*

'The Talisman', (1) *Westerly* 3, October 1970; (2) *New Country*

'The Wedding', *Hungerford: Short Fiction*

'The Willow of Beam Creek', *Hungerford: Short Fiction*

'The Woomera', *Hungerford: Short Fiction*

'The Voyager', *Westerly* 4, 1967

'Tourist with Haiku', (1) *A Knockabout with a Slouch Hat*;
(2) *Straightshooter*

'Wong Chu and the Queen's Letterbox', (1) *Westerly* 21, 1978;
(2) *The Strength of Tradition*; (3) *Hungerford: Short Fiction*;
(4) *Home and Away*; (4) *West Coast Writing.*

POETRY

T. A. G. Hungerford's poetry includes:

'On an Island Beach'—published in *Stand-To* (1950)

'In the Hills, in Kowloon'

'Old Fremantle Gaol'

'Abrolhos'

'Sea-Horse'

'The Warning Bird'

'Joe Go in Springtime', in *Summer Shorts*

'Anzac Day' (reproduced in chapter 15)

'Dark Stranger' (reproduced in chapter 15)

RADIO AND STAGE

Help Me Cut Up a Cat. Radio play, 1972 (also the title of one of the novellas under composition in 2003).

Looking After Bert. Radio play, 1976. Won fifth prize in national competition for radio play and broadcast on the ABC.

The Prudent Shepherd. 1979. Written for actor Adele Cohen. Not performed.

The Day It All Ended. Stage play. Inspired by Bill Warnock. Not performed.

Prisoner of the Skin. Stage play. Performed but never staged. Written for Maggie Anketell.

Waiting for Andy. Stage play. Performed by WA Theatre Company, 1989.

The Ambush. ABC Radio National, *Radio Eye*, 2002–03. Purchased by Radio Netherlands.

OTHER WORKS

The Best Boxer

A Million Square, with Richard Woldendorp, Thomas Nelson, Melbourne, 1969.

Fremantle: Landscape and People, photographs by Roger Garwood, Fremantle Arts Centre Press, Fremantle, WA, 1979.

'Oil Transfusion for the Western Third' (typescript), Battye Library, Perth, 1953.

Screen scripts from Antarctic trip, a documentary *Antarctic Journey* and a radio script.

Queen's Tour booklet (ANIB).

Why I Live Where I Live, photographs by A. Porges, Swan Cottage Homes, Bentley, WA, 1996.

REFERENCES

T. A. G. HUNGERFORD'S OWN COLLECTIONS

A Knockabout with a Slouch Hat, FACP, Fremantle, WA, 1985.

Red Rover All Over, FACP, Fremantle, WA, 1986.

Stories from Suburban Road, FACP, Fremantle, WA, 1983.

Straightshooter, FACP, Fremantle, WA, 2003.

Wong Chu and the Queen's Letterbox, FACP, Fremantle, WA, 1977.

ANTHOLOGIES
FACP – Fremantle Arts Centre Press
UQP – University of Queensland Press
UWA Press – University of Western Australia Press

Bennett, Bruce (ed.), *New Country: A Selection of Western Australian Short Stories*, FACP, Fremantle, WA, 1976.

Bennett, Bruce, and Susan Hayes (eds), *Home and Away: Australian Stories of Belonging and Alienation*, UWA Press, Perth, WA, 2000.

Bennett, Bruce, and Susan Miller (eds), *Daughters of the Sun: Short Stories from Western Australia*, UWA Press, Perth, WA, 1994.

Choate, Alec, & Barbara York Main (eds), *Summerland: A Western Australian Sesquicentenary Anthology of Poetry and Prose*, UWA Press, Perth, WA, 1979.

Coffey, B.R. (ed.), *Decade: A Selection of Contemporary Western Australian Short Fiction*, FACP, Fremantle, WA, 1982.

Coffey, B.R. (ed.), *Sunburnt Country: Stories of Australian Life*, FACP, Fremantle, WA, 1996.

Coffey, B.R., and Wendy Jenkins (eds), *Portrait: A West Coast Collection*, FACP, Fremantle, WA, 1986.

Cowan, Peter (ed.), *Hungerford: Short Fiction by T. A. G. Hungerford*, FACP, Fremantle, WA, 1989.

Cowan, Peter (ed.), *Impressions: West Coast Fiction 1829–1988*, FACP, Fremantle, WA, 1989.

Dutton, Geoffrey (ed.), *Modern Australian Writing*, Collins, London, 1966.

Hergenhan, Laurie (ed.), *The Australian Short Story: An Anthology from the 1890s to the 1980s*, UQP, St Lucia, Qld, 1986.

Hewett, Dorothy (ed.), *Sandgropers: A Western Australian Anthology*, UWA Press, Perth, WA, for the Fellowship of Australian Writers, WA Section, 1973.

Holt, R.F. (ed.), *The Strength of Tradition: Stories of the Immigrant Presence in Australia, 1970–81*, UQP, St Lucia, Qld, n.d. (?1983).

Hungerford, T. A. G. (edited for FAW, Canberra), *Australian Signpost: An Anthology*, Cheshire, Melbourne, 1956.

Kinsella, J. (ed.), *Western Australian Writing: An On-line Anthology*, http://wawriting.library.uwa.edu.au/home.html, 2003; viewed September 2004.

Porter, Hal (ed.), *Coast to Coast: Australian Stories 1961–62*, Angus & Robertson, Sydney, 1962.

Turner, Bill (ed.), *WA Short Stories*, Imprint, Broadway, NSW, n.d. (?1986).

Warnock, Bill & Diana (eds), *Summer Shorts*, FACP, Fremantle, WA, 1993.

NOTES TO APPENDIX 2

1 Peter Cowan's introduction to *Hungerford: Short Fiction* described these as 'winners'.
2 Tom Hungerford considers that these are some of his best.

NOTES

Where there are references to *Stories from Suburban Road* et seq., these are taken exclusively from *Straightshooter*, Hungerford's collection of autobiographical short stories in one volume.

PREFACE

1 Janet Malcolm quoted by Linda Simon, 'The Dangerous Art of Writing Biographies', in *Atlanta Journal-Constitution*, 3 April 1994.
2 What became the Australian Security and Intelligence Organisation (ASIO) started out in 1942 as the Allied Intelligence Bureau. The AIB was a conglomeration of the American and Australian military intelligence agencies that cooperated to gather intelligence against Imperial Japan during World War II. The AIB continued its work until the end of the war, when it was disbanded. In 1949 ASIO was established. (Source: www.asio.gov.au; viewed 9 May 2004.) It appears that information on Hungerford before 1953 was maintained by Army Intelligence, but to date this has been impossible to verify.
3 Eric Hobsbawm, *Interesting Times: A Twentieth-Century Life*, Alfred A. Knopf, New York, 2003.

INTRODUCTION

1 'My Turn in the Barrel', *A Knockabout with a Slouch Hat*, pp. 242–3.
2 ibid., p. 343.
3 'They have sown the wind and they shall reap the whirlwind.' Hosea viii 7.
4 Reprinted in *A Knockabout with a Slouch Hat*, p. 222.
5 Believed to have been presented by the Australian Literature Society and funded by Colonel Richard Armstrong Crouch, a philanthropist whose good works included a gift of medieval manuscripts to the Ballarat Fine Art Gallery and founding the Prime Ministers' Walk at Ballarat. He was a distant relative of the author.
6 Interview with Phillip Adams, *Late Night Live*, 6 October 2003.
7 Last broadcast on Anzac Day 2003 (its third presentation) and destined to be frequently revived on similar national occasions.
8 Nevertheless his travel accounts, as in 'And Now…' (*Red Rover All Over*, pp. 552 ff), put him into that special category of travel writers who inform and entertain.

9   'And Now…', *Red Rover All Over*, pp. 552 ff.
10   The young boxer was devastatingly attractive to women, and in two relationships he left his companions pregnant (he later married the second lover)—Hungerford, interview with author.
11   Hungerford, interview with author.
12   David Lawrence, review of *Code Word Macau*, *West Australian*, 12 October 1991.
13   His first poem, according to 'Professor Murdoch and the Old White Road' (*Stories from Suburban Road*, p. 156), went as follows:

> There was a man from the Friendly Isles
> He was full of frowns, very seldom smiles.
> He was by the natives got
> And put into a cooking pot
> Where he found it very hot.
> So he hopped out and ran for miles.

Two more contemporary examples of Hungerford's poetry appear in the last chapter of this book.

CHAPTER 1: THE BRAVE DAYS OF OLD

1   Sir Richard Colt Hoare Bt, *Hungerfordiana: The Memoirs of the Family of Hungerford*, first published by J. Rutter, 1823, and Sir Richard George Baker, *Chronicle of the Kings of England*, Sawbridge at the Bible on Ludgate Hill, 1679.
2   Sir Richard Colt Hoare Bt, quoted by Revd John Hungerford in *The History of Modern Wiltshire: Hundreds of Heytesbury*, John Nichol & Son, London, 1824.
3   Hungerford, interview with author.
4   *The Rambler*, No. 60 (1750), quoted by Peter France and William St Clair (eds), *Mapping Lives: The Uses of Biography*, Oxford University Press, Oxford, 2002.
5   Hungerford Society.
6   Information in this chapter was supplied by Hungerford himself unless otherwise specified.
7   Hungerford, interview with author.
8   He delivered Geoffrey Bolton, the future professor, among other eminent Western Australians. Bolton's mother spoke very highly of him.
9   Also known as the settlement of Shellborough (now abandoned).
10   Jenny Hardie, *Nor'Westers of the Pilbara Breed*, Shire of Port Hedland, 1981.
11   Busselton Historical Society.

12 Hungerford obtained the following information on his parents mainly from a sister of his mother then living in Albany, Western Australia.

13 Hungerford, interview with author.

14 Professor Geoffrey Bolton, interview with author; also J. K. Crowley, *Australia's Western Third*, Macmillan & Co., London, 1960.

15 Mollie Hungerford, interview with author.

CHAPTER 2: HALCYON YOUTH

1 Hungerford, interview with author.

2 ibid.

3 ibid.

4 ibid.

5 ibid.

6 ibid.

7 ibid.

8 ibid.

9 ibid.

10 'Long Before Now', *Red Rover All Over*, p. 363.

11 Hungerford, interview with author.

12 'Professor Murdoch and the Old White Road', *Stories from Suburban Road*, p. 161.

13 Sir Charles Court reminiscing of his own childhood in interview with author.

14 Hungerford, interview with author.

15 ibid.

16 ibid.

17 ibid.

18 Beatrice Cotton, an Englishwoman, had a strong influence on Tom Hungerford as he was growing up. It was she who gave him a love of dogs, dating from her own animals. He enjoyed discussing life and politics with her. She was secretary of the Royal Automobile Club and introduced him to the club when he agreed to stop biting his nails. She taught him to play good bridge. She was to die while Hungerford was in the USA, having tried to stay alive until he returned to Western Australia. He was greatly upset by her death.

19 'Long Before Now', *Red Rover All Over*, p. 355.

20 ibid.

21 ibid.

22 Interview with Phillip Adams, *Late Night Live*, 6 October 2003. See note 13 in the Introduction for an example of his early output.

23 Hungerford, interview with author.

24 ibid.

25 ibid.

26 'The Lady Who was Diddled by the Judge', *Stories from Suburban Road*, p. 138.

CHAPTER 3: TICKETY-BOO

1 Hungerford, interview with author.

2 ibid.

3 ibid.

4 ibid. Hungerford commented that Dick Halliday, state school coach for swimming, was impressed by his coming second in the state Inter-School Competition of 1930.

5 Later Mary MacKinnon, wife of Graham MacKinnon, a Liberal minister in the Brand–Court administrations of the 1960s and '70s.

6 In 1998 Hungerford was interviewed on behalf of the Australian Association of Dance Education in West Australian, to contribute to a series History of Dance Education in Western Australia (Battye Library).

7 'Before the war there was a very fine dance band, Victor Silvester's, renowned for its strict dance tempo [on 78 rpm records]. Now the woman came out to Australia to conduct examinations of teachers in dance studios. Mary said she would put me in, and I topped the class.' Hungerford, interview with author.

8 'The Day It All Ended', *Stories from Suburban Road*, p. 195.

9 ibid., p. 186.

10 R. M. Bennett, 'Expansion of the Australian Army During the Early Part of WWII—The Raising of the 2nd AIF', Manpower Policy Branch, Department of Defence, Canberra, June 1974 (unpublished).

11 John Rickard, *A Cultural History of Australia*, Longman Cheshire, Melbourne, 1988.

CHAPTER 4: APOCALYPSE NOW

1 Hungerford, interview with author.

2 Hungerford was correct. C. Lloyd, *Professional Journalist: A History of the Australian Journalists' Association* (Hale & Iremonger, Sydney, 1985) confirmed that although journalists were excluded from the list of essential occupations granted a 'reserved' status for the duration of the war, almost all other newspaper workers were exempted from call-up. Journalists over the age of 30 were later placed on reserve.

3 Bennett, 'Expansion of the Australian Army During the Early Part of WWII—The Raising of the 2nd AIF'.

4 'World War II: Japanese policy, 1939–41', *Encyclopedia Britannica*, 2001 (electronic edition).

5   Western Australia's final contribution was 62,000, or more than 13 per cent of all Australian enlistments. Bennett, 'Expansion of the Australian Army During the Early Part of WWII—The Raising of the 2nd AIF'.

6   For an entertaining account of Hungerford's first few days in the army, see 'Boots, Boots, Boots', *A Knockabout with a Slouch Hat*, p. 202.

7   ibid.

8   Hungerford, interview with author.

9   ibid. His army Service and Casualty record (National Archives of Australia, Canberra) states that he was made up to acting corporal on 26 September 1941 and acting sergeant from 2 March 1942.

10 Hungerford, interview with author.

11 ibid.

12 ibid.

13 Service and Casualty record.

14 www.specialoperations.com, viewed 27 February 2003.

15 Hungerford, interview with author.

16 ibid.

17 ibid.

18 Service and Casualty record.

19 Hungerford, interview with author.

20 *Hungerford: Short Fiction by T. A. G. Hungerford*, selected and introduced by Peter Cowan, Fremantle Arts Centre Press, Fremantle, WA, 1989.

CHAPTER 5: THE DOGS OF WAR

1   Dennis, P., et al., *Oxford Companion to Australian Military History*, Oxford University Press, Melbourne, 1995, pp. 585–8.

2   Tom Hungerford, interview with author.

3   ibid.

4   ibid.

5   He took the reprimand to heart: see note 10 in chapter 6.

6   Service and Casualty record.

7   Hungerford, interview with author. He had been made up to sergeant again.

8   Don Astill, *Commando White Diamond: Memoir of Service of the 2/8 Australian Commando Squadron: Australia and the South West Pacific 1942–1945*, Australian Military History Publications, Loftus, NSW, 1996, p. 5.

9   There is a good description of Bannah in 'The Darwin Jack-up', *A Knockabout with a Slouch Hat*, p. 219.

10 Hungerford, interview with author.

11 ibid.

12 'World War II: The Allies' first decisive successes', *Encyclopedia Britannica*, 2001 (electronic edition).

13 Service and Casualty record.

Chapter 6: The Jungle

1 Tony Sweeney, *Malaria Frontline: Australian Army Research during World War II*, Melbourne University Press, 2003, pp. 28–9.

2 Service and Casualty record.

3 'Bougainville Island', *Encyclopedia Britannica*, 2001 (electronic edition).

4 Astill, *Commando White Diamond*, pp. 31–6.

5 Hungerford, interview with author.

6 Astill, *Commando White Diamond*, p. xi.

7 The US general who commanded the Southwest Pacific Theatre in World War II, later administered Japan during the Alllied occupation and led United Nations forces in Korea during the first nine months of the Korean War (*Encyclopaedia Britannica*).

8 Hungerford, interview with author; and 'Interview with Sgt Hungerford 2/8th Cdo: Revision on Bougainville', Australian War Memorial (hereafter AWM), author unknown, undated.

9 Referred to in this account as 'OC', since the convention is that 'CO' refers to a battalion commander.

10 'A wonderful man,' commented Hungerford. The two built up a close relationship: Hungerford was older than most of the men and briefed Winning on the different personalities in the 2/8th when Winning assumed command. Hungerford later saw fit to deliver a reprimand to a young commissioned officer who was not enforcing the strict rule that after sundown everyone had to work outside with their sleeves down, to obviate mosquito attack. Winning later told Hungerford that he would have been promoted to sergeant major of the 2/8th if he had not shown up the officer, Lieutenant Atholl 'Ap' Jones.

11 Hungerford, interview with author.

12 ibid.

13 'The Rosary', *A Knockabout with a Slouch Hat*, p. 234.

Chapter 7: Alarums and Excursions

1 Hungerford, interview with author.

2 Hungerford recalled the Kanaka as 'Karim' when he reminisced, but the official records give his name as Kumba.

3 Hungerford, interview with author.

4 Lieutenant 'Ap' Jones, referred to above—see note 10, chapter 6.

5   Hungerford, interview with author. On a personal basis, Ap Jones and Hungerford got on well together, so there was no personal animosity on Hungerford's part, although it can be speculated that Jones might have been the source of the report to ASIO that damned Hungerford (see note 13, chapter 8), although Hungerford thinks not.

6   See the poem 'Anzac Day' in chapter 15 for an example.

7   Hungerford, interview with author.

Chapter 8: Anticlimax

1   'The Rosary', *Stories from Suburban Road*, p. 237.

2   Hungerford spoke informally of a Japanese prisoner being inappropriately handled by his Australian escort when he attempted to stop to drink from a stream; a minor example of misbehaviour, given the stories of Japanese brutality towards Allied prisoners of war that circulated at the time.

3   Sir Charles Court, interview with author.

4   Hungerford, interview with author.

5   ibid.

6   Major Winning had told Hungerford that he was putting him up for a decoration—these were allocated to each unit—and asked him whether he would like a British Empire Medal or a mention in dispatches. 'What for? I hadn't done any deeds of valour! He said I'd held the unit together. I said the MID...This is the man who believed in me; he didn't see me as a communist or a cunt.' Hungerford, interview with author.

7   ibid.

8   Service and Casualty record.

9   Hungerford, interview with author.

10 *Daily News*, Perth, June 1945.

11 Hungerford, interview with author.

12 Service and Casualty record.

13 Hungerford, interview with author. A distorted version of this anecdote was reported to ASIO (or to Army Intelligence, which passed it on to ASIO in 1955). Someone who had served with Hungerford reported that the latter had been 'removed' from the infantry battalion as a professional troublemaker and transferred to the canteen service. In fact, as recounted, he volunteered for the transfer.

14 Morotai Protests, AWM 124361 et seq., Australian War Memorial. This incident must have occurred before Hungerford arrived on Morotai as it was separate from that in which he was to be a ringleader.

15 'Incident in Morotai', *A Knockabout with a Slouch Hat*, p. 244.

16 Hungerford was told it could have been as many as 3,000, but he thought this figure was inflated.

17 'Incident in Morotai', *A Knockabout with a Slouch Hat*, p. 245.

18 As retold to the author by Hungerford. In 'Incident in Morotai' (*A Knockabout with a Slouch Hat*) he relates the lead-up and subsequent conversations somewhat differently.

19 'Incident in Morotai', *A Knockabout with a Slouch Hat*, p. 247.

20 Hungerford, interview with author. An earlier record of those days (a typed manuscript held by the author) suggests he was more conciliatory in his response.

21 Nevertheless the intelligence authorities were busy. See note 13. Another ASIO report commented in part: 'Hungerford is recorded as a ringleader in the "protest parade" held by Australian troops in 1945, such parade being considered at the time as due to planned Communist agitation.' (Secret Memorandum, 9 January 1956, Director-General ASIO to Regional Director for ACT, in National Archives of Australia.)

22 Hungerford, interview with author.

23 ibid.

24 ibid.

25 ibid.

26 ibid.

27 This according to an ex-ASIO operative, who knew him personally and who urged later that Hungerford's name be taken off the list, but ASIO continued to maintain interest in Hungerford decades later. Anonymous source.

28 Service and Casualty record.

29 Later Hungerford was also to visit the test site at Maralinga, in South Australia, one of few Australians to have witnessed 'post-Armageddon' in two locations.

30 This according to Hungerford. Another (anonymous) source was less sure that such marriages were a success and, because of the prohibition on such marriages until the Korean War, they would have had to have been covert.

31 Hungerford, interview with author.

32 Service and Casualty record.

CHAPTER 9: REORIENTATION

1 Hungerford, interview with author.

2 ibid.

3 ibid.

4 Service and Casualty record.

5 'The Last Camp', *A Knockabout with a Slouch Hat*, p. 283.

6 A recollection of one of Hungerford's friends who had met Peg in the 1960s.

7 Hungerford, interview with author.

8 Hungerford's application to join the AWM, AWM archives.

9 Anonymous, interview with author.

10 Hungerford, interview with author.
11 Charles Frank Norton, a gifted New Zealander, worked as a marine painter, teacher and gallery director (director of the Western Australian Art Gallery, 1958–76). He served as an Australian official war artist during World War II and the Korean War (AWM records and the author's recollections).
12 Anecdotal information from AWM staff and Hungerford himself, who was used to controlling his own working life.
13 ibid.
14 Hungerford, interview with author.
15 Anecdotal information from AWM staff and Hungerford.
16 Hungerford, interview with author.
17 'Me and the National Capital', *A Knockabout with a Slouch Hat*, p. 289.
18 Anecdotal information from AWM staff.
19 'The Last Camp', *A Knockabout with a Slouch Hat*, p. 290.
20 Correspondence with Hungerford, AWM archives.
21 Hungerford, interview with author.
22 ibid.
23 ibid.
24 Geoffrey Dutton, review of *The Ridge and the River*, *The Argus*, 3 May 1952.
25 Douglas Stewart, review of *The Ridge and the River*, *Bulletin*, 7 May 1952, p. 2.
26 Hungerford, interview with author, quoting Vance Palmer's review of *The Ridge and the River*.
27 Osmar White, review of *The Ridge and the River*, *Herald* (Melbourne), 3 May 1952.
28 Eric Lambert, *The Veterans* (Frederick Muller Ltd, London 1954), reviewed by Hungerford in *Stand-To*, May–June 1955.
29 'A Sort of Boswell', *A Knockabout with a Slouch Hat*, p. 310.
30 Professor Geoffrey Bolton, interview with author.
31 'Australian Prime Ministers', http://primeministers.naa.gov.au, viewed 18 May 2004.
32 'A Sort of Boswell', *A Knockabout with a Slouch Hat*, p. 317.

CHAPTER 10: IN HIS ELEMENT

1 From 'Hughes', a draft typescript by Hungerford held by the author.
2 Hungerford, interview with author.
3 ibid.
4 ibid.
5 ibid.
6 Jim Gibbney, *Canberra 1913–1953*, Australian Government Publishing Service, Canberra, 1988.
7 The author heard this tale from the man himself, whom he met after the latter's retirement to the UK, in 1993.
8 Hungerford, interview with author.

9   ibid. There would have been no reference to 'a couple of mutinies'. ASIO records refer only to Hungerford's role at Morotai, not the Northern Territory jack-up, so the story understandably has improved in the telling.

10 However, one entry is a speech made by Hungerford over Canberra radio (reproduced as a fine piece of rhetoric as appendix 1 of this book), which finally gave the lie to his being a communist. In fact, Hungerford had voted Liberal for much of his life, in spite of his left-leaning inclinations in such matters as Indigenous affairs and refugees. ASIO was still following Hungerford around in 1972, the latest record from then being available under the thirty years rule.

11 Walter Crocker had been a member of the British colonial service as a district officer in Nigeria and, after a subsequent career in the Australian diplomatic service, was appointed lieutenant governor of South Australia. The author knew him personally.

12 This according to Hungerford. The facts according to the ASIO file appear to be different. Hungerford had been cleared for this posting and was apparently acceptable to Crocker, once another candidate withdrew, but he was posted to New York while the Djakarta posting was being finalised. Crocker concluded that his embassy could have used the services of local Indonesian journalists for publicity purposes (ASIO records). It is likely that as both had reputations as mavericks, they might well have clashed if Hungerford had been posted to Djakarta.

13 Hungerford, interview with author.

14 ibid.

15 ibid.

16 Cheshire, Melbourne, 1956.

17 Hungerford, interview with author.

18 Marjorie Barnard, review of *The Ridge and the River*, undated typed sheet provided by Hungerford to the author.

19 Hungerford, interview with author.

20 Geoffrey Dutton, review of *Riverslake*, publication unknown, found in Hungerford's ASIO file.

21 Geoffrey Tubbutt, review of *Riverslake*, publication unknown, found in Hungerford's ASIO file.

22 Hungerford, interview with author.

23 ibid.

24 ibid.

25 'Red Rover All Over', *Red Rover All Over*, p. 377.

26 Hungerford, interview with author. See 'Red Rover All Over', *Red Rover All Over*, pp. 379–84, for a fuller account of the visit to Hermannsburg.

27 This was Piers Akerman, the well-known journalist based in Sydney. Although Akerman has always respected Hungerford and his approach to writing, Hungerford is less charitable about Akerman. The latter was then

WA bureau chief for *The Australian* and News Ltd. See chapter 13 for details of their encounter.

28 Antarctic Territory website, www.antdiv.gov.au, viewed 9 May 2004.

29 'The Land Beyond the Ice', *Red Rover All Over*, p. 404.

30 ibid., p. 408.

31 Robert Carrier might have approved of his improvised recipe for basic Glacé Icing, which is just sifted sugar and water, but the proportions of each are essential.

32 Hungerford, interview with author.

33 'The Land Beyond the Ice', *Red Rover All Over*, p. 409.

CHAPTER 11: THE NEW WORLD

1   Hungerford, interview with author.

2   'Give My Regards to Broadway', *Red Rover All Over*, p. 449.

3   Plainly a favourite saying of Hungerford's: his character 'Dusty' Miller uses a variant of this in 'Boots, Boots, Boots', *A Knockabout with a Slouch Hat*, p. 205.

4   Hungerford, interview with author.

5   'Give My Regards to Broadway', *Red Rover All Over*, p. 458.

6   Hungerford, interview with author.

7   ibid.

8   ibid.

9   ibid.

10 ibid.

11 ibid.

12 Recounted by a fellow member of the consulate staff.

13 Hungerford, interview with author.

14 ibid.

15 ibid.

16 ibid.

17 ibid.

18 It was also noted in passing by the writer friend that, as with his other writings, there is a reticence about Hungerford's private emotional life that has been seen as limiting what he has been prepared to put down on paper. Hungerford is an intensely private man.

19 Hungerford, interview with author.

20 ibid.

CHAPTER 12: THE BACK OF BEYOND

1   Hungerford, interview with author.

2   ibid.

3   ibid.

4   For a full and entertaining account of the man, see A. G. Evans, *C. Y. O'Connor: His Life and Legacy*, UWA Press, Perth, 2001.

5   'The Great Iron Ore Caper', *Red Rover All Over*, p. 498.

6   A Wesfarmers publication of the time.

7   Richard Woldendorp, interview with author.

8   Anonymous, interview with author.

9   'The Great Iron Ore Caper', *Red Rover All Over*, p. 498.

10 Richard Woldendorp, interview with author.

11 Anonymous, interview with author.

12 'The Great Iron Ore Caper', *Red Rover All Over*, p. 483.

13 Hungerford, interview with author.

14 ibid.

15 ibid.

16 ibid.

CHAPTER 13: FROM ORIENTAL INTERLUDE TO PREMIER'S VOICE

1   Hungerford, interview with author.

2   'Stopover in Macau', *Red Rover All Over*, p. 521.

3   ibid., supplemented by casual enquiry and *Encyclopedia Britannica*, 2001 (electronic edition).

4   Hungerford, interview with author.

5   *Encyclopedia Britannica*, 2001.

6   Hungerford, interview with author.

7   ibid.

8   ibid.

9   'Any confidences that Court, or indeed Tonkin, wished to discuss were with their ministers, and we were given the results.' It is interesting to compare the nature of the access that Hungerford had to the Western Australian premiers he served with contemporary government press advisers. 'It was before the days of "spin", and I think that political leaders are much more closely entwined with their top spin doctors and speak to them more.' Hungerford, interview with author.

10 Piers Akerman, email to author.

11 ibid.

12 Hungerford, interview with author.

13 Actually, this might not have been the case. A reliable and well-placed source of the time maintained that the development was vetoed by the Whitlam government.

14 A photocopy of an old photograph at the Battye Library shows part of the building: M. Pitt Morison and J. White (eds), *Western Towns and Buildings*, UWA Press, Perth, 1979.

15 Professor Geoffrey Bolton, interview with author.

16 Hungerford, interview with author.

17 ibid.

18 Sir Charles Court, interview with author.

19 Hungerford, interview with author.

Chapter 14: Living the Life

1 Hungerford, interview with author.

2 Anonymous, interview with author.

3 ibid.

4 ibid.

5 Hungerford, interview with author.

6 See the list of Hungerford's works in appendix 2.

7 Hungerford, interview with author.

8 Hungerford, interview with Gail O'Hanlon, Battye Library, Perth, 1998.

9 Andrew Sant, review of *Stories from Suburban Road*, *Australian Book Review*, May 1984, pp. 20–1.

10 From 'Hughes', a Hungerford manuscript held by the author. For a full account of Hungerford's time with Hughes, see 'A Sort of Boswell', *A Knockabout with a Slouch Hat*, p. 307.

11 Laurie Clancy, *Australian Book Review*, August 1985, pp. 18–19.

12 Alex Harris, review of *Red Rover*, *West Australian*, 10 January 1987, p. 44.

13 The short stories included are listed in appendix 2 of this book.

14 Hungerford, interview with author.

15 'And Now…', *Red Rover All Over*, pp. 567 et seq.

16 Hungerford in letter held by the author. Hungerford had been asked to climb large stone steps inside an ancient Yemeni citadel, to dine at the top. The damaged ankle, knee and hip protested.

Chapter 15: Epilogue

1 Anonymous, interview with author.

2 ibid.

3 'Oh Mr Gallagher, Oh Mr Shean', *Stories from Suburban Road*, p. 108.

4 Anonymous, interview with author.

5 ibid.

6 ibid.

7 ibid.

8 Recounted by one of those present.

9 He is also at home on air. In the interview conducted over the telephone on *Late Night Live* with Phillip Adams (6 October 2003) there was a knock at his door. Hungerford asked Adams to fill in while he answered the door and was back to continue the interview, with complete aplomb.

INDEX

A comprehensive list of T. A. G.
Hungerford's writings can be found in
appendix 2. Only his books, collections
of short stories and two poems are
listed here.